1812
THROUGH FIRE AND ICE
WITH NAPOLEON

A French Officer's Memoir of the
Campaign in Russia

Eugène Labaume

Captain of the Royal Geographical Engineers; Ex-Officer of the Ordnance of Prince
Eugene; Chevalier of the Legion of Honour, and of the Iron Crown.

Helion & Company

Helion & Company Limited
26 Willow Road
Solihull
West Midlands
B91 1UE
England
Tel. 0121 705 3393
Fax 0121 711 4075
Email: publishing@helion.co.uk
Website: http://www.helion.co.uk

This edition published by Helion & Company Limited, 2002

Designed and typeset by Helion & Company Limited, Solihull, West Midlands
Dustjacket designed by Bookcraft Limited, Stroud, Gloucestershire
Printed by The Cromwell Press, Trowbridge, Wiltshire

Originally published as *Relation circonstanciée de la campagne de Russie, en 1812*, Paris 1814.
Translated into English by E. Boyce, and published in London 1815, as *A Circumstantial Narrative of the Campaign in Russia*. This edition taken from the 1817 English edition published in Hartford, Connecticut by Silas Andrus. This edition's spelling has been retained throughout this reprint.
This newly-typeset edition © Helion and Company 2002.

ISBN 1 874622 75 2

British Library Cataloguing-in-Publication Data.
A catalogue record for this book is available from the British Library.

For details of other military history titles published by Helion & Company
contact the above address, or visit our website: http://www.helion.co.uk.

We always welcome receiving book proposals from prospective authors.

Contents

Preface

I relate that which I have seen. A witness of the greatest disasters that ever befell a great nation; a spectator and an actor in every scene of this sad and memorable expedition. I present the reader with no fictitious narrative, artfully arranged, and heightened by false colouring. The events that passed around me were daily recorded, and I now simply endeavour to communicate the impressions which I then felt. It was by the light of the burning of Moscow, that I described the sack of that unfortunate city. It was on the borders of the Beresina, that I traced the recital of that fatal passage.

It is scarcely possible to conceive what difficulties I had to surmount in the progress of my work. Compelled, like my companions in arms, to struggle with the most urgent necessities, pierced by the cold, tormented with hunger, a prey to every accumulated horror; uncertain at the rising of the sun whether I should see its setting rays, and doubtful at night, whether I should witness the morrow's dawn; every thought seemed concentrated in the ardent desire to live, that I might perpetuate the memory of what I had seen. Animated by this irresistible feeling, I retraced, each night, the events of the day, sitting beside a wretched fire, under a temperature of ten or twelve degrees, and surrounded by the dying and the dead. The knife with which I had carved my scanty morsel of horse flesh, was employed in cutting a raven's quill, and a little gun-powder, mixed with some melted snow, in the hollow of my hand, served me for ink and ink-stand.

I have composed this work without personal ill will and without prejudice; yet I must confess, that during the recital of the most horrible enterprise, which the genius of ambition had ever conceived, I could often scarcely restrain my indignation against the author of all our misfortunes. But the respect with which his former well-earned reputation had inspired me, and the memory of the glorious victories that I had witnessed, and in the honours of which I had shared, compelled me to speak of that conqueror with moderation and reserve.

Having constantly before me the mournful image of a crowd of warriors, doomed to perish miserably in remote deserts, I was sustained by the hope of rendering my feeble homage, to a courage acknowledged even by their enemies; and to exploits the more heroic, since their object was no longer the safety of their country, nor even of their lives, but the preservation of their fame. I shall account myself most happy, if my reader is convinced, that in the midst of so many disasters, our brave soldiers were always worthy of themselves; that they stained not their ancient renown, and that, always formidable to their enemies, they were conquered by the elements alone.

Part I

Book I

Wilna

If we were to look into our annals for the most brilliant period of our glory, we should find that France had never been more powerful than after the treaty of Tilsit. Spain, under the name of an ally, was, in reality, one of our provinces, whence we were supplied with money, men, and ships. Italy, wisely governed by a prince who was at once a skilful warrior and an able politician, being subject to, and obeying the same laws, as the French empire, enjoyed an equal share of prosperity with ourselves; and saw with pride that her legions, transported to the Baltic, had given proofs of the noblest courage, in order to procure for France, a peace as glorious as it was beneficial. Germany, alarmed by our colossal aggrandizement, far from opposing our successes, endeavoured merely to insure her own existence, by a submission to all the great changes which subverted the German constitution. England, the only constant opponent of an ambition so fatal to mankind, saw, in the prosperity of Napoleon, a new cause of fear to herself, and of terror to the continent. Jealous of the honour of circumscribing that boundless ambition, she anxiously represented to the sovereigns of the north, how much of it was their interest to arrest the rapidly increasing progress of our excessive power. Vain efforts! these sovereigns had not yet acquired the requisite degree of conviction, that they must all be united to crush the giant who wished to devour them. Napoleon's passion for invasion, suggested to him on his return from Tilsit, the idea of declaring an unjust war on Spain, which had not only tarnished his laurels, but afterwards furnished his enemies with the long wished for occasion of subverting his power.

A weak prince nominally presided over that unhappy peninsula; but a perfidious minister, treacherous towards his country, and ungrateful to his king and benefactor, in reality governed the state with a partial hand; and by the most abject deference to the evil counsels of foreigners, degraded the nation, whose rights he seemed to have usurped only to drag it into long and shameful servitude. The credulity of the father, and the moderation of the son, alike promoted his criminal views. He incensed them against each other, and parties were soon formed. The artful Napoleon profited by the discord, which was thus produced, to excite a civil war, and to kindle that flame which was necessary for the execution of the most unjust and abominable project, a project which presents in the

1

history of a civilized nation, an example of atrocious ingratitude, unparalleled even amongst barbarians.

Spain, notwithstanding its proximity to France, was little known; and the character of its inhabitants was still less understood. This fatal ignorance misled the conqueror, and induced him to attempt an unfortunate invasion; the miseries of which will, however, be easily forgotten, when we consider that, like the campaign of Moscow, it was the primitive cause of those events which led to the happy deliverance of the world.

It does not enter into my plan to recapitulate an ill fated aggression, which made enemies of two nations equally generous, and who, always united by a reciprocal esteem, would yet have retained the most friendly sentiments, had it not been for the perfidious politics of the tyrant. The struggle which ensued, memorable for its obstinacy and its vicissitudes, will furnish the historian with an interesting subject, and the military man with ample matter for meditation. I shall only briefly observe, that Providence appears to have excited in Napoleon the idea of these two unjust wars, to convince the Spaniards and Russians that an allegiance with the vicious will unavoidably prove fatal. This instrument, which the Almighty had employed to accomplish his purpose, was now precipitated from error to error, to show that tyranny is a crime against the common and inalienable rights of man, and that it may, at all times, be successfully opposed by those who march united under the banners of justice.

Whilst Napoleon vainly endeavoured to chase the English from the peninsula, a new storm was gathering in Germany. Austria, whom he had so often humbled, could not tamely submit to the disgraceful yoke under which her defeats had placed her. The resistance of the Spaniards, and the powerful armaments of England, offered her a favourable opportunity for again having recourse to arms, and endeavouring to recover the territories which she had lost, and that political preponderance of which she had always been so jealous.

The new war against Austria only opened a new field of triumph to the French. Landshut, Eckmuhl and Ratisbon, having been attacked, with brilliant success, prepared the way at the end of four months, for one of the most memorable victories. The field of Wagram saw the prodigies of Austerlitz renewed, and secured to France the most glorious campaign, and the most decisive results.

The treaty of Vienna which gave us peace, brought several wealthy provinces under our domination. It aggrandized Wirtemberg and Bavaria, and seemed to promise to Poland her complete re-establishment. But that treaty, dictated by a power that grasped at every thing, might, like those which preceded it, have contained the seeds of fresh contention, if the most august and most unexpected alliance, had not crowned the prosperity of the fortunate Napoleon. Of all the blessings which chance had bestowed upon him, that marriage was undoubtedly the greatest; since it secured forever the destiny of a man, who having risen from the humblest rank in society, had now become allied to a powerful monarch. But seduced by a prosperity so dazzling, he was yet dissatisfied; and forming new, and romantic, and impious projects, he hazarded all that he had acquired. He wearied his good genius, and provoked his fate. To his own folly alone is it to be attributed, than that which was so well calculated to cement his power, became the cause of his ruin.

That period ought to have been esteemed the happiest of Napoleon's life. What more could the wildest ambition desire? From a private individual he saw himself raised to the first throne in the world; his reign had been one continued series of victories; and to complete his happiness, a son, the object of his most ardent wishes, was born to succeed him. The people, though oppressed under his government, became accustomed to it, and seemed desirous to secure the crown to his family. All the foreign princes, who were subjected to his power, were his vassals. They maintained his troops, and supplied him with money, to gratify his luxury and his pleasures. In short all obeyed him. Nothing was wanting to make him happy! nothing, if *he* could be happy, who possessed not a love of justice. To that sentiment Napoleon had ever been a stranger, and, consequently, knew not either enjoyment or repose. Agitated by a restless spirit, and tormented by ungovernable ambition, the very excess of his fortune was his ruin. Aiming at that which it was impossible to obtain, and ignorant of human nature, he forgot every principle of honor and humanity – he forgot himself.

The sovereign of the German empire, tired of a resistance so long fatal to his arms, fancied for a moment, that he obeyed his fate, in yielding to a man to whom every one had submitted. He sacrificed his glory, and even his offspring, to obtain peace; thus realising those fabulous times, when magnanimous princes devoted their daughters to appease the wrath of some dæmon, who ravaged their country.

All seemed to disposed to submit to the great changes which Napoleon had effected; and the common people, whose limited conceptions seldom penetrate into the dark minds of ambitious monarchs, thought that the surprising alliance between this man and an archduchess, must satisfy all his immoderate desires. They also expected, that the tender feelings of a parent, would teach him, that a throne is not so firmly cemented by ambitious conquests, purchased by blood and by tears, as by wise institutions, which, making a government beloved, insure its duration. The being never existed who possessed ampler means for promoting the happiness of mankind. Nothing was required but justice and prudence. The nation expected these from him, and granted him that unlimited confidence, which he afterwards so cruelly abused. Posterity will hesitate to decide, whether Napoleon be more culpable on account of the crimes which he has committed, or the good that he might have done, but on which he bestowed not a single thought.

Instead of considering with calmness and moderation, how he might best employ his vast resources, he ruminated on projects beyond the power of man to execute; forgetting what innumerable victims must be sacrificed in the vain attempt. Continually tormented by spleen and melancholy, the least contradiction irritated him. The very idea that there existed a nation sufficiently great and generous to despise his proposals, and resist his fatal influence, lacerated his bosom, and poisoned the happiest moments of his glory.

In the hope of conquering that invincible enemy, he vainly endeavoured to grasp the extremities of Europe. Scarcely did he think that he had secured him on one side, than he escaped on the other. Infuriated at the disappointment of his chimerical plans, he aspired at universal despotism, for no other reason, than because a nation isolated from the continent, and profiting by its happy situation, had refused to submit to his intolerable yoke.

From that time he dismissed his ministers, whose wisdom he despised. In his estimation, talent consisted only in a blind submission to his absurd pretensions; and it was necessary for the greatest men to become the most abject slaves. Despot over his people and his armies, and a slave to his own ungovernable passions, he carried his ambitious views to the extremities of the globe, and aspired to the empire of the world. Misled by his rash and hasty temper, he adopted a false line of politics, and converted in the north, as he had done before in the south, the most useful and powerful of his allies, into a dangerous enemy.

In his senseless dreams he overstepped the natural boundaries of France. He allotted to her a chimerical and romantic destiny, and terrified himself with the groundless apprehension, that Russia might place herself on the ancient throne of Constantine, and command the two seas by which Europe is surrounded. He then assumed the prophet, predicting distant disasters to his country, and sacrificing the present generation to the uncertain happiness of posterity.

Blinded by an excess of prosperity, he fancied that the neighbouring powers beheld him with envy; and, judging of others by himself, he imagined that Russia must look with secret jealousy on the union between the most ancient and the most modern empires. Full of this idea, he pursued his plans of devastation; and desiring, as he said, that his dynasty might soon become the most ancient in Europe, he endeavoured to sanction his usurpation by dethroning every legitimate prince in order to bestow their crowns on his brothers, who, too effeminate to second him in his tyranny, or rival him in his exploits, only shone like pale satellites around an ill-boding star.

The treaty of Tilsit appeared but a truce to those who knew Napoleon's character. Every one who compared the constantly growing power of the two great empires, predicted an approaching rupture, and foresaw, in their systematic plans of aggrandizement, the future destruction of the gigantic edifice which both were erecting. The distance which had formerly separated them, had likewise separated their interest; but the conquests of France, having rendered her a neighbour of Russia, every thing presaged that a terrible struggle must, ere long, ensue between those rival powers, the shock of which would convulse the world.

For more than two years, Russia and France had maintained a war-like attitude; but at length Napoleon having reinforced the garrison of Dantzic, consisting of a strong body of troops, and completed the cavalry, the artillery-train, and the military equipages, forbore no longer to overwhelm Russia with reproaches. Forgetful that since the treaty of Tilsit, he had not only invaded Holland and the Hanse-towns, but likewise the duchy of Oldenburg, which belonged to the sister of Alexander, he imputed to the latter as a crime, that he had renewed a commercial intercourse with England.

From that moment, France made immense preparations. Numerous legions hastened from the banks of the Tagus to those of the Oder; and the same soldiers who, not long ago, had encamped on the fertile plains of Lombardy, saw themselves, in less than three months, transported to the barren sands of Poland.

Nothing, however, had yet transpired respecting these great movements, except the famous *senatus-consulte*,[1] which organized the empire into *cohortes, bans,* and *arriere bans.*[2] Thus France was on the point of being engaged in the most bloody contest which it had ever sustained, and one half of Europe was marching against the other, while Napoleon had not deigned to afford the least intimation of it to the senate; nor had that body ventured to demand from him any reason for a war, in which France was about to exhaust her treasures and her blood.

Under these circumstances all eyes were turned towards Prussia, anxious to discover which party she would espouse. Her fortresses, and her

1   Sitting of the Senate, 10th of March 1812.
2   Three classes into which the men were divided from 25 to 60 years of age, for the defence of the frontiers and the coasts.

whole territory were occupied by our armies; nevertheless, an alliance with us appeared so opposite to her true policy, and so prejudicial to her interests, that, in spite of the constraint and the subjugation in which we held her, she long hesitated to declare herself. At last, to the surprise of the world, we learned that she had decided in our favour.[3] They, however, who knew in what manner Napoleon contracted all his alliances, observed that Prussia did not declare for us till Berlin was pressed on all sides, and the duke of Reggio (Oudinot) was on the point of entering it as a conqueror. The king of Prussia was shortly after compelled to abandon his capital, and leave the command of it to the French generals.

At this time appeared another treaty of alliance, between France and Austria, by which it was stipulated, that each of the two contracting powers should furnish the other with an auxiliary corps of thirty thousand men, in case of attack. Napoleon, pretending that he was threatened by Russia, claimed and obtained the promised succour, which was put under the command of the prince of Schwartzenberg. Thus Napoleon tyrannized over kings, as Robespierre tyrannized over the people. No one could remain neutral under either. The love of peace was regarded as a treason, and moderation considered as a crime.

Innumerable troops traversed every part of Germany, and bent their course towards the Oder. The king of Westphalia (Jerome Bonaparte) at the head of his guards and of two divisions, had already crossed that river, as well as the Bavarians and Saxons. The first corps was at Stettin, the third marched in that direction; and the fourth, having arrived at Glogau, replaced the Westphalians, who proceeded towards Warsaw.

The composition of our army was curious and imposing. Were I to enumerate the different troops, it would remind my reader of the description of Homer, when he speaks of the various nations who marched to the conquest of Troy. In the month April the grand army consisted of eight corps of infantry, each of them containing at least three divisions (the first had five divisions) and one body of cavalry. To these were joined the imperial guards, composed of about fifty thousand men; and three great corps of cavalry under the name of the reserve. The total of our forces may have amounted to three hundred thousand infantry and sixty thousand cavalry. More than a thousand pieces of cannon, distributed amongst the different corps, constituted our artillery.

The Prince of Eckmuhl (Davoust) had long commanded the five divisions which constituted the first corps of the army. The second was intrusted to the duke of Reggio (Oudinot). The third to the duke of

---

3   Treaty of alliance (24th Feb. 1812) between his majesty the emperor and king, and his majesty the king of Prussia.

Elchingen (Ney). The fourth, known by the name of the *army of Italy,* and which contained the royal guards, was commanded by the prince viceroy (Eugene Beauharnois.) Prince Poniatowski, at the head of his Poles, formed the fifth corps. The Bavarians, incorporated into the sixth, were under the orders of count Gouvion St. Cyr. The Saxons were counted as the seventh corps, commanded by general Regnier. The Westphalians, marching under the orders of their king (Jerome Bonaparte) took rank in the army as the eighth corps. Only a skeleton of the ninth was formed, but it was destined for the duke of Belluno (Victor); and lastly the tenth corps, commanded by marshal the duke of Tarentum, was composed of Prussians under general Grawert, and included no French, except the division of general Grandjean.

The Russian army opposed to us, was divided into two corps, under the denomination of first and second army of the west; the one commanded by general Barclay de Tolly, and the other by prince Bagration. The number of divisions amounted to forty-seven, amongst which eight consisted of cavalry. The emperor Alexander, who, on the 26th of April, arrived at Wilna with all his staff, had been long prepared to repel our attacks. But those who had studied our system of war, strenuously advised that monarch not to hazard a battle, being well assured that Napoleon's ambition would lead him into savage countries which, during the rigour of winter, would become the grave of his armies.

Although Prussia had declared for us, prudence required that we should mistrust an alliance exacted by force. The French garrisons, in the different fortified places guarded them with the utmost care, particularly Glogau, where the fourth corps was assembled. Its vicinity to Breslau, whither the king of Prussia had retired with the remainder of his troops, naturally awakened our fears, and induced the. governor to take every precaution against a *coup de main,* which might have proved fatal to the enterprises of France.

The fourth corps, which arrived from Italy, under the denomination of *the army of observation,* seemed, from its title, to be destined alternately to advance in front of the grand army, and to observe its flanks, and lastly, to rejoin it when great events required its assistance. Having had the, honour to belong to this corps, I shall more particularly describe its exploits during this memorable campaign. Its operations, when separated, from the grand army, were more interesting than. those of any other corps, and it was generally united to the main body when circumstances induced Napoleon to concentrate his forces.

The viceroy (Eugene Beauharnois) before he was appointed to the fourth corps, which had in the interim been under the orders of the duke of Abrantes (Junot) was called to Paris, where his frequent conferences with the emperor led to the belief that he was destined to higher functions than those which attached to the command of one corps of the army. The rumour had long been spread that Napoleon, desirous of terminating in person the Spanish war, had announced in council that he intended to confide the government of the empire to a young prince, if circumstances should oblige him to absent himself from the capital. But these brilliant hopes, which since the repudiation of his mother seemed to have no foundation, were soon destroyed. The viceroy, having received his instructions seven or eight days after his arrival in Paris, took the road to Poland, and arrived at Glogau on the 12th of May.

While he remained at Glogau, he reviewed the troops which had been placed under his orders, and was particularly pleased with the fine appearance of the fifteenth division, consisting solely of Italians, and amounting to thirteen thousand men. The soldiers who composed it were so excellently disciplined that general Pino, though first captain of the royal guards, deemed it an honor to command them.

The fourth corps was to assemble at Plock. The Bavarian army was there already; and the prince viceroy arrived in this town by way of Posen, a few days before his army. He employed this time in reconnoitering the banks of the Narew, and in uniting the lines of defence formed by this river, with those of the lakes which extend from Angerburg to Joannisburg. His highness particularly examined the fortress of Modlin, whither the king of Westphalia had also proceeded. The conference between these princes appeared to indicate that the banks of the Bug and of the Narew would be the theatre of war. But a few days afterwards, all eyes were directed towards the emperor who had arrived at Thorn. The viceroy went to pay his respects to him, and on his return made the necessary dispositions to effect a movement on the fourth of June.

On that day our corps marched for Soldau, which it reached on the 6th. The troops were allowed a halt of two days, which were employed in constructing ovens for the use of the army. We then marched to Villemberg, where we likewise remained two days; and three days afterwards we arrived at Rastembourg, a neat little town surrounded by lakes. It afforded a valuable supply of provisions to the army, being the largest and most populous town we had passed through since our departure from Glogau. From Rastembourg we marched to Lotzen, and afterwards to Oletzko, the last town in East Prussia.

Two leagues further on we entered Poland, and soon perceived the striking difference between these two countries. In the one the houses are clean and well built; in the other, they are dirty and of a clumsy construction. The inhabitants of the former are civil and hospitable; those of the latter consisted chiefly of filthy and disgusting Jews. Many of the petty seigneurs were too indigent to maintain the proper splendour of their rank: but the higher orders of the nobility are brave, magnificent, and generous. Unsullied honour and ardent patriotism will ever constitute them true heroes. The peasantry are few in number, and this defect in the population, joined to the barrenness of the soil, accounts for the uncultivated state of the country. The sandy plains of Poland, planted only with bad rye, seemed doomed to lasting sterility.

We arrived at Kalwary, a considerable town filled with Jews. At Marienpol we found a similar population. Tired of beholding the numbers and the disgusting appearance of these people, we used to say that Poland was but another Judea, in which a Polonese was rarely to be seen.

During this march, Napoleon left Thorn, and visited the fortress of Dantzic, which his thirst for dominion made him regard as one of the most important in his empire. Thence he went to Osterode, and passed rapidly through the towns of Leipstadt and Kreutzbourg, in the neighborhood of Heilsberg, Eylau and Friedland, which had been the theatre of his greatest military exploits. On his arrival at Koningsberg, he made every preparation for his great enterprise. He reviewed numerous divisions, visited the fortress of Pillau, and a few days afterwards marching with the centre of his army, traversed the Prégel as far as Gumbinnen.

Napoleon hoped to intimidate Russia by his preparations, and to compel her to submit to his dictates, while he disregarded every thing which could possibly lead to a friendly understanding with Russia, or to the maintenance of peace. Russia, with an excess of moderation, seldom to be met with in great powers, consented that France should retain a garrison in Dantzic; but she required, and with justice, the evacuation of Prussia, that a country unoccupied by the troops of either power might be left between these two great empires. These wise and moderate conditions were called by Napoleon, *arrogant and altogether extraordinary demands;* [4] and on the formal refusal of Russia to listen to the embassy of count Lauriston without these preliminaries, Napoleon was absolutely enraged, and exclaimed, in a tone of phrenzy which the slightest contradiction always excited, 'The vanquished assume the tone of conquerors. *A fatality involves them; let their destinies be fulfilled.*' Leaving Gumbinnen that very instant, he went to Wilkowiski, 22d of June, 1812, and issued the following proclamation in his general orders:

Soldiers,

The second Polish war is begun. The first terminated at Friedland and at Tilsit. At Tilsit, Russia vowed an eternal alliance with France, and war with England. She now breaks her vows, and refuses to give any ex-

---

4 Second bulletin of the grand army.

planation of her strange conduct until the French eagles have repassed the Rhine and left our allies at her mercy.

Russia is hurried away by a fatality! Her destinies will be fulfilled. Does she think us degenerated? Are we no more the soldiers who fought at Austerlitz? She places us between dishonour and war. Our choice cannot be difficult. Let us then march forward. Let us cross the Niemen, and carry the war into her country. This second Polish war will be as glorious for the French arms as the first has been; but the peace we shall conclude will carry with it its own guarantee, and will terminate the fatal influence which Russia, for fifty years past, has exercised in Europe.

This proclamation reached us at Kalwary. Unbecoming real greatness, it was only remarkable for its excessive boasting, and for the prophetic tone of its contents: yet, although it was but a monotonous repetition of the same ideas so often expressed, it excited the ardour of our soldiers, always ready to listen to anything flattering to their courage. Elated with the idea of treading on Russian ground, they proudly contemplated the commencement of the second Polish war, and were eager to leave behind them a river at which they had closed their victorious career, at the termination of the first war. The word Niemen inflamed their imagination. They burned to pass it: and this desire was the more natural as independent of the spirit of conquest the miserable state of Poland every day augmented our sufferings and privations. To silence our complaints, the territory of Russia was always held out to us as the promised land.

The army opposed to ours, was composed of six corps. The first, twenty thousand strong, and commanded by the prince of Wittgenstein, occupied Rossiena and Keïdanouï. The second corps, consisting likewise of twenty thousand men under the orders of general Bagawout, guarded Kowno. The third, consisting of twenty-four thousand men, under general Schomoaloff, was posted at New-Troki. The fourth corps, commanded by general Tutschkoff, was stationed between New-Troki and Lida. These four divisions together with the, guards, formed what the Russians called, the *First Army of the West*. The second army comprised the fifth corps, amounting to forty thousand men, and the sixth corps, called that of Doctorow, of eighteen thousand men. This second army, commanded by Prince Bagration, was encamped at Grodno, Lida, and throughout Wolhynia. General Markoff organized in this province, the ninth and fifteenth divisions, which were to form the seventh corps, and which acted in the sequel, under the orders of general Tormazow, against the duchy of Warsaw.

Such was the position of the Russians beyond the Niemen, when the king of Naples (Murat) who commanded our cavalry established his headquarters within two leagues on this side of the river, (23d June). He had with him the two corps of cavalry, commanded by generals Nansouty and Montbrun, each composed of three divisions. The first corps took post at the opening of the great forest of Pilwisky. The second corps and the guards marched in the rear. The third, fourth, and sixth corps, advanced by Marienpol, and marched at a day's distance from each other. The king of Westphalia, with the fifth, seventh, and eighth corps, directed his march to Grodno, up the Narew, and facing the army of prince Bagration.

The pontoons under the orders of general Eblé, arrived the same day at the Niemen. Napoleon, disguised as a private Polish soldier, and in company with the general of the engineers Haxo, then visited the line of the Niemen, and from the heights which command Kowno, discovered the most advantageous point. About eight o'clock at night, the army was put in motion. Three light companies of the division of Morand (first division of the first corps) passed the Niemen, and protected the construction of three bridges, which were thrown across the river.

At day-break, that is to say, about one o'clock in the morning, we were close to Kowno. General Pajol having pushed forward the advanced guard, occupied the town with one battalion and drove before him the enemy's cavalry, which retired as we advanced. On the 24th and 25th, the army continued to cross the river at the three bridges. In the meantime, Napoleon having arrived at Kowno, caused another bridge to be thrown across the Wilia, near that town; while the king of Naples (Murat) marched towards Zismori, and the marshals, prince of Eckmuhl (Davoust) and duke of Elchingen (Ney) went the one to Roumchichki, and the other to Kormelov.

The following day (27th June) our light cavalry was within ten leagues of Wilna. The day after, about two o'clock in the morning, the king of Naples continued his march, supported by the division of cavalry of general Bruyères, and by the first corps. The Russians fell back on all sides behind the Wilia, after burning the bridge and their magazines. A deputation consisting of the principal inhabitants of Wilna, now delivered to Napoleon the keys of the town. He entered about noon, and proceeded immediately to the advanced posts of general Bruyères, to ascertain the direction in which the enemy had retreated. They were pursued on the left of the Wilia, when Octave de Segur, captain of hussars, was wounded and taken prisoner in a charge of cavalry. This distinguished officer was the first in this campaign, who fell into the hands of the Russians.

The point which Napoleon had chosen to pass the Niemen was difficult to defend, Kowno being commanded by a high mountain on our side, which completely overhung the town. But if this position had been even less advantageous to us, it was not the intention of the Russians to oppose our first efforts. It is said that the emperor Alexander had made every preparation to dispute the passage of the Niemen but that at the moment at which the attack was to have commenced, general Barclay de Tolly, throwing himself at the feet of his master, entreated him not to combat a formidable army which nothing could resist; adding that Napoleon should be suffered to pass like a torrent, keeping their forces unbroken in reserve, to be employed against him, when famine and the inclemency of the season had thinned his ranks. I will not vouch for the authenticity of this anecdote: but it will not be thought improbable when it is recollected that the emperor Alexander, after having remained six weeks at Wilna, inspecting his armies and reconnoitering the principal points which were capable of defence, suddenly abandoned this line without fighting, and ordered a retreat across the Dwina and the Nieper.

On our arrival at Wilna we read the proclamation which the emperor of Russia had issued when he learned that the French troops had passed the Niemen. It paints so truly the magnanimity and the equity of Alexander, that on comparing it with the proclamation of Napoleon published at Wilkowiski, and breathing a spirit of unbounded arrogance and injustice the reader may obtain a perfect knowledge of the characters of these two conquerors, on whom the eyes of the world were then fixed. It was thus worded:

Wilna, the 25th of June, 1812.

We had long observed, on the part of the emperor of the French, the most hostile proceedings towards Russia; but we had always hoped to avert them by conciliatory and pacific measures. At length, experiencing a continued renewal of direct and evident aggression, notwithstanding our earnest desire to maintain tranquillity, we were compelled to complete and to assemble our armies. But even then we flattered ourselves that a reconciliation might be produced while we remained on the frontiers of our empire, and, without violating one principle of peace, were prepared only to act in our own defence. All these conciliatory and pacific measures could not preserve the tranquillity which we desired. The emperor of the French, by suddenly attacking our army at Kowno, has been the first to declare war. As nothing, therefore, could inspire him with those friendly sentiments which possessed our bosoms, we have no choice but to oppose our forces to those of the enemy, invoking the aid of the Almighty, the witness and the defender of the truth. It is unnecessary for me to recall to the minds of the generals, the officers, or the soldiers, their duty and their bravery. The blood of the valiant Sclavonians flows in their veins. Warriors! you defend your religion, your country, and your liberty! I am with you. God is against the aggressor.

(Signed)   ALEXANDER.

While the whole of our army was concentrated near Wilna, the second Russian corps, under general Bagawout, effected its retreat across the Dwina. Prince Wittgenstein likewise was retreating to Wilkomer, since the duke of Reggio (Oudinot) by marching on Janow and Chatoui had forced him to abandon Samogitia. On the 28th they met near Develtovo. A smart cannonade commenced; but prince Wittgenstein being driven from his positions and pursued by our troops as far as the Dwina, passed the bridge thrown over this river with so much precipitation, that he had not time to burn it.

The Russians being repulsed beyond the river, the fifth, seventh, and eighth corps, under the orders of prince Poniatowski, and the king of Westphalia (Jerome Bonaparte) took possession of Grodno, and closely pressed the second army of the west, under prince Bagration. Intrenched, however, in a strong position, he resisted all their attacks; and by a happy employment of his numerous corps of cossacks, commanded by the Hetman Platoff, he would, no doubt have long defended the provinces confided to him, if, after the evacuation of Wilna, he had not been ordered to join general Barclay de Tolly. Prince Eckmuhl (Davoust) was instantly detached from our centre to occupy the road to Minsk, and prevent their junction.

On the 29th of June, the fourth corps, which had hitherto remained in observation behind the Niemen came in sight of this long desired river. On arriving at Pilony, the place appointed for our passage, we found the viceroy, the duke of Abrantes (Junot) and all the staff, who, notwithstanding the rainy weather were busy in constructing a bridge. The artillery of the royal guards was posted on an eminence commanding the opposite shore. This was a wise, but useless precaution; for, on reconnoitering beyond the Niemen we learned that every thing was perfectly tranquil on that side.

We now dismissed all apprehension with regard to the success of our passage, for an aid-de-camp of the viceroy, sent with a message to Napoleon, had informed us, that our troops, after having passed the defile from Kowno to Roumchichki, without opposition, were arrived at Zismori; that even the positions between Rouikontoui and Wilna had been but slightly defended by the Russians; and that having, moreover, constructed no redoubts on the heights, within two leagues of this town, the emperor had entered it on the 28th instant, preceded by the Polish uhlans of the eighth regiment, commanded by prince Radzivil. The report of this officer mentioned, that the suburbs had suffered a little from the rapacity of our soldiers, but order having been speedily re-established, every thing returned to its natural course. He likewise added, that this great and populous town afforded ample supplies for the army, and was favorably disposed towards the views of Napoleon.

The following day, the thirteenth and fourteenth divisions, under generals Delzons and Broussier, quietly effected their passage; and the day after (1st July) the royal guards, followed by the division of Pino, effected theirs. Thus all the Italian troops passed the Niemen in one body, in presence of their viceroy. They expressed their sense of this honour by spontaneous acclamations; and the prince must, in his turn, have felt great satisfaction at beholding the soldiers whom he had raised, marching undismayed into an enemy's country, and at a distance of six hundred leagues from their native soil, preserving the same discipline and the same fine appearance, as if manoeuvring in front of his palace.

Scarcely had we reached the opposite shore, when we seemed to breathe a new air. However, the roads were dreadfully bad, the forests gloomy and the villages completely deserted; but the imagination, inflamed by a spirit of conquest, was enchanted with every thing that it saw, and cherished illusions which were but too soon destroyed.

In effect, our short stay at Pilony, while the rain beat tempestuously, was marked by such extraordinary disasters, that any man, without being superstitious, would have regarded them as the presage of our future misfortunes. In this wretched village, the viceroy himself had no house to shelter him; we were heaped upon one another under some wretched sheds, or exposed to all the inclemencies of the weather. An extreme scarcity made us anticipate the horrors of famine. The rain fell in torrents, and overwhelmed both men and horses. The first escaped, but the badness of the roads completed the destruction of the latter. They were seen dropping by hundreds in the evirons of Pilony. The road was covered with dead horses, overturned waggons and scattered baggage. It was in the month of July, that we suffered thus from cold, and rain, and hunger. So many calamities excited in us sad foreboding of the future, and every one began to dread the event of an enterprise the commencement of which was so disastrous; but the sun re-appeared on the horizon, the clouds dispersed, our fears were scattered with them, and from that moment we thought that the fine season would last forever.

After a march of two hours through marshy ground, we arrived at the town of Kroni (1st July) in which the *chateau* and all the houses are built of wood. I make this observation here, because most of the villages in Russia are thus constructed. Whenever I find them otherwise I shall remark it. We found some brandy in Kroni, which the soldiers seized with great avidity. This place not being inhabited by any Jews, the houses were all deserted, which convinced us that the enemy, in order to ruin the country through which we were to pass, and deprive us of all means of subsistence, had carried along with them the inhabitants and the cattle.

The next day (2d July) we received orders to march to Zismori, to regain the great road which the emperor had taken. Arrived in this large town, we found only some Jews, still overwhelmed with terror at the horrible tumult which the passage of our troops had occasioned. The first orders were to halt here, but on the arrival of the viceroy, the staff continued their route to Melangani, leaving the division of Pino at Zismori, and those of generals Delzons and, Broussier in the environs of Strasounoui.

The following day (3d July) we proceeded to Ricontouï, a miserable village, with a little *chateau* built of wood on the left, and on the right, a church erected on an eminence. The prince did not stop here, but took up his quarters at a *chateau* placed near the branching off of the cross-road leading to New-Troki.

Our corps had pleased itself with the hope, that it was destined for Wilna. Sadly was it disappointed, when on the morrow (July 4th) our advanced-guard took a direction towards New-Troki. Every one complained of the change in our route. They said that a fatality attached to our corps; that harrassed with fatigue, we were suddenly and unnecessarily prevented from entering a town where we had expected to repose ourselves after our long and tedious march. Our commanders endeavored to console us for this disappointment, by assuring us that we should certainly visit Witepsk and Smolensko, two towns which would soon make us forget Wilna.

After four tedious hours, during which we had traversed nothing but forests and miry foot-paths, we arrived near New-Troki, situated on an eminence and surrounded by lakes. This delightful place formed a striking contrast with the road we had just quitted, and every one admired its fine situation and the charming effect which was produced by a large convent on the summit of a mountain that overlooked the town. Others, were struck with the wild appearance of the impenetrable forests and the clearness of the waters, which are said never to freeze. They who had acquired any taste for the beauties of nature, were never tired of admiring this romantic spot. In the middle of the lake was an old ruined castle, whose darkened walls projected on one side over the surface of the water, and on the other seemed to touch the gilded horizon.

Troki appeared at first a delightful spot, but the illusion ceased the moment we entered it. We had scarcely approached the first houses, when a crowd of Jews, followed by women, children, and old men with their beards reaching to their girdles, threw themselves at our feet, and implored us to deliver them from the rapacity of the soldiers, who plundered and destroyed every thing which fell into their power. We could grant them nothing but our pity. The town in which we were quartered had no magazines, and our soldiers, having been long deprived of their rations, subsisted now only on pillage. This caused the greatest confusion. And the fatal want of discipline which it produced was the more pernicious, as it is an infallible sign of the approaching ruin of an army.

The houses of the Russians at Troki, had been all deprived of their furniture by the inhabitants, who had carried every thing away with them in their flight; and the houses of the Jews, which were disgustingly dirty, had been pillaged by the soldiers. Thus an abode which we had expected to find so agreeable, was, in the highest degree, unpleasant and uncomfortable. We had not even straw to sleep upon; and the forage for the horses was procured from a distance of nearly four leagues.

As it was probable that we should remain some days at Troki, the emperor having halted at Wilna, the viceroy went to him, and they had some long conferences together. Several officers also obtained leave to go there, and had an opportunity of witnessing the artifices to which Napoleon resorted to ensure his conquest. He excited the enthusiasm of the people by the most magnificent promises, and obtained from them the greatest sacrifices. The nobles also exerted themselves to the utmost of their power in promoting the views of the conqueror. By his means, they hoped to ensure the independence of Poland; and to restore to their country the glory which she had possessed in the times of the Jagellons, the Cassimirs, and the Sobieskies.

The sight of the Polish standards, floating on the walls of the ancient capital of the dukes of Lithuania, excited the enthusiasm of all the inhabitants, and recalled the most pleasing and brilliant recollections to the minds of those who cherished the memory of the ancient glory of their beloved country. Nothing, however, more forcibly reminded them of their former greatness, than to meet again on the borders of the Wilia, those warriors who had devoted the time of their exile to immortalize the Polish name on the banks of the Nile, the Tiber, the Tagus, and the Danube. The air was rent with joyful acclamations. Crowds every where followed their steps. All wished to see them, to engrave on their hearts the image of their brave compatriots; and all glowed with the noble desire of marching under the same banners.

Napoleon, having given audience to the whole body of the university, questioned the principal on the different branches of science which were taught in that celebrated institution. He afterwards reorganized the civil administration of the town, which had been completely subverted by the departure of the chief functionaries, and by the loss of all the books and registers that belonged to the archives of the place. After the example of France he divided the invaded provinces into different districts, nominating inspectors, receivers, commissaries of police, and above all, intendants to facilitate the payment of his numberless requisitions. But he principally endeavored to stimulate the Lithuanians to make levies en masse, for the formation of new corps. He offered arms to all the peasants who were inclined to revolt against their masters; and strove, as at the commencement of our revolution, to cause a civil war between the people and the nobility.

These projects certainly caused some sensation in the city where the emperor commanded; but, in the towns and the country, nothing was produced favourable to the projected revolution. Napoleon, however, continued to invite the Lithuanians to assist him; and to impose on them, he endeavoured to astonish the vulgar. He spoke with equal fluency, and at the same audience of the public spectacles, and of religion, of war, and of the arts. He was seen on horseback at all hours of the day; and after having superintended the erection of some new bridge or fortification, he immediately entered his cabinet, and showed himself perfectly master of the most complicated scheme of politics or finance; and often he affected to assist at a ball or a concert, on the eve of the most important battle.

The commission which was formed for the general administration of all Lithuania, consisted, at first, of only five members: but Napoleon added to their number in proportion as his partisans increased. The day on which that commission was instituted, three proclamations were instituted. The first which was addressed to the people, announced the installation of the provisional government of Lithuania, and enforced the gratitude which was due to him who had delivered Poland from the grasp of its oppressors. The next exhorted the clergy to second the zeal of the nation, and to obtain, by their fervent prayers, the favour of Almighty God. The third, the object of which was to recall the Lithuanians who were in the service of Russia, contained the following words:

Polanders,
    You are under Russian banners. It was permitted you to serve that power while you had no longer a country of your own. But all is now changed. Poland is newly created. You must combat for her complete re-establishment, and compel the Russians to acknowledge those rights of which you had been despoiled by injustice and usurpation. The general confederation of Poland and Lithuania, recalls every Polander from the Russian service. Generals of Poland, officers and soldiers listen to the voice of your country. Abandon the standards of your oppressors. Hasten and range yourselves under the eagle of the Jagellons, the Casimirs

and the Sobieskies! Your country requires it of you. Honour and religion equally command it.[5]

The committee of the government established at Wilna, which lent itself to the views of Napoleon, merely to lighten those calamities, which the horrors of the war had brought on the people, was indefatigably zealous in every thing which could promote the interest of the administration. The department of Wilna was already formed, and the conquered territory was divided into eleven sub-districts. That organization, apparently advantageous, produced, however, no kind of benefit. The country was pillaged, the villages deserted, and all the peasants fled into the woods. We saw only a few miserable Jews, covered with rags, who from a spirit of avarice, chose rather to expose themselves to the insults of our soldiers, than abandon their infectious habitations. In short, to give some faint idea of the disorder which prevailed in the midst of this pretended organization, I shall only mention, that when the sub-prefect of New-Troki came from Wilna, to take possession of his government, he was stopped by our troops, and plundered of every thing. Even his own escort robbed him of his provisions and clothes; and at length he arrived on foot, in a condition so wretched, that every one regarded as a spy the man who was destined to be our first administrator.

Thus the brilliant hopes with which the Polanders had at first flattered themselves, began to fade, when it was perceived, that our chief was actuated solely by the puerile ambition of placing a new crown on his head; and, that while he was unable to consolidate any thing he talked incessantly of conquering immense provinces, and of subjecting to the same laws and the same sceptre, countries which differed so widely in their customs and their climates. Blind to the want of discipline which prevailed in his army, he occasioned the ruin of the rich, and the despair of the poor; and reduced the Lithuanians to consider those as their greatest aggressors, who had promised to become their deliverers. He thus exposed us to the hatred of the people; and made us the first and the saddest victims of his tyranny.

While this happened at Wilna, Warsaw might have exhibited the sublimest spectacle, if she had not been under the baneful influence of a man who trifled with the fate of nations; and whose plans, never the offspring of mature reflection, were always frustrated, when their execution required calmness and prudence. The unhappy Polanders, relying on his flattering promises, assembled in their capital (June 28), and formed a diet. The committee digested an eloquent report, in which the orator stated the importance of the work which had been entrusted to their

5   See Lithuanian Courier, July 7, 1812.

care. He reminded his auditors, in an energetic manner, that Poland, placed in the centre of Europe, had formerly been a distinguished empire, mistress of a country extensive and fertile, and equally celebrated for her valour and her refinements; that for many centuries, she had with unwearied courage, repulsed from her borders, those barbarous tribes who attempted in vain to subjugate the civilized world; that the honour of filling their throne had ever been an object of universal desire; and that if some little divisions had arisen among themselves, they had only obscured for a short time their own horizon, without carrying the tempest abroad. He enumerated at length all that their beloved country had suffered from the ambition of Russia, who had outraged a powerful nation by frequent dismemberments. He dwelt particularly on the last period when Poland was annihilated by a triple partition, and Warsaw heard, amidst the shouts of a ferocious conqueror, the lamentable cries of the inhabitants of Praga, given, without mercy, to the sword and to the flames. He showed that Russia, continually trampling upon Poland, gradually approached nearer to Germany, and already aspired at her conquest; and, finally, he demonstrated that such a fatal superiority of power, must ultimately destroy the rights of every nation, and subject the whole world to its empire.

After this rapid exposition of facts, the speaker made a less animated, but not a less judicious, enumeration of the weighty reasons which ought to unite Poland to France.

Europe requires some rest after twenty-five years of violent agitation. Her system will remain incomplete, nor will the reward of her struggles and her blood be secure as long as the regions of the north are permitted to vomit forth those hordes, to the true character of which it becomes us to be no longer blind.

They are no more those whom necessity alone forced to quit their savage abodes, and to seek in other lands the comforts which their own inhospitable climate denied. A blind instinct once served the instead of the arts which civilize or defend other countries. But now the refinements of polished nations are united to the barbarism of former times. The Russian has supplicated from the European, and he has now learned from him all the arts of attack and defence and he has made them the instruments of desolation and destruction. He is in some respects the equal of the European, and he may soon become his master. In Russia, superstitious and submissive slaves unhesitatingly obey the orders of a government to whom every outrage is familiar. For a century past they have been busily employed in undermining all those banks which have restrained a torrent that threatens destruction to the world. How often have they overflowed them, urged either by their own ambition, or invited by imprudent princes to whom they brought slavery instead of assistance. Russia, in the course of fifty years, has twenty times overwhelmed the south of Europe with her arms. The empire of Constantinople is almost subverted, and her crescent shorn of half its splendour.

Animated by his subject he thus continued:

Henceforth the children of the Piasts and the Jagellons will be proud to bear a name which was the glory of their ancestors; a name at which they grew pale, whom fraud and injustice have, for a short time, made our masters. Let us not doubt that this country once so rich in heroes, will recover all her wonted glory. She will produce new Sigismonds, and new Sobieskies. She will shine with more brilliant and purer lustre; and surrounding nations, compelled to do us justice, will acknowledge that nothing was wanting in Poland for the growth of every virtue, but the cultivation of the soil by the free and unfettered hands of her own children.

Then addressing the venerable old man[6], who, from his services and his virtues, presided at the assembly, he concluded with the following beautiful apostrophe:

Nestor of the Polish patriots, when you left them, you carried with you the gods, which had escaped the overthrow of your country. They return to it to-day, to receive eternal adoration; and to dwell in it as in a temple, around which the whole nation, instructed by their misfortunes, and awakened to vigilance by the surprises from which they have suffered, will not cease to maintain a constant guard; which they will enrich with every virtue that has adorned the Polish character, and which they pledge themselves to defend at the hazard of their lives.

After this harangue the orator submitted another report to the diet, in which he explained the motives that had induced the committee to draw up the act of confederation; declaring that it was the wish of the nation to offer the crown to the king of Saxony; who, too wise and too virtuous to object, would condescend they hoped, to accept it, and unite with Divine Providence in restoring the arms of Lithuania to their escutcheon, and in spreading through the fertile countries of Wolhynia, and the extensive plains of Podolia and the Ukraine, the cheering sounds of, *Long live Poland! Long live our Country!*

The committee then produced the act of confederation, the chief articles of which consisted, in uniting every part of ancient Poland, in the formation of the new kingdom : in recalling the Polanders from the Russian service; and lastly in sending a deputation to the emperor Napoleon,

---

6   Prince Czartoryski, grand marshal at the diet.

soliciting him to extend his powerful protection over the cradle of Polish liberty.

The deputation was admitted to Napoleon the night before his departure from Wilna. They submitted to him the act of confederation, of which we have just spoken. The conqueror gave them evasive promises. Perhaps he was offended that the noble Polish nation had not thrown itself at his feet, to obtain the honour of becoming a part of the great empire. The liberty which they demanded, appeared to disquiet and to surprise him. He feared that the assembly which he had convoked, and which seemed now so willing to second his views, might, hereafter prove less submissive to his wishes. It is the peculiar character of tyrants, to be suspicious even when they are doing good; to take umbrage, at the objects of their own protection; and to be alarmed at the independence of others even if it has been their own work. Napoleon, therefore, made no decisive promises, but exacted, as preliminaries, enormous sacrifices, and a devotion to his interest, with which the Polanders could not comply, without putting to the hazard their hopes of future happiness. He demanded that the provinces subjected to Russia, should declare themselves against her, even before his arrival, and that Gallicia should form no part of the confederation, because he had guaranteed to Austria the integrity of her states.

If all these extensive projects had been conceived by a prudent head, more anxious for the welfare of mankind, than the gratification of its own ambition, there is no doubt that, although gigantic, they might have been realized. Napoleon had attained so high a degree of power, that it was not necessary for him to resort to war to accomplish any purpose. By a policy prudent, skilful, and, above all, conciliatory, he might have made more lasting, and even more extensive conquests, than he had gained by force of arms. Posterity will perceive that he was dazzled by too much prosperity, and employed incalculable means to accomplish his own downfall, while he might have succeeded to the utmost of his wishes, without hazarding or compromising any thing. An enemy to whatever required patience and reflection, he knew nothing but force; and heaven permitted him to be crushed by that very power, which, till then, had been his only law.

The brave Polanders, despairing for their country, considered all their plans as chimerical, when they perceived that Napoleon, more ambitious and less virtuous than Charles XII, aspired at the Polish crown, and only promised them his assistance, that he might profit by their resentment against Russia. Thus, that fortunate conqueror, restless, even on the most splendid throne of Europe, was led astray by the excess of his conquests, and strangely imagined that he could not cement his fortune better than by subverting the whole world, and renewing in the north the horrible wars of the middle age, when nations, exasperated against each other, delivered themselves up to every excess of barbarity.

Book II

Witepsk

Whilst Napoleon remained at Wilna, Marshal Davoust proceeded to Minsk, in pursuit of prince Bagration, who endeavored to effect a junction with the army of Barclay de Tolly. By that manoeuvre we prevented the Russian prince from marching on the Dwina, and forced him to proceed towards Mohilow on the Nieper, whither he was pursued by the first corps, and the cavalry of general Grouchy. All our other corps, which formed the centre, directed their course towards Dinabourg. With regard to the fourth corps, the two French divisions, and the royal guards, took the road of Paradomin in their march to Ochmiana; whilst the viceroy, the division of Pino, and all the cavalry, marched to Rudniki.

This latter movement was rendered necessary in consequence of information which we had received, that the Hetman Platoff, at the head of four thousand cossacks, having been separated from the corps of Bagration, was expected on the road of Lida, where he would endeavour to effect a junction with the Russian army, which had evacuated Wilna. At this news the viceroy put himself in motion, but the road to Rudniki was so bad, that the cavalry of the royal guard was obliged to pursue a different route. It is not possible to form an idea of the difficulties which presented themselves on that road, which was entirely formed of the trunks of fir-trees, placed on the marshy ground. The horses in passing over these pieces of wood frequently trod between them, and, falling in this situation, inevitably broke their legs. If, to avoid these difficulties, we turned to the right or left, we were in danger of sinking into morasses from which there was no possibility of escape.

The staff, after having lost some horses belonging to our escort, at last succeeded in extricating itself from this dangerous passage, and arrived at Rudniki in the middle of the night. The following morning (July 8th) we marched towards Jachounoui, where we regained the great road. Thence we proceeded to Mal-Solechniki. The prince, however, would not stop there but pursued his route to Bol-Solechniki, where he intended to remain during the night, and hoped to receive some tidings of the cossacks, whom he had orders to pursue. The following day we continued our march, and arrived at a castle not far distant from Soubotniki.

The viceroy was obliged to halt here, for the bad roads having impeded the march of the thirteenth and fourteenth divisions, as well as the

Italian corps, we had nothing but the light cavalry with us. The order which had been sent for hastening their progress, was, by some mistake, returned to the chief of the staff, so that these troops having received no instructions, had retained their position, while we believed that they were following us. At length, seeing that they did not arrive, some intelligent officers were sent out in all directions, who succeeded, after a long search, in extricating the division of Pino from the marshes of Rudniki, and conducting the guard towards Ochmiana. The viceroy in the mean time, after having searched in vain for the cossacks, returned and marched towards Jachounoui, where he joined the thirteenth and fourteenth divisions. On the following day (July 12th), they all took the road towards Smorghoni, where they effected a junction with the rest of the troops who composed the fourth corps.

The town of Smorghoni is large and populous, yet all the houses, with the exception of two or three, are built of wood. A little river, with a bridge thrown over it, divides the castle from the town. The inhabitants consist chiefly of Jews, who carry on considerable commerce. For this reason, though the town contained little that was remarkable, the halt which we made in it was delightful to the whole army, for it enabled us to procure a supply of bread and beer.

During the day that we reposed at Smorghoni, we erected a bridge over the Narotsch, that we might proceed in a direct line to Vileïka. But the work was hardly finished when the orders were changed, and the majority of the troops marched to Zachkevitschi, where they remained that night.

The road from Zachkevitschi, to Vileïka is very sandy, and lies through a thick forest. A little before we arrived here, we crossed the Wilia over a floating bridge. The river at this place is neither very broad nor deep, but its banks are extremely steep, particularly the one opposite Vileïka. On entering the town, general Colbert, who commanded the advanced-guard, took some magazines which had been abandoned; and as a short time only had elapsed since the enemy had quitted that position, the viceroy redoubled his vigilance, for fear of a surprise, and selected with the utmost care, an advantageous situation for his troops to encamp.

Whilst we marched towards Vileïka, the king of Naples (Murat), assisted by the second and third corps, drove the first western army from one position to another behind the Dwina, and at last forced them to retire into the intrenched camp of Drissa. On our right, prince Eckmuhl (Davoust) continued the pursuit of prince Bagration, and arrived without fighting as far as Borisow, on the Berezina. On our left the marshal duke of Tarentum likewise obtained important advantages and took entire possession of Samogitia.

The conduct of the enemy in thus continually flying before us was accounted for in different ways. Some thought it was the effect of weakness, others believed it to be the result of a well-digested plan. 'What is become of those Russians,' asked the former, 'who, for more than fifty years, have been the terror of Europe, and the conquerors of Asia? The power of Russia seems to be merely fictitious, invented by hireling writers, and deceitful travellers. It exists only in imagination, and the phantom vanishes the moment we attack it.' They, however, whom experience had taught to wait the result of time, affirmed that it was unwise to despise an enemy whom we had not yet combatted; that his flight was calculated to diminish our force, and to deprive us of the means of recruiting it, by drawing us further from our own country. 'The Russians', added these intelligent reasoners, 'derive their most powerful succours from their climate. Why should they seek to fight us when they know that the winter will compel us to abandon all our conquests?'

At last the Russians themselves explained the motives of their retreat, by the following proclamation distributed on the borders of the Dwina:

French Soldiers!

You are forced to march to a new war. You are told that it is because the Russians do not render justice to your valour. No, comrades, they truly appreciate it. You will see it on the day of battle. Consider that if it be necessary, army will succeed to army, and that you are four hundred leagues from your resources. Do not allow yourselves to be deceived by our first movements. You know the Russians too well to suppose that they fly before you. In proper time they will accept the combat, and you will find it difficult to retreat. We advise you as fellow-soldiers to return in a body to your native country. Do not believe the perfidious suggestion that you are fighting for peace. You shed your blood to gratify the insatiable ambition of a sovereign who does not wish for peace. He might have obtained it long ago; but he sports with the lives of his brave subjects. Return to your homes, or if you wish it, seek an asylum in Russia; there you will forget the names of conscription, levies, *bans* and *arriere-bans,* and that military tyranny which does not allow you for one minute to shake off the oppressive yoke.

This proclamation contained such palpable truths, that its publication astonished every one. Some, however, regarded it as a forgery, and thought that it was written to prepare the way for that despicable answer of a French grenadier, which would certainly have become a subject of pleasantry to the army, and of contempt to foreigners, if we had not long known that an implicit obedience to his chief is the first duty of a soldier;

and that every Frenchman faithful to his banners, esteemed it a point of honour strenuously to combat all those whom his commanders should represent as the enemies of his country.

Continuing our march we arrived at Kostenevitschi, a miserable little village, where, excepting the post-house and vicarage, there were only a few wretched barns covered with thatch. The royal guard encamped round the village, but the viceroy established his head-quarters two leagues further on.

The following day (July 17), after a march of five leagues over a tolerably good road, we reached the town of Dolghinow, the inhabitants of which consisted almost entirely of Jews, a circumstance by which we were enabled to procure a few bottles of brandy. Our incessant marches, and the long period during which we had been deprived of that liquor, induce me to mention a circumstance apparently so insignificant; but, from the importance which we attached to it, the reader may judge of the extent of our wants, and the difficulty of supplying them.

We proceeded thence to Dokzice, a distance of about seven leagues. That town the inhabitants of which were likewise Jews, contained a handsome square, near which stood a church, and a wretched *chateau*, built of wood. The extremities of the town are situated on two eminences, between which runs a little marshy rivulet. On the day that we halted here we suddenly perceived a thick smoke arising behind the *chateau* in which the prince was quartered. The flames soon spread on every side, and consumed in an instant several neighboring houses; but the soldiers rendering the most timely and efficacious assistance the fire was quickly subdued, and all our apprehensions vanished.

Near Smorghoni we had left the road to Minsk and the Nieper, and had turned to the left, to approach to Dwina, and to follow the movements of the centre of the grand army, which had taken that direction. General Sebastiani, who commanded the advanced-guard, assisted by the corps of the duke of Reggio (Oudinot), repulsed the cossacks as far as Drouïa; but the enemy, which was shut up in the intrenched camp, at Drissa, having been informed that our cavalry was badly guarded, threw a bridge over the river, and detached five thousand infantry and as many cavalry, commanded by general Koulniew. An engagement soon commenced, and general Saintgeniez, being taken by surprise, was made prisoner, while the rest of the brigade did not escape without considerable loss.

As we approached Berezina, where we intended to encamp that night, the road gradually descending, brought us unawares to the river of the same name, which runs through one of the most marshy plains in Europe. We were convinced of this when we arrived at the town, the houses of which extended in a long line over an absolute morass. Beyond Berezina the road is continued over a kind of turf, on which were placed a quantity of fir branches, to give some firmness to a mere bog. A few intervals were left for the waters to drain off.

From the Berezina, as far as the Oula, the country was wet and marshy. The road from one river to the other forms a line of twenty or twenty-five leagues, passing continually through marshes and immense forests. Gloubokoé was our first station, and Kamen the second. The first of these towns is remarkable for a beautiful castle of wood; and the latter for a kind of mountain in the very centre of the place, which overlooks the plain.

At Botscheïkovo we approached the borders of the Oula (July 23d). This river is united to the Berezina by the canal of Lepel, which gives facility to the commerce of all the neighboring provinces. This canal is yet more important, as it forms a communication between the Nieper and the Dwina; and thus uniting the Baltic and the Mediterranean, it enlivens the interior of Lithuania, and enriches her with productions of the most distant climes. The banks of this river are very high and steep. On the left side beyond the bridge, appears a magnificent *chateau*, which we thought the most beautiful that we had seen since our arrival in Poland.

We could not, however, restrain our astonishment at the rapidity with which we were allowed to proceed in our march without opposition. We advanced daily without any impediment, and with almost as much security as when we traversed Bavaria, and Saxony. The tranquility in which our adversaries permitted us to continue was incomprehensible, and every one formed the most opposite and frequently the most erroneous conjectures. At Kamen, however, we learned, from several officers, who had been sent to Ouchatsch, where the emperor was, that the enemy, having quitted their trenches at Drissa, had ascended the Dwina, towards Polotsk and Witepsk, through fear of being cut off by our corps, which had taken a direction towards the latter town. The orders which they brought us, made us likewise believe that we should soon meet with considerable resistance. These conjectures were presently changed into certainty when, on reconnoitering the mouth of the Oula, and the road to Bézenkovitschi, we discovered that the cossacks hovered on our flanks. The viceroy immediately ordered the advanced-guard and the light cavalry, to Bézenkovitschi, where the Russians were assembled in much force, under general Osterman (July 23d).

The prince soon afterwards mounted his horses accompanied by his aids-de-camp, and followed the movements of the advanced-guard. When he arrived at Bézenkovitschi, the enemy retreated, and crossed the Dwina with his cavalry, and some pieces of artillery. While we were in that town, the Russian sharp-shooters, who were concealed in the houses of the village, on the opposite side of the river, kept up an incessant fire upon us. Colonel la Croix who was passing down the principal street leading to the river, received a shot which broke his thigh. This accident produced a painful sensation through the whole army. Every one pitied this worthy officer, and lamented that we were deprived of his valuable services, by a fatality which frequently takes from the most deserving all power to distinguish themselves. After having reconnoitered the position of the enemy the viceroy returned, for the night, to the castle of Botscheïkovo. In the evening he had a long conference with general Dessoles, the chief of his staff, which made us presume that we should march in the night; but the order was not given till the following morning.

(July 24th.) After five hours' march, and crossing a small river, called Svetscha, our troops arrived at Bézenkovitschi. This little town was already filled with troops, particularly with the two divisions of cavalry under generals Bruyères and Saint Germain, who had come by the way of Oula. This great mass of troops marching towards Witepsk, terrified not the enemy, who was separated from us by the Dwina. His cavalry proudly manoeuvred and fired on our soldiers when, they approached to seize the ferry-boat, which had been carried to the opposite shore.

The viceroy, however, having resolved to cross the Dwina at this point, caused a battery of two pieces of cannon to be erected, to protect the sappers who had been ordered to construct a bridge and the marines of the royal guard, who, plunging into the water, attempted to reach the boat. These guns, and a few sharp-shooters placed on the shore, intimidated the Russians so much, that they quitted the houses in which they had concealed themselves and allowed us quietly to take back the boat, and to complete the bridge which the engineers were erecting.

In the meantime a division of Bavarian cavalry, under general Preysing, having discovered a ford about two hundred paces below the bridge, effected their passage. Scarcely had they crossed the river, when they ranged themselves in order of battle, supported by some companies of light troops, which had been sent over in the boat. In an instant they advanced to charge the enemy, who fled at their approach, setting fire to every thing which he was compelled to leave behind. We particularly admired, on that occasion, the manner in which the Bavarians advanced. The precision of their evolutions, and the skill with which they disposed their out-posts, may be quoted as models for those who may be called to execute similar manoeuvres.

While we were contemplating these operations, it was reported that the emperor was approaching. The courier who had brought the news was quickly followed by another, who confirmed it. Soon afterwards arrived the saddle-horses, the officers of ordnance, and the generals of the guard; in short, the town, already full of troops, presently became absolutely crowded. In the midst of this tumult Napoleon appeared. He proceeded immediately to that part of the river at which they were erecting the bridge. In a dry and sarcastic manner he blamed its construction, which was certainly very defective: but, having determined to proceed to the other side, he crossed the bridge, and mounting his horse, joined the Bavarians, who had halted on the plain. Then marching with them, he advanced nearly two leagues from Bézenkovitschi. Napoleon, doubtless, executed this manoeuvre with a view of attracting the enemy's attention to this point, that he might find less opposition when he attacked Witepsk, on the opposite bank. He likewise hoped to annoy the Russian army in its retreat, which was now ascending the Dwina, after having abandoned the intrenched camp at Drissa.

It is impossible to imagine the confusion which reigned at Bézenkovitschi, and which increased on the arrival of the staff. In the night the tumult became still more dreadful. The crowd of troops which flowed in from all parts, and the quickness with which they were ordered to proceed, left no doubt that we were on the eve of a battle. The cavalry commanded by the king of Naples (Murat) formed the vanguard, and the fourth corps followed immediately to support them.

(July 25th). Orders were given to march to Ostrowno; and the staff was on the point of setting out, when we heard a strong cannonade. At this moment an aid-de-camp of general Delzons arrived in great haste to inform the viceroy (Eugene Beauharnois) that the enemy had been overtaken near Ostrowno, and that a vigorous engagement had just commenced. The aid-de-camp had scarcely finished his report, when the noise of the cannon was redoubled. His highness immediately commanded the baggage of the headquarters to halt; and, accompanied only by his staff, hastened to Ostrowno, where he joined the king of Naples, who had with him the divisions of cavalry of Bruyères, and Saint Germain, supported by the thirteenth division of infantry. But when they arrived at Soritza, the affair had already been successfully decided. Twenty pieces of cannon, which had fallen into our power, and the vast numbers of dead that were left on the field of battle, proved, both the resistance of the conquered, and the valour of the seventh and eighth hussars, who had on that occasion, covered themselves with glory.

It was three o'clock in the morning (July 26th) when the viceroy arrived at Ostrowno, with the king of Naples. The fourth corps were encamped near him, and the cavalry, placed in front, watched the manoeuvres of the enemy. At six o'clock his majesty and the prince, accompanied by their respective staffs, marched towards the out-posts, and passing over the ground where the engagement had taken place the night before, they heard that Ostermann's corps, consisting of two divisions, was drawn up in order of battle. The prince immediately ordered the thirteenth and fourteenth divisions to support the cavalry commanded by the king of Naples. The hussars who were sent out to reconnoitre, having met with much opposition at the entrance of a forest, returned with the intelligence that the enemy seemed determined to dispute our passage. We heard on all sides the fire of the sharp-shooters; and the cannon of the Russians, placed on the road, enfiladed our columns which had advanced. General Danthouard ordered our artillery to be brought forward without delay, and it was in this exchange of balls, that captain Ferrari of the eighth hussars, formerly aid-de-camp to the prince of Neufchatel, had his leg shot off. Meanwhile, the king of Naples, hastening wherever his presence could be useful, ordered an attack to be made from our left, to disperse the enemy's cavalry, which occupied the extremity of a wood. But, notwithstanding this manoeuvre was well planned, it had not the desired effect. The detachment of hussars, entrusted with execution of it, was too weak and was soon compelled, though without loss, to retreat before the numerous squadrons who rushed on to the charge.

While we were thus manoeuvring on our left, the Russians attempted to force our right. The viceroy perceiving it, caused the thirteenth division to proceed towards that point, who advancing rapidly on the road, stopped the progress of the enemy; and the artillery of our regiments, being advantageously placed on some eminences, made us feel certain that our line could not be forced.

Our right seemed well defended, when a sudden attack was made, and dreadful cries were heard, both on the left and in the centre. The enemy, advancing in great force, had vigorously pushed back our sharp-shooters, placed in the forest, and compelled the artillery to retire precipitately; while the Russian cavalry, profiting by a little plain on our left, furiously charged the Croats, and the 84th regiment. Happily, however, the king of Naples came up in time to check their progress. Two battalions of the 106th, which had been kept in reserve, supported the Croats; while general Danthouard, in whom were united the most brilliant talents and undaunted bravery, seconded by colonel Demay, and captain Bonardelle, reanimated the courage of the artillery, and, by skilful evolutions, replaced them in the position which they had quitted but for a moment.

The affairs of the left and of the centre being reestablished, the king of Naples and prince Eugene proceeded to the right wing and put it in motion. The enemy, lying in ambuscade before a forest, opposed a vigorous resistance to the 92d regiment, which, notwithstanding its being placed on an advantageous eminence, remained inactive. The viceroy instantly despatched the adjutant-commandant Forestier, to urge them forward; who, with some difficulty, succeeded in making them advance. Their march, however, appeared too slow to the impetuous valour of the duke of Abrantes (Junot). That intrepid general, who, in other campaigns had acted as commander in chief, hastily quitted the viceroy and put himself at the head of this regiment, on which every eye was now fixed. His presence, or rather his example, electrified every heart; and the brave 92d, led on by general Roussel, marched instantly to the charge, overthrew every thing that opposed them, and penetrated at last into the forest, where the enemy was protected by intrenchments almost impregnable.

On looking to the extremity of our right, we perceived a Russian column, which had been sent to turn our flanks commencing its retreat. The king of Naples, with that enthusiasm which is peculiar to great minds, ordered the cavalry to charge upon that column, and to compel it to lay down its arms. The difficulties of the ground made the soldiers hesitate for a moment but the king, perceiving at a glance, that the execution must be as prompt as the thought itself, drew his sword from its scabbard, and eagerly exclaimed, 'Let the bravest follow me.' This trait of heroism filled us with admiration. All pressed forward to second him; but deep ravines and impenetrable thickets impeded our progress, and gave the enemy time to escape, and to rejoin the corps from which they had been detached.

The success of the combat was certain; but we dared not venture to cross the extensive forest before us, on the other side of which were the hills of Witepsk, where we knew the forces of the enemy were encamped. While we were deliberating on the means of effecting that important passage, we heard a great tumult behind us. No one could guess the cause, and uneasiness was added to our curiosity; but when we perceived Napoleon surrounded by a brilliant suite, our fears were dissipated; and the enthusiasm which his presence always excited made us hope that he would add to the glory of that eventful day. The king of Naples and the prince hastened to meet him, and informed him of the event of the engagement, and the measures which they had since adopted. But Napoleon, desirous become more intimately acquainted with every circumstance, quickly proceeded to the most advanced posts of our line, and viewed from an eminence, the position of the enemy, and the nature of the ground. His eye penetrated into the Russian camp. He guessed their plans, and immediately ordered new dispositions, which being executed with precision and rapidity, the army was soon in the middle of the forest. We followed at a quick pace and reached the hills of Witepsk as the day began to close.

The thirteenth division, which assisted in this manoeuvre, experienced much resistance from the enemy in crossing the woods. He retired slowly, and disputed every step; while his numerous sharpshooters made us pay dearly for the ground which we had gained. It was in one of these unfortunate recontres, that a Russian dragoon, coming up to general Roussel, fired at him with a pistol, and killed him on the spot. As the Russians seldom place dragoons among their sharp-shooters, it occasioned the report that general Roussel had been murdered by one of our own men; but we were afterwards assured that we had not to reproach ourselves with the death of that brave general, who was truly worthy of our regret, both on account of his military qualities and his private virtues.

Brussier's division (the fourteenth) followed the great road, and arrived very late at the position which had been appointed for it between the road and the Dwina. The fifteenth division and the Italian guard, forming the rest of the infantry of the fourth corps, were left in reserve, a little behind the fourteenth.

After the different corps had taken their respective positions, Napoleon established his headquarters in the village of Koukoviatschi. The king of Naples and prince Eugene were encamped in an uncomfortable little *chateau* near the village of Dobrijka, surrounded by the corps under their command.

On the following morning, at the dawn of day, (July 27th) our troops marched towards Witepsk. The Russians, retiring on that town, fired some cannon, which, however, did us little injury. They afterwards occupied a large plain near the town, which commanded the roads by which we could approach. We could easily observe the lines of the enemy from the hill on which we were placed, and particularly his numerous cavalry, arranged in order of battle at the extremity of the plain.

The division of Broussier, constituting the advanced-guard, crossed, by means of a miserable bridge, the rivulet which separated us from the plain, and drew up on a height opposite the eminence, which was occupied by the Russians. The sixteenth regiment of chasseurs, having descended the hill, was vigorously charged by several squadrons of the cossack-guard, and it would have experienced a total defeat, if it had not been disengaged from the enemy, towards the left, by the light troops of the ninth regiment, commanded by captains Guyard and Savary. These brave men attracted, on this occasion, the attention of the whole army, which, encamped on the surrounding heights, as on an amphitheatre, witnessed their exploits, and rendered them the applause that was justly due to their valour.

The sixteenth chasseurs, retiring upon the fourteenth division, were protected by the 53d regiment, commanded by colonel Grosbon. That division forming a square, presented to the enemy an impenetrable front, and all their repeated and furious attempts to break it, proved ineffectual. This circumstance threw a little confusion into our ranks; but Napoleon being at hand, it could not continue. Placed on an eminence, from which he could see all the manoeuvres, he calmly made every disposition which he thought was necessary to secure the victory. He ordered a regiment of cavalry to retire, to open the passage of the bridge to the thirteenth division. This retrograde movement spread terror amongst our train, which was composed of workmen, sutlers and victuallers, a class of people who are easily alarmed; and who, always afraid of losing their booty, are rather prejudicial than useful to an army.

The thirteenth division having advanced, filed to the right. The viceroy marched at their head, and conducted them behind the fourteenth division, to an eminence which overlooked the plain on which the enemy was encamped.

These heights, not being guarded, we advanced without difficulty, and took our position on the summit, opposite the Russian camp, separated only by the river Loutchesa, the steep shores of which formed a ravine so deep, that it was impossible to come to a general action. We pretended, however, to commence the engagement by detaching some light troops, who succeeded in passing over the ravine and established themselves in a little wood. But not being supported, they proceeded no further, and returned to their corps, as soon as the fire of the batteries had ceased, and the divisions were no longer under arms.

This suspensions, when the armies were in sight of each other, excited universal astonishment and every one enquired, 'Where is the emperor? What are his intentions?'

During these discussions we were joined by the first corps, and the imperial guard. Some thought that Napoleon waited for the junction of all his forces before he began a serious attack; others affirmed that marshal Ney, and the cavalry of general Montbrun, advancing from the other side of the Dwina, would turn the position at Witepsk, and thus cut off the retreat of the Russians. But this manoeuvre was, doubtless, impracticable, since it was not executed.

On that night the troops bivouacked on the places where they had taken their positions, and the soldiers of the different corps, mingling together, related to each other the share which their respective divisions had borne in the honor of the day. From these accounts it appeared, that the combat, though glorious, had not been bloody. Amongst the small number who were killed, was the ingenious colonel Liedot, a man truly worthy of the corps to which he belonged. During the expedition to Egypt, he distinguished himself by his courage; and in the construction of some fortifications in Italy, he proved that the military art is no obstacle to the development of the most profound conceptions.

The boldness with which the Russians retained their positions, and the function of a great part of our troops at the same point, induced us to believe that a general action would take place on the following day. What was, therefore, our astonishment, when we perceived at the dawn of day (July 28th) that the enemy had effected his retreat! Our whole army went immediately in pursuit, except the imperial guard, which was established at Witepsk, where the emperor seemed inclined to remain.

This town, the capital of the government of that name, situated on a plain between some rising ground, and the shores of the Dwina, contained twenty thousand inhabitants, and presented, from the beauty of its situation, a most delightful aspect. Poland and Lithuania had during more than two months, and through a space of more than three hundred leagues, offered nothing to our view but deserted villages, and a ravaged country. Destruction seemed to precede our steps and in every direction the whole population was seen flying at our approach, leaving their habitations to hordes of cossacks, who destroyed every thing which they could not carry away. Having long experienced the most painful deprivations, we regarded with envious eyes, those well-built and elegant houses where peace and abundance seemed to dwell. But that repose which we had so eagerly anticipated, was again denied us, and we were compelled to renew our pursuit of the Russians, leaving on our left this town, the object of our most ardent wishes and our dearest hopes.

As we followed the movement of the advanced guard, we were astonished at perceiving the perfect order with which count Barclay de Tolly had evacuated his position. We wandered in all directions over an immense plain, without perceiving the faintest trace of his retreat. Not one carriage, not a single dead horse, not even a solitary vehicle, indicated the road which the enemy had taken. While we remained in this uncertainty, which, perhaps, was without a parallel, colonel Klisti, scouring the neighbouring country to endeavour to find some peasant, discovered a Russian soldier sleeping under a bush. This rencontre was extremely fortunate, and the viceroy profiting by it, questioned the prisoner, who gave us some information as to the route that the column to which he belonged had taken.

The prince, doubting the accuracy of the intelligence, advanced to reconnoitre, but not having met with any thing worthy of attention, we returned at full speed towards the high road which leads from Witepsk to the source of the Dwina. The whole road was covered with cavalry. The king of Naples soon joined the viceroy, and after some consultation, they ordered their respective corps to proceed. The heat was excessive, and the clouds of dust raised by the horses rendered our march insupportably fatiguing. We were soon obliged to stop, and halted at a church built of wood, where the king of Naples and the prince had a long conference together.

The cavalry had filed off in pursuit of the Russian army, and we soon heard that they had come up with them. The rest of the troops immediately hastened their march and overtook the enemy. The cossacks who formed the rear-guard retreated on the advance of our artillery, and only halted to fire a few cannon shot whenever they found a favourable opportunity. They continued manoeuvring till they were beyond Aghaponovchtchina, where our corps and the cavalry encamped. Near this village, on an eminence towards the left, was a wretched *chateau* built of wood, where the emperor (who, being informed that we had overtaken the Russians, immediately left Witepsk to join us) established his quarters.

Never did a bivouac present a more military appearance than ours at Aghaponovchtchina. Napoleon, the king of Naples and the prince, were in one tent. The generals, placed in miserable huts which their soldiers had hastily constructed, were encamped with their officers by the side of a rivulet, the miry water of which was preserved with the greatest care. During the three days that we had been on the field of battle, water and roots had constituted our only nourishment. Our divisions were encamped on the eminences which surrounded the *chateau*, and the enemy could see our numerous fires, the brilliant light of which dissipated the obscurity of the night.

Early on the following morning (July 29th) we again proceeded in search of the Russians. The emperor, however, returned to Witepsk, where he proposed to remain a sufficient time to execute his plans relative to Lithuania. When the king of Naples arrived at the separation of the roads of Janowitchi and Sourai, he left us, taking with him the whole heavy cavalry, and the fourteenth division. The viceroy, still pursuing his way, marched towards the Dwina, followed by the thirteenth and fifteenth divisions, the royal guard, and the brigade of light cavalry commanded by general Villasa.

We were on. the point of entering Sourai when we were informed by some chasseurs that an enemy's convoy, feebly escorted, was endeavouring to pass the river to arrive at the road to Weliki-luki. The viceroy immediately ordered his aid-de-camp, Deseve, to follow the chasseurs, and seize on the convoy. This order was fully executed : for, after two hours, the aid-de-camp returned with the intelligence that the convoy was ours.

The town of Sourai, although entirely built of wood, was the best that we had seen. Its population, consisting chiefly of Jews, was considerable, and their industry procured us many comforts of which we stood in the greatest need. The magazines were tolerably filled, which was, in truth, a fortunate circumstance, for every thing seemed to indicate that we should make some stay in this little town.

Sourai, without being a military position, was a very important place. It is situated at the junction of the Casplia with the Dwina, and at the point where the high roads to Petersburgh and Moscow divide. These form two *têtes-de-pont,* which perfectly command the road to Witepsk. During our stay here several geographical engineers arrived, and executed some plans of the river and the surrounding country.

The thirteenth division which had followed us, was encamped about a league behind Sourai; a part of the fifteenth, and the foot guard, were quartered in the town. The horse guard, commanded by general Triaire, proceeded to the other side of the Dwina, and sent off a strong detachment on the road to Weliki-luki. During that march, the adjutant of the palace, Boutarel, discovered that the road, as far as Ousviat, formed a continued defile across the woods. In the immediate vicinity of that small town, the country was totally different, and the provisions which the dragoons brought from that expedition, proved that this neighbourhood offered abundant resources for the cantonment of the troops.

On our arrival at Sourai, the viceroy being informed that another Russian convoy, with a strong escort had taken the road towards Veliz, ordered Baron Banco, colonel of the second regiment of Italian chasseurs, to take with him two hundred chosen men, and proceed immediately in pursuit. After nine hours' march, this detachment arrived at Veliz, just as the convoy was issuing from the town, and crossing the bridge over the Dwina. The chasseurs instantly charged the escort. Five times they were repulsed by the infantry, and by numerous detachments of cavalry, much stronger than their own. But the bravery of the Italians triumphed at length over the obstinate resistance of the enemy, and they succeeded in taking all the baggage, and compelling five hundred Russians to lay down their arms. This victory cost us some wounded men ; among these were six officers, one of whom died of his wounds.

While Napoleon was at Witepsk, endeavoring to organize Lithuania, and the centre of the army was inactive between the Nieper and the Dwina, we learned that the prince of Eckmuhl (Davoust) had been attacked at Mohilew. Bagration, profiting by the leisure which the combat at Borisow had allowed him, crossed the Berezina, at Bobruisk, and marched towards Novoi-Bickow. On the 23d July, three hundred cossacks attacked us, at the dawn of day, and took about a hundred prisoners from the third chasseurs, among whom was the colonel. An alarm was spread in our camp. The drum was beat, and our soldiers flew to arms. The Russian general Sieverse, with two chosen divisions, directed all the attacks. From eight in the morning until five in the evening the firing continued on the skirts of the forest and on the bridge which the Russians wished to force. At five o'clock the prince of Eckmuhl caused three chosen battalions to advance; he placed himself at their head, overthrew the Russians, forced their position, and pursued them more than a league. The loss must have been equal on both sides, but prince Bagration, satisfied with the reconnaissance which he had made, retired on Bickow, where he crossed the Nieper and proceeded to Smolensko, at which place the two Russian armies were to form a junction.

General Kamenski, with two divisions, endeavoured to join prince Bagration; but, being unable to effect it, he returned to Wolhynia, and uniting himself to the ninth and fifteenth divisions, formed by count Markoff, and then commanded by general Tormasow. These four divisions, forming a considerable army, marched towards Kobrin, and attached themselves to the seventh corps. They surrounded the Saxon general Klengel, who had with him only two regiments of infantry, and two squadrons of cavalry. Obliged to yield to superior force, he did not surrender till after an obstinate combat, hoping to the last, that he might be reinforced by general Regnier; but that officer, though he advanced as rapidly as possible, did not arrive till the capitulation had been signed more than two hours.

Notwithstanding we sustained these losses on our right, the successes of our left wing more than counterbalanced them. The duke of Tarentum, commanding the Prussian corps, pushed forward several strong detachments on the road to Riga, and by the skilful dispositions of generals Grawert and Kleist, gained very signal advantages over the Russians. A few days afterwards, general Ricard took Dunabourg, which the enemy had abandoned, after having made great preparations for its defence. But the enterprise most glorious to our arms, was performed by the second corps. The duke of Reggio (Oudinot) having pushed forward his advanced guard towards Sebei, met prince Wittgenstein, who having been previously reinforced by the corps of prince Repnin, furiously attacked him. The engagement took place near the castle Jakoubovo.

The division of Legrand sustained a severe engagement till ten o'clock at night, when, by the valour of the 26th light infantry, and the 56th of the line, the Russians were repulsed with considerable loss. Notwithstanding this, they ventured on the morrow to attempt the passage of the Dwina. The duke of Reggio (Oudinot) ordered general Castex not to oppose them. The enemy fell into the snare, and on the 1st of August, advancing towards Drissa, drew up in order of battle, facing the second corps. Fifteen thousand men, forming half of Wittgenstein's army, had crossed the river, when a masked battery of forty pieces of cannon was opened upon them, and kept up a constant and destructive fire for half an hour. At the same moment the division of Legrand advanced to the attack, and the enemy beginning to fall into confusion, the division of Verdier made a furious and irresistible charge with fixed bayonets. The Russians were driven into the river. Three thousand men, and fourteen pieces of cannon remained in our power. Pursuing their scattered troops on the road to Sebei, we counted two thousand dead, among whom was general Koulniew, a very distinguished officer of the light troops.

At that time a rumour was spread, that the emperor Alexander had been assassinated at Veliki-luki by his courtiers, who were indignant at his offering to treat with us. It was asserted that Napoleon had exultingly announced this as a positive fact at one of his audiences at Witepsk. We afterwards ascertained, that this false report had been circulated to counteract the effect of the energetic proclamation which the emperor Alexander had issued to the Russian people; in which he had commanded every inhabitant of his immense empire to take arms against a perfidious enemy, who, after having violated the boundaries of their country, was advancing to destroy their ancient capital, and to annihilate the glory of its illustrious founders. All these infamous falsehoods completely failed of success. They did not even reach a population, which, flying at the approach of the French army, could neither experience the effects of an artifice so mean, nor be, corrupted by our flattering promises. In truth, the object of every promise made by our deceitful chief was to delude and to betray; it was to kindle the most frightful discord, by exciting the people against the nobility; and stifling in their hearts that faithful attachment which was due to their sovereign.

Book III

Smolensko

After the battle of Veliz, the viceroy feeling the necessity of reinforcing the detachment of chasseurs that had been left there, reinforced them with the whole brigade of general Villata and with one battalion of Dalmatians. Veliz, situated at the junction of two principal roads, from Petersburg and Smolensko, was exposed to the frequent attacks of the cossacks; it was also the extreme point to which the French army had penetrated. The population of this small town, consisting entirely of Jews, procured us little more than enough to supply the absolute necessities of life. The environs contained only a few miserable hovels. While the soldiers gave themselves up to the indulgencies which such circumstances could afford, colonel Banco, who perfectly understood the Russian language, was informed by some spies, that the enemy intended to attack the brigade. On receiving this intelligence, general Villata secretly made every proper disposition to repel the enemy, while he publicly affected to think himself in complete security. At daybreak the cossacks suddenly appeared before the town, hoping to find the garrison buried in sleep; but the Dalmatians, who were under arms, issuing from their ambuscade, fired a well directed volley on them, which did considerable execution. The enemy, frightened by this unexpected reception, immediately took to flight, and abandoned the hope of surprising a town so bravely defended. The soldiers showed themselves on this occasion, worthy of the rewards which their former valour had procured them.

The fourth corps, after resting ten days in the town of Sourai, marched on the 9th of August, towards Janowitschi, to join the fourteenth division. On the evening before this movement took place, colonel Labedoyére, aid-de-camp to prince Eugene, was sent to the king of Naples. At his return from his mission, he confirmed the news of a desperate engagement having taken place between the enemy and our troops, under general Sebastiani, near Inkovo, in which we had been defeated with considerable loss. The reports of the different officers agreed that our cavalry had severely suffered, and that, besides several pieces of cannon, a fine light company of the 24th infantry had been captured. It was likewise said, that had it not been for the bravery of the Polish lancers, our losses would have been infinitely greater. On this occasion, some blamed general Sebastiani; but the greater part attributed the fault to general Montbrun, who disregarding the information he had received, and urged on by his natural bravery, had hazarded a battle against a much superior force of the enemy.

The viceroy having halted on the 10th of August at Janowitschi, the pioneers of the fourth corps, under the direction of general Poitevin, endeavoured to the bridge over the little river that passes through the town. It was, however, so completely out of condition, that they were obliged to abandon it, and the baggage and cavalry passed the river at a ford where the bottom was very muddy, and the banks exceedingly steep.

On our march towards Liozna, we crossed a plain gently undulated with little hillocks. We afterwards passed several small woods, and a rivulet that runs near a hamlet situated about half way to the castle of Velechkovitschi, where the army arrived on the 11th of August, and the soldiers encamped on the heights which surround the *chateau*. The following day the road was dreadfully miry, as far as Liozni, and leading through wet and marshy meadows, it presented almost insuperable obstacles to our convoys, and particularly to our artillery; it is true, that two days before it had rained abundantly. I should remark that these were the only violent storms which we experienced; for, during the rest of the campaign, we were very little incommoded by rain.

Near Liozna, a large and dirty village, we crossed (August the 12th) a wretched bridge thrown over a deep and winding river, which separates the town from the *chateau*, at the distance of three quarters of a mile towards the west where prince Eugene had established his quarters. But a communication was established by means of another bridge. Our troops availed themselves of the camp that had been formed by the duke of Elchingen's (Ney's) corps, and which was situated near this, bridge, between the town and the *chateau*.

Several obstacles arising from the nature of the country, prevented us from taking the direct road to Liouvavitschi; and even the road which we pursued was not exempt from difficulties. We were forced to pass through several defiles, and over many swampy meadows, and to cross roads which were cut through the middle of the forest. We arrived at last at Liouvavitschi, the approaches to which were as miry as the interior of Liozna.

This town was composed of a great many wretched houses built entirely of wood. To arrive there, we crossed a ruinous bridge. The road was so dreadfully deep and clayey, that it was with the utmost difficulty the horses could proceed. These unwholesome marshes are the result of the situation of Liouvavitschi. Several rivers surround the town, and form extensive and dangerous morasses, which never dry.

As we entered Liouvavitschi, we saw all the cavalry of the king of Naples returning from the environs of Roudnia and Inkovo; but, instead of
following the road to Razasna, they turned to the left, to pass the Nieper
at a higher point than that which had been marked out for us.

The thirteenth and fourteenth divisions encamped before the town;
the fifteenth remained on the heights which were to the left, with the
cavalry of the Italian guard; while the infantry of the same guard, being
generally stationed at the headquarters, encamped in the suburbs near
the *chateau* occupied by the viceroy.

The re-union of the whole army on the borders of the Nieper,
plainly announced the intention of crossing that river, and attacking
Smolensko by the left bank, the fortified part of which city was on this
side. The order was, in fact, to go to Razasna, where bridges had been
thrown across to facilitate the passage.

Before our arrival at this river, we passed over an almost desert country. No village was to be seen on the road, and we rarely found any
houses at which it was possible to stop. About half way on our route, was
a dangerous marsh, where we were forced to leave part of our baggage.
After many difficulties, we reached the Nieper, which is called also the
Borysthenes by the Greeks, a name which excited in our minds the
sublimest ideas. The illusion, however was soon destroyed, when we saw
a shallow and insignificant stream. The river is so narrow, and its banks
so steep, that it was not seen till we were on its very brink; while the very
steepness of the banks renders the passage extremely difficult.

Near Razasna, all the different corps of the grand army, some coming from Orcha, and others from Babinovitschi, effected their junction.
This immense crowd of men thronging to the same point, while it augmented our privations, redoubled the confusion and disorder that
reigned on the great road. The stragglers sought in vain to recover their
proper regiments. They who were entrusted with the most important orders, could not fulfil their mission, so much were the roads encumbered.
Hence arose a dreadful tumult on the bridges and in the defiles.

The fourth corps having arrived (August the 15th) at a small town
called Liadoui (remarkable as being the last place where we found any
Jews), we crossed a little river very near it, above which is a considerable
eminence which entirely commands the town. We continued our march
as far as Siniaki, a miserable hamlet consisting only of a few houses, and
situated about two hundred yards from the road. The viceroy intending
to encamp in this place, gave orders for the troops to halt. In the meantime, the other divisions of the grand army marched towards Smolensko,
and the cannonade which we heard made us presume that the town was
vigorously attacked.

The next day (August the 16th) we remained in the same position, and during the whole of the day, great numbers of troops passed by us towards the city. Towards six o'clock in the evening we quitted Siniaki, and after three hours march arrived at Krasnoë, a small town with some houses built of stone, and where the viceroy established his posts of communication. We did not, however, stop here, but continuing our march, crossed a small river near Katova, above which was a rising ground. The prince pitched his tent under a large avenue of trees surrounded by his division. At day break (August the 17th) we continued our route, and bivouacked as before, three miles beyond the post of Korouitnïa in a wood of birch trees near a lake. Our camp offered a most picturesque appearance. The viceroy having caused his tent to be pitched in the middle of the wood, the officers slept in their carriages, and those who had none cut down branches of trees to construct little huts, whilst their comrades lighted the fires to cook the provisions. As for the soldiers, some went on a foraging party, others washed their linen on the banks of a limpid stream, while the rest, after a long march, amused themselves in making war against the few ducks and geese that had escaped the rapacity of the cossacks.

We here learned that Smolensko, after a long contested battle had been set on fire by the Russians and abandoned to their conquerors. This was an omen of mournful presage to us, and proved to what extremities they will proceed who are determined not to bow to a foreign yoke. The next day we approached this unhappy town; but the viceroy ordered us to halt in a wood, near the castle of Novoidwor, about three miles from the town, and went to join the emperor.

I was encamped with the whole of the fourth corps, in this thick forest, when one of my comrades returning from Smolensko detailed to me, in the following words, the circumstances of the battle at which he was present:

> The position that we had occupied until the 13th of this month, made the enemy suppose that we should attack Smolensko by the right bank of the Borysthenes, but the emperor, by a prompt and unexpected manoeuvre, caused the whole of the army to pass to the opposite side. The same day the king of Naples (Murat) who still commanded the advanced-guard, and supported by the duke of Elchingen (Ney) arrived at Krasnoë, and, as you know already, gave battle to the twenty-fifth Russian division, amounting to five thousand infantry, and two thousand cavalry. In this gallant affair we took several pieces of cannon, and some prisoners. After this success, Napoleon, as early as the 16th, in the morning, appeared before Smolensko. This town is surrounded by an ancient wall, with battlements of eight thousand yards in circumference, ten feet

thick, and twenty-five high, and at certain distances, flanked with enormous towers in the form of bastions, the greater part of which were mounted with heavy pieces of cannon.

The Russians still expecting the attack to take place on the right bank of the Borysthenes, kept a considerable portion of their troops on that side of the river, but when they saw us arrive by the left bank, they thought themselves turned, and retreated with the utmost rapidity to defend Smolensko, by the principal point at which we were about to attack them. They maintained themselves with the greater obstinacy, as Alexander, when he quitted the army, had recommended them to give battle in order to save Smolensko.[1]

After employing the 16th in reconnoitring the place and its environs, the emperor confided the left to the duke of Elchingen (Ney) inclining towards the Borysthenes; the prince of Eckmuhl (Davoust) had the centre; the prince Poniatowski the right; and further on was the cavalry of the king of Naples; while the guard and ourselves composed the reserve. The eighth corps, under the command of the duke of Abrantes (Junot) was also expected; but that general, making a false movement, lost his way.[2]

Half the day was passed in reconnoitring. The enemy occupied Smolensko with thirty thousand men, the rest were in reserve on the right bank, communicating by means of bridges, constructed below the town. But Napoleon, perceiving that the garrison availed themselves of every moment of time to strengthen their fortifications, ordered prince Poniatowski to advance, having on his left Smolensko, and on his right the Borysthenes. He recommend him to construct some batteries to destroy the bridges, and by that means intercept the communication between the two banks. The prince of Eckmuhl (Davoust) who still kept the centre, attacked two intrenched suburbs each defended by seven or eight thousand infantry. General Friand finished the investiture of the place, taking his position between the first division and the Poles.

Towards mid-day the light cavalry of General Bruyères repulsed the Russian horse, and took possession of an eminence near the bridge. On that point was established a battery of sixty pieces of cannon, the fire of which was so well directed on the divisions of the enemy which remained on the other bank, that they were compelled to retire. Against this battery were opposed two of the enemy's consisting each of twenty pieces of cannon. The prince of Eckmuhl (Davoust) who was charged with the storming of the town, confided the attack of the suburbs on the right, to general Moran; and those on the left to general Gudin. After a severe fire of musketry, these two divisions forced the positions of the enemy, and followed them with wonderful intrepidity as far as the covered way, which they found strewed with dead. On the left the duke of

1   See the Thirteenth Bulletin.
2   See the Thirteenth Bulletin.

Elchingen (Ney) forced the intrenchments occupied by the Russians, and constrained them to take refuge in the town, in the towers, or on the ramparts, which they defended with obstinacy. General Barclay de Tolly then perceiving that an assault on the town was likely to be attempted, reinforced it with two new divisions and two regiments of infantry of the guard. The battle continued the whole of the night; but soon after the evening had commenced, thick columns of smoke were seen to rise from different quarters. As the darkness increased, the flames were distinctly observed spreading with incredible rapidity in every direction. The whole city was soon on fire, and, in the middle of a fine summer's night, presented to our view the same spectacle that the eruption of Mount Vesuvius offers to the inhabitants of Naples.

At one o'clock the ruins of the town were abandoned. Our first grenadiers prepared to mount the breach at two o'clock in the morning, when, to their surprise, they approached without opposition, and discovered that the place was entirely evacuated. We took possession of it, and found on the walls many pieces of cannon which the enemy could not take away.

Never can you form an adequate idea of the dreadful scene which the interior of Smolensko presented to my view, and never during the whole course of my life can I forget it. Every street, every square, was covered with the bodies of the Russians, dead or dying. The flames shed a horrible glare over them. Ah! how much have those princes to answer for, who, merely to gratify their own ambition, expose their people to such calamities.

The next day (August 19th) we entered Smolensko, by the suburb that is built along the bank of the river. In every direction we marched over scattered ruins and dead bodies. Palaces, still burning, offered to our sight only walls half destroyed by the flames, and thick among the fragments were the blackened carcasses of the wretched inhabitants, whom the fire had consumed. The few houses that remained were completely filled by the soldiery, while at the door stood the miserable proprietor, without an asylum, deploring the death droll, and the loss of his fortune. The churches alone afforded some consolation to the unhappy victims, who had no other shelter. The cathedral, celebrated through Europe, and held in great veneration by the Russians, became the refuge of the unfortunate beings who had escaped the flames. In this church, and round its altars, were seen whole families extended on the ground. On one side was an old man just expiring, and casting a last look on the image of the saint whom he had all his life invoked; on the other was an infant whose feeble cries the mother, worn down with grief, was endeavoring to hush, and while she presented it with the breast, her tears dropped fast upon it.

In the midst of this desolation, the passage of the army into the interior of the town, formed a striking contrast. On one side was seen the abject submission of the conquered - on the other the pride attendant upon victory; the former had lost their all - the latter, rich with spoil, and ignorant of defeat, marched proudly on to the sound of warlike music, inspiring the unhappy remains of a vanquished population with mingled fear and admiration.

The grand bridge across the Nieper, which had been burnt, and that communicated with the other part of the town, in which there did not remain a single house, was promptly repaired. In the meantime, the cavalry of general Grouchy, with the fourth corps, and all their artillery crossed a ford at the extremity of the suburb by which we entered. In this interval the other bridges were constructed, which so accelerated the passage, that the same day the artillery and cavalry of the king of Naples were on the road to Moscow, in pursuit of the enemy.

All the fourth corps having succeeded in crossing the river, encamped on the heights that surround the town, near the post road from Porietsch to Petersburgh. This was a position of the greatest importance, and every one was astonished that the enemy had not defended it better. Had they made a stand here, our march would have been considerably retarded; the principal road to Moscow would have been cut off, nor could we have retained possession of the town, which this position completely commanded.

While the centre of the army pursued its triumphant career, general Gouvion St. Cyr gained some important victories on the banks of the Dwina. After the battle of Drissa, prince Wittgenstein, being reinforced by twelve battalions, resolved to act on the offensive against the duke of Reggio (Oudinot). The latter, seeing himself on the point of being attacked, united the Bavarian corps (the sixteenth) to that which he already commanded. The engagement actually took place on the 16th and 17th of August; but at the moment the duke of Reggio was taking measures to repel it, a grape shot struck him in the shoulder, and so dangerously wounded him that he was compelled to quit the field of battle, and to give up the command to general Gouvion St. Cyr.

The latter disposed every thing for the attack the next morning at day break; and, the better to deceive the Russians, he ordered all the baggage, and a great part of the artillery and cavalry, to retire on the left bank of the Dwina, in sight of the enemy, and, ascending the river, to repass it at Polotsk without being seen. The enemy, deceived by this skilful manoeuvre, believed that we were retreating, and advanced in pursuit; but, instead of finding us disposed to quit the ground, we presented ourselves ranged in order of battle, and our artillery, advantageously placed, commenced a destructive fire on them. At the same time our infantry, under the protection of our cannon, attacked the left and centre of the corps commanded by general Wittgenstein. The two divisions of generals Wrede and Roy, having combined their movements with great bravery and skill, marched out of Spas together. The division of Legrand, in position on the left of this village, was connected with that of general Verdier, one of whose brigades observed the right of the enemy; and the division of Merle covered the front of the town of Polotsk.

The enemy, although surprised at seeing us so well disposed, advanced with great resolution, confiding in their artillery; but, towards the evening, prince Wittgenstein, seeing his centre and his left forced, retired in echelon after furiously defending every position. By this obstinate resistance he succeeded in saving his army, which, notwithstanding the arrival of powerful reinforcements, endeavored in vain to resume offensive operations. We should have taken a great number of prisoners, had not the woods facilitated their escape. Those who fell into our hands had been left wounded on the field of battle, and by their numbers we were enabled to judge of the severe loss which the Russians had sustained. Several pieces of cannon added to the trophies of this glorious day.

In truth, this victory was dearly purchased by the loss of several brave Bavarian officers, especially of generals de Ray and Sierbein. The first was particularly regretted. The soldiers lost in him a father, a chief whose talents and consummate experience were held in veneration by the whole Bavarian army. Generals, officers and soldiers, rivalled each other in contributing to the success of the day. Among the first, Count Gouvion St. Cyr rendered a just tribute of praise to generals Legrand, Verdier, (wounded), Merle, Von Wrede and Aubry; the latter, who was general of the artillery, particularly distinguished himself in his department. The count closed his report by invoking the benevolence of the emperor towards his officers. He thus did justice to all except to himself, on which point he observed a profound silence; but his modesty was the more conspicuous, and this virtue, which belongs only to great minds, was a few days afterwards rewarded on the field of battle with a marshal's staff.

While our corps on the left gained these important victories on the Dwina, those of the centre distinguished themselves in combats no less glorious.

The Duke of Elchingen (Ney), having passed the Nieper (19th August) above Smolensko, joined the king of Naples in pursuit of the enemy. After marching a league, he met part of the rear-guard, consisting of six thousand men. Their position was carried in an instant, and the bayonet covered the field battle with their dead.

This corps which protected the retreat of the Russians, having been forced hastily to retire, took post on the rising ground of Valantina. The first line, however, was broken by the eighteenth regiment, and towards four o'clock in the afternoon, a fire of musketry commenced with the whole rear-guard, then consisting of fifteen thousand men. The duke of Abrantes (Junot), who had lost his way on the right of Smolensko, could not reach the road to Moscow time enough to cut off the retreat of the rear guard.[3] The first columns of the enemy therefore returned to the charge, and brought four divisions successively into the field. The Russians were the more interested in defending this position, as, besides its real strength, it had always been regarded as impregnable, from the defeats which the Poles had uniformly sustained here in their ancient wars. Thence the Russians, superstitiously connected with this plain, the idea of certain victory, and, decorated it with the pompous title of the *Sacred Field*.

If the enemy attached the highest importance to the preservation of this position, it was not of less moment for us to carry it, that we might be enabled more effectually to annoy his retreat, and to obtain possession of all the baggage, and the waggons with the wounded from Smolensko, the evacuation of which had been protected by the rear-guard.

At six o'clock in the evening the division of Gudin, sent to support the thirteenth corps against the numerous troops which the enemy recalled to his succour, appeared in column before the centre of the enemy's position. Supported by the division of Ledrue, they instantly carried it. The seventh light infantry, the twelfth, twenty-first, and one hundred and twenty-seventh, which composed the division of Gudin, charged with such impetuosity that the enemy immediately fled, persuaded they were engaged with the imperial guards. But so much bravery cost us the life of the gallant general who commanded them. He was one of the most distinguished officers in the army, and was equally regretted for his private virtues, and his military skill and intrepidity. His death, however, was well avenged. His divisions made a dreadful carnage of the enemy, who fled towards Moscow, leaving the *Sacred Field* covered with their dead. Among the rest were found the bodies of generals Skalon and Balla; and it was asserted that the general of cavalry, Koff, being mortally wounded, was considered by the Russians as a loss equally great with that which we had to deplore.

3   See 13th and 14th bulletins of the campaign.

At three o'clock on the morning of the following day, the emperor distributed rewards on the field of battle to the regiments which had distinguished themselves. To the one hundred and twenty-seventh, a new regiment, which had contributed much to the glory of the day, Napoleon granted the carrying of an eagle; a privilege which they had not before enjoyed, because they had not been present in any engagement. These rewards, bestowed on a spot rendered famous by victory, and in the midst of the dying and the dead, exhibited a scene of grandeur that assimilated our exploits to the heroic deeds of ancient times.

At Smolensko, the fourth corps changed the chief of its staff. General Dessoles, who had till then filled that situation, disgusted to see his services remain unnoticed, desired to enjoy in retirement the esteem which his talents had procured him. The army, recollecting that he had shared in the glory and the disgrace of Moreau, approved his determination, well knowing the difficulty which he would find in obtaining a rank that could put him on a level with those who had outstepped him in his career, and who would always be preferred before him. The emperor, yielding to the entreaties of this skilful general, granted him an honourable retreat, and appointed baron Guilleminot his successor, who was well known to the viceroy, by having exercised the same functions for a short time after the battle of Wagram.

During the four days that Napoleon remained at Smolensko, he reviewed the different corps which had distinguished themselves since the opening of the campaign. In this respect none was more justly entitled to honorable distinction than the fourth corps. It was at length granted us, and the chiefs of each division, with the exception of general Pino, who, with the fifteenth, was gone to Witepsk, received orders to put their soldiers under arms. (22d of August.)

The whole of our army, in its best accoutrements, was drawn up on a vast plain, a little beyond that on which we were encamped. Its fine appearance, and, above all, the recollection of the brilliant affair of Witepsk, gained our corps the rewards due to its bravery, and which were worthy of the munificence of the chief who deigned to grant them.

It had hitherto been believed, that Napoleon, desirous only to re-establish the kingdom of Poland, would terminate his conquests by the capture of the two towns of Witepsk and Smolensko, which, by their position, completely defended the narrow passage comprised between the Nieper and the Dwina. Every one considered these towns as our destined winter quarters, and if the ambition of our chief had suffered him to limit the operations of this campaign to the taking of Riga, the fortifying of Witepsk and Smolensko, and, more particularly, the organization Poland, the whole of which he had now conquered, he would, doubtless, in the following spring, have forced the Russians either to subscribe to his conditions, or to run the risk of the almost certain destruction both of Moscow and Petersburg. But, instead of adopting so wise a plan, Napoleon, blinded by excess of prosperity, and at a distance of six hundred leagues from France, with worn-out horses, and destitute of provisions, magazines, or hospitals, ventured upon the great road to Moscow. As a last proof of his imprudence, he left in his rear a Russian army, cantoned in Moldavia, and which was ready to march against us on the ratification of the treaty of peace, which had been already conclude with the Porte.

This army having ceased hostilities against the Turks, was then commanded by admiral Tschikakoff, who constantly sent fresh troops to reinforce the army of Wolhynia, which was opposed to the corps of prince Schwartzenberg. Napoleon had flattered himself that the Austrians, in obedience to his orders, would have repulsed the corps of Tormasow, Ertel, and Essen, as effectually as we had beaten that of Barclay de Tolly, and that consequently, our allies ravaging the Ukraine, would penetrate into the governments of Kiew and Kaluga, and join us on our entry into Moscow. But the manoeuvres of the Russian generals frustrated this great plan. Victors and vanquished, by turns, they defended every position; and, taking advantages of the chances of war, returned continually to the ground which they had abandoned. The fortress of Bobruisk therefore continued to hold out, and the Austrians never saw the banks of the Nieper.

Leaving Smolensko (23d August) we went to Volodimerowa, a village situated on the main road. On an eminence to the right, surrounded by marshes, is a *chateau* built of wood. Arrived on this height, at a distance of about five leagues from Smolensko we halted. It was then the intention of the prince to march to Doukhovchtchina, and afterwards to fall on Doroghobouï, where the centre of the grand army was quartered; but general Grouchy, who had preceded us with his cavalry, announced that he had repulsed the enemy more than twenty leagues. The viceroy (24th August) who could now dispense with pushing on to Doukhovchtchina, determined to search for a path that would conduct him straight to the high road leading to Doroghobouï. He found this route after following an excellent road, traced by the Russians themselves, in effecting their retreat.

On this march we traversed a fertile and luxuriant country. We saw, for the first time in Russia, cattle grazing in the fields, inhabitants remaining undisturbed in their villages, and houses that had not been plundered. The soldier, possessing abundance, forgot his fatigues, and regarded, not the length of his march which continued several hours. At length, towards the evening we arrived at Pologhi, a village at a small distance from the road which we were seeking. On the following morning (25th of August) we crossed the Wop, a small river that would have at tracted our attention more could we have foreseen how fatal it would one day prove to us. We might, however, have formed an idea of what it would be in winter, from the difficulty we found in passing it in the midst of summer. Its bed was very deep, and the banks so steep, that the artillery crossed it with great difficulty and only by doubling the number of horses to each piece.

Continuing our route, we again came in sight of the Nieper, whose marshes covered with wood nearly reached the hill on which lay the road we sought. Proceeding about a league we perceived the high turrets of the beautiful *chateau* of Zazélé, appearing at a distance like a considerable town. Close by was a lake, where the cavalry of general Grouchy refreshed themselves. They had arrived before us, and were encamped round the *chateau* of Zazélé.

The viceroy despatched some officers from this place to Napoleon who was at Doroghoboui; but although general Grouchy had pushed his advanced guard along the high road, we doubted whether it were cleared as far as that town. The aids-de-camp, therefore, crossed the Nieper below Zazélé, and pursuing the post road from Smolensko, they arrived safe at Doroghoboui, where the staff of the grand army had established their head-quarters.

This town, situated on an eminence, offered a military position capable of effectually stopping the progress of any army marching on the two high roads from Smolensko to Moscow. Yet, notwithstanding these advantages, it was very feebly defended owing to the great losses which the had sustained in the battles of Smolensko and Valontina. Our corps was entering Doroghoboui, when an aid-de-camp from Napoleon brought despatches to the viceroy. Having read them, the prince gave orders to select the most advantageous situation in the neighborhood to encamp his divisions. The want of water having obliged us to push on to Mikailovskoë, we established ourselves near this village. The cavalry was in the rear, the infantry of the royal guard in the centre; and, on the flanks, were the two French divisions, which formed part of our corps.

At a league from Mikailovskoë (27th August) we passed through two villages, situated in a marshy valley. Shortly after, we entered the plain through which runs the Nieper, and followed the road to Blaghové where we intended to cross the river. On our right were some cultivated hills, with several villages. The smoke issuing from the houses made us conjecture that they had not been abandoned. We saw at a distance their peaceable inhabitants standing on the summit of the hills anxiously observing whether we came to trouble the peace of their cottages.

The sources of the Nieper not being far distant, the river is here little larger than a brook. We forded it with ease, and the artillery had no other difficulty than to climb its banks, which, like all the rivers of Russia, are extremely steep and high, to contain the great masses of water produced by the melting of the snow.

The viceroy always present at the passage of a river, did not quit this till all the troops had crossed. The fourth corps still forming the extreme point of the left of the grand army, we marched over almost unbeaten tracks. To prevent our wandering, the prince ordered general Triaire, commanding the advanced-guard, to post dragoons along the road. This wise precaution proved beneficial to the detachments, and especially to the stragglers, who now, having no doubt which road they ought to pursue, arrived all safely at Agopochina. Before this measure was adopted, these unhappy beings, when left in the rear from fatigue and sickness, found themselves in the midst of thick forests, or on immense plains intersected by numerous paths, all equally beaten, and not knowing the language of the country, nor meeting with a single person to direct them, they wandered about in these vast solitudes, and perished, sooner or later, by famine, fatigue, or the sword of the enemy.

The village of Agopochina, where we halted, is remarkable for a large *chateau*, and a noble church, built of stone. The four sides are ornamented with peristyles. The sanctuary, constructed according the Greek ritual, is very rich, and adorned with several paintings, which reminded us of those which the Greeks brought from Constantinople, when, in the fourteenth century, they first established their schools in Italy. From this village, the commandant Sewlinge, who had lately joined our staff, was sent with important despatches to the king of Naples. The king not having received these despatches, and the commandant never returning, we felt the painful conviction that he had fallen into the hands of the cossacks.

The next day, (28th August) we continued to flank the left of the high road marching always nearly in line with the corps of the centre. The track which we followed had never before been traversed by an army. It was narrow, cut by frequent ravines, and often so contracted, that it resembled a path, traced merely to divide the grounds. Arrived at a village the name of which was unknown, we found three roads; one straight before us, one on our right, and a third on our left. We followed the latter, which conducted us, after a march of three hours, to an abandoned *chateau*, within a league of Béreski.

Early in the morning (29th August) we left this *chateau*, in a thick fog. The frequent halts which the viceroy made, and the reconnoitring parties which he sent to the right, as if to listen whether cannon were firing on the high road, convinced us that he was impatient to know whether Napoleon met with any obstacles in his march.

We approached Viazma. This small town, which, in Russia, may be reckoned a great one, was in a very advantageous situation for the enemy, being situated among the numerous branches of the river Viazma. It is surrounded by ravines, and stands on a beautiful eminence, commanding the plain and the defile, through which passes the high road from Smolensko. The Russians did not profit much by these advantages, they but feebly defended the place, and, after a slight resistance, set fire to the principal buildings and retired. When we arrived, Viazma was a prey to the flames; and, although accustomed to conflagrations, we could not help regarding with pity, this unhappy town, so lately peopled by ten thousand inhabitants. Though newly founded, it contained more than sixteen churches. The houses, all new, and elegantly constructed, were enveloped in clouds of smoke, and their destruction excited greater regret, as they were the noblest which we had seen since we quitted Smolensko.

The viceroy halted on the plain more than two hours. Placed on a rising ground we observed distinctly the progress of the flames, and heard the guns firing on the enemy beyond the town. A numerous cavalry, which arrived from every quarter, encamped in the environs. Prince Eugene, having received the emperor's orders, now passed the little river Viazma, which runs by the town of the same name, and proceeding to the left, he overtook the troops which he had sent before him, and whose march had been retarded by the passage of the Viazma. We met with yet another branch of the Viazma, the approach to which was so muddy, that it was impossible to ford it at any point. It was therefore necessary to march along the bank till we found a wretched bridge by which we crossed the river. Hence we came to a little hill, from the top of which we perceived at a distance a beautiful *chateau*, consisting of four pavilions, and a noble church. On entering it, we learned that the village was called Novoe, and that the *chateau* had been plundered by the light cavalry.

We halted in this village (30th August) having on our left the royal guards, and the fourteenth division with the thirteenth in front. The artillery of these divisions was placed in batteries facing the different roads on which it was possible that the enemy might appear.

As we commenced our march (31st August) we were rejoined by the Bavarian cavalry under general Preysing. The viceroy and the staff accompanied us. We saw on the road two neat *chateaux* completely ravaged. We halted at the second, and passed through a delightful garden with beautiful walks tastefully arranged. The pavillions had been newly decorated, but they offered now an image of the most frightful desolation. The furniture was broken to pieces; fragments of the most precious china were scattered about the garden, and many exquisite paintings had been torn from their frames, and were dispersed by the winds.

The viceroy had pushed his march beyond the *chateau* of Pakrovo; but observing that the infantry was far in the rear, he returned to the *chateau* in which some provisions were found, and especially a quantity of oats in the straw, and excellent forage.

Since the affair at Witepsk, the fourth corps had not met the enemy, and had not even seen any of those detachments of cossacks which, in the first Polish campaign, continually harrassed our troops, and intercepted the baggage; but after we passed Viazma, more circumspection was necessary on our march.

Although the enemy had not presented himself to observe our movements, we were nevertheless certain that he would soon appear; and, the next day (1st September) being about half way on our accustomed march, our cavalry was stopped by the cossacks. Two or three cannon-shots were the sign of this rencontre. The viceroy immediately put the cavalry of the Italian guards in order of battle, preceded by a considerable number of sharp-shooters. These drove before them the enemy's squadrons, who retired in proportion as we advanced, without opposing any resistance. They continued to retreat as far as Ghiat, of which the emperor had just taken possession. Above this town is a small river, which they crossed, and immediately, as if to observe us, drew up in order of battle on an eminence that commands the plain by which we arrived. The viceroy, after having made me reconnoitre the fords which might facilitate the passage of the river, ordered the Bavarian troops to cross it at a point that had been explored and which was exactly between two little villages, occupied by the cossacks. The enemy, however, no sooner perceived this movement, than they abandoned the villages and the heights, which the Bavarian cavalry, followed by their artillery, soon took possession. Arrived on these height we saw the enemy flying on all sides. They were closely pursued; but as night approached, our corps established itself in the little village of Paulovo, at the distance of half a league from Ghiat.

The emperor having passed three days in this town, we halted likewise at Paulovo and Woremiewo (2d and 3d September). Here the emperor, in the general orders of the day, granted some repose to the troops, which he commanded them to employ in provisions, in cleaning their arms, and preparing for the battle, which the enemy seemed willing to accept. Lastly, the marauding detachments were ordered to return on the following evening, if they wished to participate in the honour of the engagement.

Book IV

The Moskwa

After the capture of Smolensko, the emperor Napoleon was not ignorant that Russia, having concluded a peace with the Turks, would
soon have the whole of the Moldavian army at her disposal: nevertheless,
he followed up his successes without disquieting himself respecting the
future. But the news which he received at Ghiat, that general Kutusoff,
the renowned conqueror of the Ottoman power, had arrived from the
banks of the Danube, and taken the command of the Russian army,
hitherto under the orders of count Barclay de Tolly, ought to have convinced him that he would soon be attacked.

This general, who was regarded by the Moscovites as the hope of
their country, arrived at Czarévo-Saïmiche, (29th August). The officers
and soldiers hailed as their chief this venerable warrior, already celebrated in the annals of Russia; and the inhabitants of Ghiat informed us
that the sight of him had inspired the army with hope and joy. In fact, he
had scarcely arrived, when he announced that the Russian army would
retreat no further. That he might better defend Moscow, within four
days march of which we were now arrived, he chose a strong position between Ghiat and Mojaïsk, where he could advantageously await one of
those decisive battle which often determine the fate of empires. Each
party was sanguine in its expectation of victory. The Moscovites con-
tended for their country, their homes, and their children. Our soldiers,
accustomed to conquer, and filled with those grand and heroic ideas,
which continued success naturally inspires, eagerly demanded the fight;
and such is the superiority that courage gives over mere numbers, that on
the eve of the battle we calculated what, on the morrow, would be the
fruits of our approaching victory.

During the stay of Napoleon at Ghiat, our headquarters were transported from Paulovo to Woremiewo, where was a beautiful seat, belonging to prince Kutusoff. The staff had just entered the village, when the
viceroy, accompanied by several officers, arrived to examine the environs
of the place. Scarcely had he been gone a quarter of an hour, when he discovered that the whole plain was filled with cossacks, who advanced as if
they would charge the group that surrounded the prince Eugene; on seeing some dragoons, who formed his escort they fled precipitately, and
appeared no more in the neighbourhood of Woremiewo.

While we remained in this village, some soldiers of the hundred and sixth regiment, going on a foraging party, fell in with a post-chaise occupied by a Russian officer and surgeon; the former on being interrogated by an officer of the staff, declared that he came from Riga, his native country, and was going to the head-quarters of Kutusoff, who had for some days superseded Barclay de Tolly. Although this officer was descended from a good Lavonian family, and was decorated with several crosses and medals, the viceroy would not see him, justly suspecting that he had purposely exposed himself to discover our manoeuvres. Several peasants who were surprised on an unfrequented road, and particularly in the neighborhood of Mojaïsk, where the enemy had intrenched themselves, almost reduced this suspicion to a certainty.

Having passed two days at Woremiewo, we left it on the 4th of September, and passed through some forests, where they informed us the cossacks had been seen. The reports of the advanced-guard confirming this news, caused the viceroy to halt in an extensive plain, where our whole corps was assembled. The prince, placing himself at the head of the cavalry, ordered the infantry to follow, while the guard, placed as a reserve, brought up the rear. In this order we advanced to meet the enemy. When we reached the little village of Louzos, we found ourselves impeded by a rivulet. The cossacks, who were assembled on the opposite side, appeared to be forming themselves into squadrons to oppose our passage; but the viceroy ordering the cavalry to mount the ravine, the Russians, fearing lest they should be charged in the rear, fled with precipitation.

On gaining the heights, we discovered before us several villages on fire, and hearing a brisk cannonade, we imagined that we were not far from the road which Napoleon had taken. Near the post-house, called Ghridneva, was another immense ravine that crossed the main road; and on the opposite side was a steep hill, on which the Russians had established some batteries, after an obstinate engagement which had taken place there during the day.

When the enemy perceived that the fourth corps was forming on their right, they dispatched a numerous cavalry to reconnoitre our position, which retired when our artillery opened upon them. This cavalry appeared for a moment disposed to maintain itself on the edge of a wood; the viceroy, therefore ordered colonel Rambourg, of the third Italian chasseurs, to march upon that point, and bring them to action. The cossacks observed this movement without being intimidated; and when the chasseurs were on the point of charging them, they rushed from the wood, crying 'Houra! houra!' – a cry, since become too celebrated, and which these barbarians always use when they attack their enemies. The Italian chasseurs received them with great coolness. The action was smart, but of no duration, for the cossacks seeing the Bavarian light-horse advance, quitted the field, leaving some prisoners in our possession.

The Russians, nevertheless, maintained their positions on the summit of the hill, whence they kept up a galling fire on us as we advanced. Several bullets fell among a group of officers who surrounded the prince. We succeeded, however, in passing the ravine in spite of all opposition, and effected our junction, with the advanced-guard of the grand army, commanded by the king of Naples. We distinguished that monarch from afar by his white plume, as stationed at the head of his troops, he animated them to the combat by his own example.

As soon as the viceroy was informed that the king of Naples was there, he went to concert with him the necessary dispositions. The place of their conference was not changed, and both of them discoursed with the utmost sang-froid, though exposed to the fire of the batteries, and seeing those around them falling every minute by the shot of the enemy.

At the approach of night we returned to Louzos, where we had no other shelter than some miserable barns, covered with thatch. Hunger redoubled our sufferings, and we had nothing to satisfy its cravings. The surrounding hamlets, which had been sacked by the cossacks, could yield us no relief. At the same time we were close to the intrenched camp of Mojaïsk, where Kutusoff hoped to accomplish our defeat; and this he would certainly have effected, if he could only have detained us a few days before his formidable lines.

The position of Ghridneva, which the Russians had defended on the preceding evening, was evacuated during the night. The king of Naples, ardent in pursuit (5th September) rapidly advanced. The fourth corps, which continued to flank the left wing of the army, always kept at the distance of about a league from the main road. On leaving a wood infested by the cossacks, we passed through a village that had been pillaged by these barbarians. The horrible desolation which marked their career enabled us easily to follow their steps. Being arrived at the foot of a hill, we discovered some of their squadrons on the top, ranged in order of battle, round a noble *chateau*, which overlooked the neighboring plains. The viceroy immediately ordered the Bavarians to advance on this point, who, notwithstanding the difficulties of the country, reached the summit in the greatest order. As our allies advanced the enemy retired; and, as they descended the other side of the hill, our artillery-men directed upon them the cannon which had been planted on the terrace of the *chateau*. We pursued them through the wood, and being arrived at an open place, we saw long columns of Russians defiling, who, pursued by our troops, took up a position on an extensive plain at the summit of a hill about half a league distant, and where it was said, prince Kutusoff intended to hazard a decisive battle. On our right, we saw, below us, the abbey of Kolotskoï. The massy towers of this building gave it the appearance of town. The colored tiles, with which it was covered, reflected the rays of the sun through the thick dust caused by our immense cavalry and served to heighten still more, the gloomy and savage aspect which the whole surrounding country presented. The Russians intending to arrest here, had devastated in the most frightful manner, all the plain, on which we were forced to encamp. The corn, though yet green, had been cut, the woods destroyed, and the villages burnt. In a word, we found no food for our horses, and no shelter for ourselves.

We halted on a hill. During this time the centre of the army vigorously pursued the enemy, and obliged them to retire upon the eminence which they had intrenched. We remained inactive till nearly two o'clock in the afternoon; when the viceroy, followed only by his staff, reconnoitred the approaches to the Russian position. He had scarcely commenced, when our dragoons, placed as sharp-shooters, announced the approach of Napoleon. Immediately the name of the emperor passed from mouth to mouth, and every one awaited his arrival with the greatest impatience. He soon made his appearance followed by his principal officers, and took his station on an eminence whence he could easily command the whole camp of the enemy. After having long and attentively regarded their position, and carefully observed all the adjacent country, he began to hum some insignificant tune. He then conversed a moment with the viceroy, and, mounting his horse, he went to consult the prince of Eckmuhl (Davoust).

The viceroy now ordered the thirteenth and fourteenth divisions to advance. The Italian guard, which had been left in the rear, was placed in reserve. These two divisions had scarcely reached the eminence whence they could attack the Russians, when a brisk fire of musketry commenced on our right between the sharp-shooter's of Gerard's division (third division, first corps) and those of the enemy. At first our troops advanced close to the ravine which separated us from the enemy; but superior numbers obliged them to retire.

The Russians had a redoubt towards the right extremity of our army, the destructive fire of which carried consternation through our ranks. They had constructed it to fortify their left wing, which was the weakest part of their intrenched camp. Napoleon understood this, and saw the necessity of taking that redoubt. This honour was confined to Compan's division (fourth division, first corps) and these gallant men advanced to the attack, with an intrepidity which ensured the success of the enterprise. In this interval, prince Poniatowski manoeuvred our right with his cavalry, in order to turn the position; and when he was at a convenient distance, Compan's division attacked the redoubt, and, succeeded in carrying it, after an hour's fighting. The enemy, completely routed, abandoned the neighboring woods, and, retreating in disorder towards the principal eminence, rejoined the centre of their army.

The division of Compan, in proving itself worthy of the brilliant enterprise with which it was intrusted, purchased that honour with considerable loss. The acquisition of this important position cost us the lives of one thousand two hundred of our men, more than half of whom remained dead in the intrenchments which they had so gloriously carried. The next morning, as Napoleon was reviewing the sixty-first regiment which had suffered most, he asked the colonel what he had done with one of his battalions: '*Sire*,' replied he, '*it is in the redoubt*.'

The possession of the redoubt did not in the least determine the success of the battle. Before the general engagement began, Napoleon wished to gain a position on the other side of the river which separated us from the enemy. Thick underwood concealed their numerous sharp shooters, and rendered the approach as difficult as it was dangerous. But our courageous light troops recommenced the attack with redoubled vigour; and although the day was nearly closed, the fire on both sides continued with equal fury. At the same time, several villages on fire to the right, spread around a frightful glare. The cries of the combatants, and the flames which were vomited from a thousand brazen mouths, and which carried every where desolation and death, completed the horror of the scene. Our corps, ranged in order of battle, received with intrepidity the fire of the enemy, and coolly closed the ranks, as soon as a cannon-ball had laid any of their comrades low.

In the mean time, the night becoming more obscure, abated the fire without abating our ardor; for each, uncertain of his aim, thought it better to reserve his strength and his ammunition for the morrow. Scarcely had we ceased firing, when the Russians, encamped as it were on an amphitheatre, lighted innumerable fires. The whole of their camp was one uninterrupted blaze of light, which, while it presented a grand and sublime appearance, formed a striking contrast with our bivouac, where the soldiers, deprived of wood, reposed in utter darkness, and heard no sound but the groans of the wounded.

The viceroy caused his tent to be erected on the spot where the Italian guard were placed in reserve. Couched in the underwood, we slept soundly after the fatigues of the day, in spite of an impetuous wind, and a rain excessively cold. Towards two o'clock, I was awakened by the chief of our staff, who informed me that the emperor wished for a plan of the ground which we had occupied the preceding evening. I transmitted it to prince Eugene, who immediately sent it to Napoleon. The next morning at day-break (6th of September,) the viceroy ordered me to complete the plan by inspecting the whole line, and approaching. as near the enemy as I possibly could, that I might the better discover the exact nature of the ground, on which they were encamped, and especially to observe whether there were any masked batteries, or ravines unknown to us.

After these instructions, I advanced, and discovered that the Russian camp was situated behind the river Kologha, upon a narrow eminence, and that its left was very much weakened by the loss of the redoubt, which we had taken the evening before. In front of the camp, and opposite to us, was the village of Borodino, an extremely strong position,[1] situated at the confluence of a little rivulet, with the Kologha. Upon this eminence were two grand redoubts, about two hundred toises from each other. That on the right had fired on us the evening before; that on the left was built on the ruins of a village, which they had destroyed for that purpose. This redoubt communicated with Borodino, by three bridges, constructed upon the Kologha. Thus, this village, and the rivulet which was in front, served the enemy for his first line.

Upon the extremity of our left, the Italian cavalry had crossed the rivulet of Borodino; but this village, placed on an eminence, was defended by a numerous corps of Russian troops. All this ground was exposed to the fire of their grand redoubts, as well as under that of several smaller masked batteries long the river. As for our right, they knew that our success the evening before, had enabled us to cross the Kologha at this point, and to push forward the greater part of our troops to the rear of the eminence, on which was placed the enemy's principal redoubt.

We passed the rest of the day in reconnoitring the position of the Russians. General Danthouard caused the redoubts, which were placed too much in the rear to be reconstructed; and on the left, they likewise threw up some epaulments, where cannon might be placed in battery. In fact, all was prepared for a decisive engagement, when, towards evening, the emperor sent a proclamation to the chiefs of the corps, with orders

---

1 Napoleon said, in his bulletin of the battle of Moskwa, 'The viceroy, who formed our left, attacked and took the village of Borodino, which the enemy could not defend.' Prince Kutusoff, on the contrary, wrote to the emperor Alexander, 'The position which I have chosen in the village of Borodino, is one of the best that can be found in a flat country. It is to be wished, that the French would attack us in this position.' We made the attack, and village was so well defended, that general Plausanne, and colonel Demay, of the artillery, officers of our corps, were killed in the commencement of the action. The Russians have given to this bloody day, the name of the Battle of Borodino.

not to read it to the soldiers till the next day, should they then come to action; for although the position was both advantageous and strong, the enemy had so often declined giving battle, that it was to be feared they would again act as they had done at Witepsk, and Valontina. Here, however, they were forced to come to action, if they would save Moscow, from which we were distant but three days' march. In addition to this, the fatigue of our soldiers, and the exhaustion of our horses, seemed to promise to the Russians an easy victory. On the other hand, we were well assured that we must either conquer or perish: and this idea inspired us all with such courage, that in spite of the numbers of the Russian army, and their impregnable intrenchments, we regarded our entrance into Moscow as certain and near at hand.

Although worn out with fatigue, we felt the want of sleep; there were many among us, so enamoured of glory, and so flushed with the hope of the morrow's success, that they were absolutely incapable of repose. As they passed the wakeful hours, and the silence and darkness of midnight stole upon them, while the fires of the sleeping soldiers, now almost extinct, threw their last rays of light over the heaps of arms piled around, they gave themselves up to profound meditation. They reflected on the wonderful events of our strange expedition; they mused on the result of a battle which was to decide the fate of two powerful empires; they compared the silence of the night with the tumult of the morrow: they fancied that death was now hovering over their crowded ranks, but the darkness of the night prevented them from distinguishing who would be the unhappy victims: they then thought of their parents, their country; and the uncertainty whether they should ever see these beloved objects again plunged them into the deepest melancholy. But suddenly, before day-break, the beat of the drum was heard, the officers cried to arms, the men eagerly rushed to their different stations, and all, in order for battle, awaited the signal for action. The colonels, placing themselves in the centre of their regiments ordered the trumpet to sound, and every captain, surrounded by his company, read aloud the following proclamation:

Soldiers,
This is the battle so much desired by you! The victory depends on yourselves. It is now necessary to us. It will give us abundance, good winter- quarters, and a prompt return to our country! Behave as at Austerlitz, at Friedland, at Witepsk, at Smolensko, and, let the latest posterity recount with pride, your conduct on this day; let them say of you, - 'He was at the great battle under the walls of Moscow.'

Every one was penetrated with the truths contained in these energetic words, and replied to them by reiterated acclamations. Some were
animated by the love of glory, others flattered by the hope of reward, but
all were convinced that imperious necessity compelled us to conquer or
to die. To the sentiment of self preservation, were added ideas of duty
and of valour. Every heart was animated, every breast proudly swelled,
and each flattered himself that this important day might place him in the
rank of those privileged men, who were born to excite the envy of their
contemporaries, and the admiration of posterity.

Such were the feelings of the army, when a radiant sun, bursting
from the thickest fog, shone for the last time on many of us. It is reported
that at this sight, Napoleon exclaimed to those around him, 'There is the
sun of Austerlitz.' The action was on the point of commencing, the armies were in sight of each other, the cannoniers at their pieces, and all
awaited in anxious silence the signal of attack. At last (7th September), at
six o'clock precisely, the firing of a cannon from our principal battery,
announced that we were engaged. Immediately our thirteenth division
marched upon the village of Borodino, to which the enemy had already
set fire. Our troops then crossed the rivulet, and arrived at the village.
Orders had been given, that they should confine themselves to the occu-
pation of this position; but, carried away by the enthusiasm natural to
Frenchmen, they crossed the river Kologha, and took possession of one
of the bridges which connected the village with the eminence. It was
then that general Plausanne wishing to moderate the ardor of the soldiers
of the one hundred and sixth ran to the bridge to recall them, when a ball
struck him in the middle of his body. Beloved during his life, his death
was sincerely regretted. On this occasion the bravery of the
ninety-second regiment deserves the highest praise. Seeing that the one
hundred and sixth had ventured too far, it crossed the bridge of
Borodino, and hastened to the succour of that regiment, which, indeed,
without its aid, must inevitably have been destroyed. While the thirteenth division possessed itself of Borodino, the fourteenth, crossing the
Kologha under the eminence, lodged itself in a ravine near the principal
redoubt, whence the enemy poured a terrible fire. On this day the viceroy, besides his own corps had under his orders the divisions of Gerard
and Morand forming the first and third of the first corps. At eight
o'clock Morand's division which had been already engaged, and formed
the right extreme of the fourth corps, was warmly attacked at the moment that it was preparing to march upon the redoubt, a movement
which ought to have been immediately seconded by Gerard's division.
Nevertheless, while general Morand sustained the efforts of the enemy's
lines, he detached upon his left the thirtieth regiment, to take possession

of the redoubt. This position being carried, our artillery crowned the heights, and seized the advantage which for more than two hours the Russians had had over us. The guns, to whose destructive fire we had been exposed during the attack, were now turned against the enemy, and the battle was lost to the Russians when they imagined that it was but just begun. Part their artillery was taken, and the rest retreated to the rear. In this extremity, prince Kutusoff saw that every thing was lost. Yet determined to make one effort more, and to maintain the reputation which he had acquired by the service of half a century, he renewed the combat, and attacked with all forces the strong positions he had just lost. Three hundred pieces of cannon, now arranged on these heights, spread devastation and death among his ranks, and his disheartened soldiery perished at the feet of those ramparts which they had themselves raised, and which they regarded as the bulwark of Moscow, their venerable and sacred city.

The thirtieth regiment, attacked on every side was unable to keep the redoubt which it had carried, not being supported by the third division, scarcely yet drawn up in order of battle. This gallant regiment, commanded by general Bonami, was there constrained to yield to the superior force which overwhelmed it, and rejoined its division with the loss of its general. That division, with general Gerard's, continued to maintain itself on the hill, and to withstand the utmost efforts of the Russians.

The enemy, encouraged by the success he had just obtained, brought forward his reserve, with the hope of striking a decisive blow; it was partly composed of the imperial guard. With all his forces concentrated, he attacked our centre, on which our right had now wheeled. For a moment we feared that our lines would have been broken, and that we should have lost the redoubt we had gained the preceding evening; but general Friand, coming up with twenty-four pieces of cannon, arrested their progress, mowing down ranks at a time, who continued two hours exposed to a fire of grape-shot neither daring to advance, nor willing to recede. While they remained in this uncertainty, we profited by it to snatch from them a victory which they had considered as their own.

The viceroy seized this decisive moment, and, flying to the right, ordered a simultaneous attack of the grand redoubt, by the first, third, and fourteenth divisions. Having arranged all three in order of battle, these troops advanced with cool intrepidity. They approached even the intrenchments of the enemy, when a sudden discharge of grape-shot from the whole of their artillery spread destruction and consternation through our ranks. Our troops were staggered at this fatal reception; but the prince knew how to reanimate their spirits, by calling to the recollection of each regiment the circumstances in which they had formerly covered themselves with glory. To one he said, 'Preserve that courage which has gained you the title of Invincible'; to another, 'Remember, your reputation depends on this day'; then turning towards the ninth of the line, he said to them with emotion, 'Brave soldiers, remember you were with me at Wagram, when we broke the enemy's centre.' By these words, and still more by his example, he inflamed the valor of his troops to such a degree, that, shouting with joy, they again marched with ardor to the redoubt. His highness, riding along the line, arranged the attack with the utmost coolness, and led it himself, at the head of Broussier's division. At the same instant a division of cuirassiers, from the centre of the army, rushed on the redoubt, and offered to our astonished sight, a grand and sublime spectacle. The whole eminence, which overhung us, appeared in an instant a mass of moving iron : the glitter of the arms, and the rays of the sun, reflected from the helmets and cuirasses, mingled with the flames of the cannon, that on every side vomited forth death, gave to the redoubt the appearance of a volcano in the midst of the army.

The enemy's infantry, placed near this point. behind a ravine, kept up so destructive a fire on our cuirassiers, that they were obliged immediately to retire. Our infantry took their place; and turning the redoubt to the right and left, recommenced a furious combat with the Russians, whose efforts rivalled our own.

The viceroy and his staff, in spite of the enemy's tremendous fire, remained at the head of Broussier's division followed by the thirteenth and thirtieth regiments. They advanced on the redoubt, and entering it by the breast-work, massacred on their pieces the cannoniers that served them. Prince Kutusoff, who had witnessed this attack, immediately ordered the cuirassiers of the guard to advance and endeavour to retake the position. These were the best of their cavalry. The shock between their cuirassiers and ours was therefore terrible; and one may judge of the fury with which both parties fought, when the enemy, in quitting the field, left it completely covered with dead. In the midst of this frightful encounter, ever glorious for the staff of the fourth corps, the young Saint Marcellin de Fontanes was wounded. He was one of the first who entered the redoubt, and received a stroke from a sabre on the nape of his neck. This wound procured him the cross of the legion of honour bestowed on the field of battle - a recompense the more flattering to him, as he was only old enough to entertain the expectation of meriting it at some future period.

The interior of the redoubt presented a horrid picture. The dead were heaped on one another. The feeble cries of the wounded were scarcely heard amid the surrounding tumult. Arms of every description were scattered over the field of battle. The parapets, half demolished, had their embrasures entirely destroyed. Their places were distinguished only by the cannon, the greatest part of which were dismounted and separated from the broken carriages. In the midst of this scene of carnage, I discovered the body of a Russian cannonier, decorated with three crosses. In one hand he held a broken sword, and with the other, firmly grasped the carriage of the gun at which he had so valiantly fought.

All the Russian soldiers in the redoubt chose rather to perish than to yield. The general who commanded them would have shared their fate, if his valour had not preserved his life. This brave soldier had sworn to die at his post, and he would have kept his oath. Seeing all his companions dead around him, he endeavored to precipitate himself on our swords, and he would inevitably have met his death, had not the honour of taking such a prisoner arrested the cruelty of the soldiers. The viceroy received him with kindness, and committed him to the care of colonel Asselin, who conducted him to the emperor.

The viceroy's attention had been entirely taken up by his centre, when it was recalled to his left by a grand movement of cavalry directed by the enemy on that point. General Delzons, who, since the morning, had been menaced by this cavalry, formed his first brigade into a square on the left of the Borodino. Several times he was on the point of being attacked; but the enemy, seeing that he could make no impression on him advanced to the extremity of our left, and commenced a brisk attack on the Bavarian light cavalry, which were for a moment thrown into disorder. The prince, who happened then to be at this point, threw himself into the middle of a square formed by the eighty-fourth, and prepared to set it in motion, when the cossacks were in their turn repulsed, and taking to flight, disengaged our left. Every thing was then restored to the greatest order.

The prince was found at all points exhorting every officer to do his duty, and reminding him, that on this day depended the glory of France. He was seen at all the batteries, causing them to advance in proportion as the enemy gave way; and, braving every peril, he himself instructed the cannoniers how to direct their fire. It was thus that, hastening to every post of danger, from the beginning of the day, his aid-de-camp, Maurice Mejean, received a wound in the thigh, and the equerry, Bellisomi, had his horse killed under him. His highness having at one time placed himself on the parapet of the grand redoubt surrounded by his officers, he remarked from the embrasures all the movements of the enemy, paying no attention to the bullets that passed him on all sides. Among the persons who composed his suite was colonel de Bourmont, whose great merit was only equalled by his rare modesty. He had dismounted with the other officers, and was leaning on the pommel of the saddle, when general Guilleminot letting a paper fall, the colonel stooped to pick it up. That motion saved him his life, for at that very instant a cannon-ball passed through the breast of his horse.

During this memorable day, the emperor remained constantly in the rear of the centre; and made, on the extremity of his right several grand manoeuvres with the Westphalians and the Poles to support the duke of Elchingen (Ney), in his repeated and desperate attempts to turn the position of the enemy. On this point the Russians obstinately withstood all our efforts, and repulsed with considerable loss the Westphalians and the Poles.

Although we had taken two redoubts, the enemy had still a third, situated on another eminence, and separated by a ravine. It was from thence that, establishing some batteries well served, they kept up an incessant fire on our regiments, some of which were sheltered by a wood, and others were behind the grand redoubt. We remained during several hours in this state of inaction; the artillery vomiting from every side flames and death. At this period general Houard was killed by grape-shot, while commanding the second brigade of the thirteenth division; companion in arms to general Plausanne, they perished on the same day. United in their lives, they were not separated in death; for, they were both interred on that field which had witnessed their gallantry.

The fourth corps, which, since ten o'clock had sustained with intrepidity the attacks of the enemy, was not the only one that had losses to deplore. Although the battle was not yet concluded there was not a corps that had not to mourn the death of one or more of its chiefs. I should make too long a digression from my subject were I to enumerate all the generals who purchased with their lives the success of this bloody day; but there were some, who, by their courage and their virtue, had gained the esteem of all the army. They excited that universal regard which brave men alone can inspire. They were the subject of general observation and applause, while living, and the circumstances of their death will be read with the liveliest interest. Among these I ought to include general Augustus Caulincourt, who was killed as he entered the grand redoubt, at the head of the fifth cuirassiers. Cut down in the flower of his age he had witnessed more combats than years. To the valour of a soldier, he united the politeness of the gentleman. He was well informed, polished, sprightly, noble, and generous. In short, he was endowed with all the qualities and all the virtues that should characterize the French soldier. Besides generals Plausanne and Houard, of whom I have just now spoken, we had to deplore the loss of the generals of brigade, Compere and Marion, as well as general count Lepel, aid-de-camp to the king of Westphalia, not forgetting, above all, the just tribute of respect due to the memory of the intrepid Montbrun. His undaunted intrepidity had long inspired us with a melancholy presentiment that such a warrior must necessarily perish on the field of battle. A worthy successor of general Lassale, he died like him; and like him he was an honour to our light cavalry. The number of generals wounded amounted to thirty, among whom were the generals of division Grouchy, Rapp, Compans, Morand, Desaix, Lahossaye, &c.

Although the day was far advanced, the fate of many an unfortunate being was yet to be decided. The cannon roared with unabated fury, and continued to overwhelm new victims. The viceroy, ever indefatigable, and unmindful of danger, was on every part of the field of battle, exposed to a shower of grape-shot and bullets. The firing still continued, and, in the evening, it was so briskly maintained that the legion of the Vistula, commanded by general Claparede, was forced to kneel down, behind the grand redoubt. We remained more than an hour in this uncomfortable position, when the prince of Neufchatel (Berthier) coming up, had an interview with the viceroy, which lasted till near dark. Their conference being ended, prince Eugene issued different orders to his divisions and the firing ceased. The enemy was then more quiet, and only fired a few shot at intervals, while the silence of the last redoubt, gave us reason to believe that the Russians were preparing to retreat on the road to Mojaïsk.

The weather, which had been very fine during the day, became, towards evening, cold and damp. The whole army bivouacked on the ground it had gained. The viceroy, who, since four o'clock in the morning had not dismounted from his horse, took the road behind the eminence occupied by the royal guard, and where his highness expected to have found his tent erected; but his people having lost their way, he and his suit were indebted to the hospitality of general Lecchi, who could only give us a supper without bread, and a tumbril for the bed on which the prince reposed. This encampment was most cruel; neither men nor horses had any thing to eat, and the want of wood exposed us to all the rigour of a cold and frosty night.

The next day (8th September), very early, we returned to the field of battle. What had been predicted the preceding evening had actually taken place. The enemy, seeing the intrepidity with which we carried his redoubts, despaired of maintaining his position; and resolved to evacuate it during the night. As we passed over the ground which they had occupied, we were enabled to judge of the immense loss that the Russians had sustained. In the space of a square league, almost every spot was covered with the killed or wounded. On many places the bursting of the shells had promiscuously heaped together men and horses. The fire of our howitzers had been so destructive that mountains of dead bodies were scattered over the plain; and the few places that were not encumbered with the slain, were covered with broken lances, muskets helmets, and cuirasses or with grape-shot and bullets, as numerous as hailstones after a violent storm. But the most horrid spectacle was the interior of the ravines; almost all the wounded who were able to drag themselves along, had taken refuge there to avoid the shot. These miserable wretches, heaped one upon another, and almost suffocated with blood, uttering the most dreadful groans, and invoking death with piercing cries, eagerly besought us to put an end to their torments.

While the cavalry pursued the enemy, the viceroy ordered his engineers to destroy the redoubt; and as the fourth corps remained encamped on the field of battle, it was presumed we should pass the night there. His highness had also ordered his suite to establish themselves in the church of Borodino, the only building that had escaped the flames, but it was filled with the wounded, and the surgeons were employed in dressing and amputating. The staff of the prince then determining to establish their quarters in the village of Novoe, near the road to Mojaïsk on the banks of the Kologha, were on the point of entering the castle, when some parties of cossacks obliged them precipitately to retreat.

In the meantime the viceroy being informed that the fifteenth division, returned from Witepsk, had at length, joined again their corps, received orders to advance. Arrived at the village, below which was the redoubt abandoned by the enemy, we left, on the right, the high road of Mojaïsk, which was pursued by the centre corps and marched along the Kolgha. On this march we were convinced that it would been impossible to have turned the right of the Russians on the preceding evening. They had not only many bodies of reserve on that side, but likewise several masked batteries along the river. Within half a league of the village of Krasnoë we found four other great redoubts, in the form of a square, which defended the road, and were not quite completed.

Quitting the field of battle, we left a detachment of all the stragglers that could be collected, to defend the position under the orders of colonel Bourmont. This difficult task was perfectly accomplished by that officer, who, after destroying the enemy's works, rejoined us in a few days. During this time he lived in the midst of the dead and the dying, and was obliged to procure his provisions at a distance of more than five leagues.

Whilst we were preparing to encamp at the *chateau* of Krasnoë, a rumour was spread of the arrival of Napoleon. This news, however, was not confirmed. On a height before us, we heard our sharp-shooters engaged with the cossacks. In one of the charges of cavalry, colonel Marboeuf was wounded at the head of his regiment.

The *chateau* of Krasnoë, and the village of this name, are situated near the Moskwa. The following morning we crossed this river, and, on its left, prepared to attack Mojaïsk; but the viceroy, with his escort, advanced only to the suburbs. Here we saw this unhappy town enveloped in flames. The inhabitants had fled, and our dragoons made only a few prisoners, found in the houses on this side of the river. Several batteries, established on an eminence beyond Mojaïsk, proved to us that we were masters of it. In effect we learned that Napoleon had taken it, after an obstinate engagement, and that the enemy in burning the town had not abandoned it without making a brave defence, leaving the streets and squares filled with the dead and the dying.

Our staff examined the environs of Mojaïsk, when the fourth corps, moving to the left, followed a high road, through a thick wood; beyond which we saw a considerable village, and, further on, we found larger one, called Vedenskoë.

On this delightful spot was a *chateau*, the furniture of which corresponded with the beauty of the exterior; but in an instant it was entirely pillaged, without any other advantage than some thousands of bottles of wine, which were seized by the soldiers.

From Vedenskoë, turning to the right, we crossed a rivulet, close to a little village, and, pursuing a road through thick underwood and briars, we arrived at a village, called Vrouinkovo, where we understood the head-quarters were to be established. On entering it, we perceived on an eminence at a distance, sonic very neat houses, and four steeples elegantly constructed. We were about to halt in this village, where abundance seemed to reign, when it was announced that the fourth corps was to proceed to a town of the name of Rouza, the steeples of which were plainly perceived. Leaving Vrouinkovo, we saw a great number of peasants with carts, loaded with their most valuable furniture and property. A sight so new excited our astonishment, and asking colonel Asselin what could be the reason of this singular assemblage, he answered me as follows:

> In proportion as our armies advanced into the interior of Russia, the emperor Alexander, seconding the wishes of the nobility, and following the example of Spain, endeavoured to make this a national war. Accordingly, the nobility and the priests have, by persuasions and by bribes, induced all the peasants who were dependent upon them, to rise *en masse* against us. Of all the districts which have adhered to this system of defence, that of Rouza has shown itself the most zealous. The whole population, animated by their seigneur, who had declared himself the chief of the insurrection, was properly organized, and ready to join the Russian army, as soon as they should receive the necessary orders.

As Rouza was at a distance of five or six leagues from the high road, the inhabitants had flattered themselves that we should not pass through their town, and had consequently remained secure and tranquil. What was their surprise, or rather their terror, when I was sent by the viceroy, and presented myself with a dozen of Bavarian light horse before the town? The peasants, dismayed, rushed from their houses, hastily harnessed their horses to the carts which you now see, and fled with the utmost precipitation.

The men, however who had been enrolled for the levy, collected at the voice of their lord, and, armed with poles, lances, and scithes, assemble in the square, and immediately advanced towards us; but this timed populace could not resist a few soldiers accustomed to battle, and presently took to flight. The chief alone evinced more firmness. He awaited us on the square, and, armed with a poinard, menaced all who summoned him to surrender. – '*How can I survive the dishonour of my country,*' cried he, foaming with rage. '*Our altars are no more! Our empire is disgraced! Take my life, it is odious to me!*' We wished to calm him, and endeavoured to wrench his poinard from him; but he became more furious, and wounded several of our soldiers, who then listening only to revenge, killed him with repeated stabs of the bayonet.

This was scarcely effected when the advanced-guard of the fourth corps entered Rouza. On my reciting what had happened [continued the colonel] they immediately pursued the peasants, who had fled with their effects and their cattle. They soon came up with them, and those whom you see here, are a part of the fugitives escaped from Rouza. Go into the town, and you will see many more of them.

As we approached the town, we saw a great number of these carts brought back by the dragoons. It was an affecting spectacle to behold these vehicles loaded with children and old people. The heart was pierced with grief to think how soon our soldiers would divide among them the carts and horses which constituted the sole fortune of these disconsolate families.

At length we entered Rouza; and as we advanced to the very centre of the town, we saw in every street, a crowd of soldiers, who pillaged the houses, unmindful of the cries of the inhabitants, or the tears of the mothers, who, to soften the hearts of their conquerors, presented their children on their knees bathed in tears, and distractedly wringing their hands, these innocent creatures begged only for their lives. This rage for plunder was justified in some, who, dying with hunger, only sought after provisions; but others, under this pretence, pillaged every thing, and even robbed the women and children of the very clothes which covered them.

The viceroy had arrived several hours with his staff only. He had left the divisions of infantry and the royal guards, who to-day encamped in our rear between Rouza and Vrouenkovo. Every one enchanted to find himself in so delightful a town as Rouza, give himself up to that security, or rather the disorder, which abundance produces after long privations; when suddenly some Bavarian light horse, who had been sent to reconnoitre, returned at full speed, reporting that several squadrons of cossacks were advancing towards the town. It would be difficult to describe the sensation produced by this news. The tranquillity that we had enjoyed, opposed to the imminent danger which now threatened, produced a most sudden transition from the liveliest joy to the deepest despair. 'The cossacks are here!' cried one; 'There they come!' cried another quite aghast. 'What can we oppose to them?' we asked one another. 'Nothing but some miserable soldiers, come hither to plunder the peasants.' This was, however, our only resource. They were immediately assembled in the square, but they were only about sixty in number, and half of them without arms.

The viceroy informed of the cause of this alarm, mounted his horse and ordered his officers to follow him. We hastened out of the town, and entered the plain; but what was our surprise, when, instead of finding several squadrons, we only perceived about a dozen horsemen, and at so great a distance that we could scarcely distinguish them. Some Bavarian light horse who were with us, advanced to reconnoitre, and reported that they were cossacks : but by their small number, and timid and cautious march we could easily perceive we had nothing to fear from them.

As these cossacks might have been detached from a considerable corps, the prince thought it necessary to confirm the order which he had already given for some troops to advance; but he modified it so far as to content himself with two battalions instead of the whole of the thirteenth division, which had at first been ordered. These two battalion encamping before Rouza dissipated our fears. Every one now returned quietly to his lodgings, where a table well served, and excellent wines, made us soon forget the alarm we had experienced towards the close of the day.

The following day we remained at Rouza. The viceroy profited by this repose to make the chief of his staff draw up a circumstantial report of the celebrated battle of the 7th of September, in which the fourth corps had particularly distinguished itself.

Whilst the thirteenth and fourteenth divisions laid before the emperor their claims on his regard, the fifteenth division, not less deserving than the rest, but deprived of the honour of fighting in the battle of the Moskwa, was likewise justly entitled to distinguished notice, in consideration of the numberless hardships which it had undergone in its expedition to Witepsk. This brave division, proceeding constantly through a marshy country, meeting only with deserted and ravaged villages, was always compelled to bivouac during the night, and generally without provisions, and every day to make the most painful and harassing marches to attack an enemy, which always fled at its appearance. For nearly twenty days it saw only the fields which we had completely laid waste; and at length, worn out with hunger, weariness, and disease, this unfortunate division, which, with its chief, was worthy of a better fate, could not reach Borodino till the day after the battle. The fatigues which it had endured, and especially, the great losses it had sustained, obliged the viceroy to leave it in reserve. It was the highest proof of esteem which the prince could bestow, to unite them with the heroes of the royal guards, the greatest part of whom had been taken from this division.

On quitting Rouza it was decided that this position, so important on account of the abundance of provisions which were still to be found there, should be maintained. The castle, situated on a small eminence, surrounded with ditches, afforded a sufficient defence for the garrison, and guarded them against a *coup de main*. This honourable command was given to captain Maison Neuve, who proved himself worthy of the confidence reposed in him. As long as the position was retained, this brave and intelligent officer rendered himself useful to the army by the skilfulness of his dispositions, and by the ease with which he appeared to comprehend every intention of the enemy.

Book V

Moscow

After the battle of the Moskwa, our triumphant army marched in three columns towards the capital of the Russian empire. Napoleon, impatient to get possession of it, pursued the enemy with his accustomed vigour, on the high road of Smolensko; while prince Poniatowski, at the head of the fifth corps marched on the right by way of Kaluga. The viceroy commanding the fourth corps, continued on the left flank, and, taking the road of Zwenighorod, proceeded towards Moscow, where the whole army was to assemble.

We could judge of the consternation which reigned in this capital, by the terror with which we inspired the country people. Our arrival at Rouza (9th of September) and the cruel manner in which we had treated the inhabitants, were no sooner known, than all the villages on the road to Moscow, were instantly abandoned. The country presented one uniform scene of horrible desolation: for most of those who fled, burnt, in despair, their houses, their *chateaux*, and the grain and forage, which were scarcely gathered. All these unhappy beings, terrified by the fatal and useless resistance of the inhabitants of Rouza, threw away the pikes, with which they had been armed, and swiftly fled to conceal their wives and their little ones in the thick forests at a distance from our route.

On approaching Moscow, we had hoped that civilization, which enervates the soul, and especially an attachment to property, so natural to the inhabitants of large towns, would have induced the people not to quit their habitations. We were convinced that the rapacity of our soldiers was principally excited by the deserted state in which we found the villages. But the country around Moscow does not belong to the inhabitants of that beautiful city; it was the property of the lords who had declared against us and their peasants, equally enslaved and oppressed with those of the Nieper and of the Volga, obeyed the orders of their masters. They had been enjoined, on pain of death, to fly at our approach, and to in the woods, whatever could be useful to us.

We perceived the execution of this fatal measure on entering the village of Apalchtchouina. The houses deserted, the castle abandoned, the furniture dashed to pieces, and the provisions destroyed, presented a spectacle of the most frightful desolation. All these ravages showed us what sacrifices a people sufficiently magnanimous to prefer independence to riches, will cheerfully make.

Near Karinskoé, a village half way toward Zwenighorod, whither we were marching, the cossacks appeared. According to their custom, they made no stand against our advanced-guard, but contested themselves with observing us, by marching on an eminence at our left, parallel to the high road. On the summit of this height, in the midst of a thick wood of birch rose the gray walls and the steeples of an ancient abbey. At the foot of the hill stood the little town of Zwenighorod, built on the banks of the Moskwa. On this point the cossacks formed themselves into several bodies, and skirmished for some time with our light troops, but they were gradually dislodged from their ambuscades, and we took post round Zwenighorod.

The abbey situated above this little town, commands the course of the Moskwa. Its embattled walls, more than twenty feet in height, and between five and six feet thick, are flanked by four great towers, with embrasures. This edifice, constructed in the thirteenth or fourteenth century, reminds us of the times when the Muscovites, filled with veneration for their priests, suffered the sacerdotal authority to take precedence of that of the nobles; and when the Czar marched, on days of ceremony, before the patriarch of Moscow, holding the bridle of his horse. But these monks, so powerful and so formidable before the time of Peter I, were brought back again to the simplicity of the apostles, when this great monarch, on founding his empire, confiscated their property and diminished their number.

To conceive a proper idea of the changes produced by this reform, it was sufficient to enter the abbey of Zwenighorod. At the sight of these lofty towers and enormous walls, we supposed that the interior contained an agreeable and commodious residence, and that we should find among these monks the wonted abundance of all richly-endowed abbeys. A large iron gate, strongly barricadoed, confirmed us in the persuasion that this convent was well supplied with every thing that our soldiers needed. We were about to force the entry, when an old man whose flowing beard was whiter than his robe, came to admit us. He was desired to conduct us to the abbot. On entering the court, we were much surprised at finding that this vast edifice did not correspond with the high opinion we had conceived of it; and that our guide instead of introducing us into the apartments of the superior, conducted us to a small chapel, where we saw four monks prostrate at the foot of an altar, constructed in the Grecian style. These venerable old men, when they perceived us, threw themselves at our feet and embracing our knees, entreated, in the name of the God whom they adored, that we would respect their church, and the graves of some bishops, of which they were the faithful guardians. 'You may judge, by our miserable appearance,' they addressed us by means of an interpreter, 'that we can have no hidden treasures; and our food is so coarse that many of your soldiers would scorn to eat it. We have no other possessions than our relics and our altars. Deign to respect them from a reverence for a religion so similar to your own.' This we promised, and our assurance was confirmed on the arrival of the viceroy, who established his headquarters in this abbey, and thereby preserved the church and the convent, from the pillage with which they were threatened.

While this asylum, formerly so peaceful, was a prey to the tumult unavoidable on such occasions, I perceived one of these pious monks, who, to conceal himself, took refuge in a cell almost under ground, the simplicity of which presented nothing to excite our avarice. This friar, sensible of my attentions to him, rewarded them by acknowledging that he spoke French, and that he wished to have the pleasure of conversing with me. Charmed with his candour, I profited by it, to inform myself of every thing relating to the sentiments and character of a nation, from whom we had conquered more than two hundred and fifty leagues of territory, without becoming acquainted with them. When I mentioned Moscow, he told me that it was the place of his nativity, and I perceived that deep sighs interrupted his speech. I judged by his silent grief that he mourned over the misfortunes to which this great capital would soon be exposed. I sympathized with him; but, anxious to know the state of affairs in that city which we were on the point of entering, I ventured at length to ask him concerning it.

The French have entered the territory of Russia with immense force [said this venerable monk]; they come to ravage our beloved country, and they advance even to the sacred city – the centre of our empire, and the source of our prosperity. Unacquainted with our manners and our character, they think that we shall bend under their yoke, and that, compelled to choose between our homes and independence, we shall, like too many others, submit to their dominion, and renounce that national pride in which consists the true power of a people. No, Napoleon is mistaken. We are too wise not to abhor his tyranny; and we are not sufficiently corrupted to prefer slavery to liberty. In vain he hopes to force us, by his numberless armies, to sue for peace. He does not remember that the population of is at the absolute control of the nobility. Out seigneurs, able at their pleasure to cause whole districts to emigrate, will order their peasants to fly into the deserts, at the approach of the invader, or, if necessary, will destroy every town and village, rather than give them up to a true barbarian, whose tyranny is more dreadful to us than death itself.

We are aware, too, that Napoleon relies much on the dissensions which used formerly to exist between the monarch and the nobles; but the love of our country has stifled every ancient feud. He flatters himself, likewise, that he will be able to arm the people against the great. Vain efforts! the people are, from religion, obedient to their masters: nor will they confide in the deceitful promises of him who burns their cottages, murders their children, devastates their country, and subverts temples. Besides, has not the whole of Europe witnessed the most striking instances of his perfidy? Is he not the scourge of Germany, of whom he professed to be the protector? Spain, too, having trusted to the sincerity of his alliance, is become one vast burying-place! The pontiff who crowned him raised him from a private station to the first throne in the world, what reward has he received for that diadem? An ignominious captivity! And even your own country, which, for the sake of a foreigner seems to have forgotten the race of St. Louis, what advantages does she derive from her submission? Incessant new taxes, to maintain a crowd of worthless courtiers, or to gratify the luxury of a family insatiable in their pleasures. In addition to this, you have prescriptions and secret executions without number. Your very thoughts are fettered, and whole generations are destroyed. In truth, your mothers have often been reduced to the sad necessity of deploring their fecundity. This [said the Venerable old man to me], this is the situation in which your tyrant has placed you : a tyrant who is the more vain and odious, because he sprung from an obscure family; and who, formerly having scarcely one domestic to serve him, is now desirous that the whole universe should crouch at his feet, and that even kings should be compelled to wait in his anti-room. If I did not fear to disgrace the majesty of that monarch who loves us as we love him, I would draw a comparison between your monarch and ours, - but such a comparison would only produce a shocking contrast, as it would place vice in constant opposition to virtue.

Struck by the energy of this priest, whose strength of mind had suffered nothing from age, I remained silent, and was at the same time charmed with his candour. Affected by the confidence with which he had honoured me, I thought I might cast off all reserve, and derive much useful information from his conversation. 'As you have just mentioned the emperor Alexander,' said I to him, 'pray tell me what is become of him? Since we passed the Wilia we have never heard any thing of him; and at Witepsk, in a public audience, Napoleon announced, with much satisfaction, that this monarch had shared the fate of his father, having fallen a victim, at Wiliki-luki, to the treachery of his courtiers.'

He cannot have much greatness of soul [answered the old man, smiling] who triumphs at the death of an enemy. But, to prove to you the falsity of that report, and to show you how much harmony exists among all classes at this critical moment, and how beloved our sovereign is, I will read you a letter, which was sent to me from Moscow, a few days after Alexander had arrived there from the army.

At these words he took out the letter, translating it to me as he went on.

Moscow, July 27[1]

This day will add new lustre to our annals, and the remembrance of it will descend to the remotest posterity, as an eternal testimony of Russian patriotism and loyalty. It will record the ardent attachment, which our illustrious nobility, and every class of citizens, feel for our beloved sovereign. After a notification published in the evening, the nobility and the merchants assembled, at eight o'clock on the following morning, at the palace Slobode, to wait the arrival of our most gracious emperor. Notwithstanding the object of this meeting had not been communicated, every one attended, full of those loyal feelings which the appeal of the father of his country to his children, in the capital of his empire, would naturally inspire. The silence which reigned in this vast assembly clearly proved their union, and their disposition to submit to any sacrifice. When the manifesto of his imperial majesty was read in the presence of the governor of Moscow, appealing to the nation at large, and calling on every one to defend his country against an enemy 'who, with craft in his heart, and seduction on his lips, was bringing fetters and indissoluble chains for Russia,' the illustrious posterity of the Pojarskies, animated by the most ardent zeal, immediately testified their readiness to sacrifice the whole of their property, and even their lives. They immediately resolved that levies should be made in the government of Moscow, to form an army of the interior, consisting of ten men out of every hundred, who should be armed to the utmost of their ability, and provided with clothing and pay. The manifesto being afterwards read in the assembly of the merchants this body, animated by the general zeal, resolved that a sum of money be levied on each of them, proportionate to their respective capitals, to defray the expense of the army of the interior. Not satisfied with this, the greater part of them were desirous of making further sacrifices. They demanded permission to open a voluntary subscription for that purpose, and in less than an hour the sum subscribed amounted to more than one million and a half of roubles.

Such was the disposition of these two bodies when his majesty, who had attended divine service at the church of the palace, appeared among the nobles. After assuring them, in a short speech, that he considered the zeal of the nobility as the support of his throne; and, acknowledging that they had at all times, and under all circumstances, shown themselves the guardians and faithful defenders of the integrity and glory of their beloved country, he condescended to give them a brief sketch of military

1   The translation of this letter having appeared in the French journals, it is given here as it was published in the Moniteur.

affairs, which then required extraordinary measures of defence. When he was informed of the unanimous decision of the two bodies, who had resolved to furnish, to clothe, and to arm, at their own expense, eighty thousand men for the defence of Moscow, he received this new proof of attachment to his person, and of love to the country, with the feelings of a father who loves his children; and who is proud of their courage. Yielding to the emotions which overpowered him, he exclaimed, 'I did not expect less: you have fully confirmed my opinion of you.'

Afterwards his imperial majesty condescended to proceed to the saloon where the merchants were assembled, and being informed of the zeal they had shown both in the resolution of levying a sum on the whole body and making an extraordinary voluntary subscription of a million and a half of roubles, he pressed his gracious satisfaction in terms dictated by wisdom itself. His speech was followed by the general exclamation of, 'We are ready to sacrifice for our father, not only our fortunes, but our lives.' These were the words of the descendants of the immortal Minin. The scene of that morning requires the pen of a new Tacitus; while the pencil of a second Apelles alone would do justice to the picture, which represented the monarch and the father beaming kindness and benevolence, receiving from his children, who thronged around him, the sacrifices which they were offering on the altar of their country.

May our enemy be informed of this! May that proud man, who sports with the fate of his subjects, learn it, and tremble! We shall all march against him. We are guided by religion, and by loyalty for our sovereign and country. We will conquer, or perish together.

After having read this letter, the pious friar informed me that the patriarch Platon, archbishop of Moscow; notwithstanding his advanced and decrepid age, watched still in the spirit and in prayer, for the welfare of his sovereign and the empire, and that he had just sent to his imperial majesty the precious image of Saint Serge, bishop of Radouègue. The monarch, added he, accepted this sacred relic, and presented it to the army of Moscow, hoping that it would be safe under the protection of this saint, who, once, by his benediction, shielded the victorious Demitri Douskoï, in his combat against the cruel Maniaï.

This is the letter of his eminency Platon, dated from the abbey Troitsa,[2] July 26th.

Moscow, the capital of the empire, the new Jerusalem, receives her Christ like a mother, in the arms of her faithful sons; and perceiving, through the mist which is raised, the brilliant glory of his power, she sings joyfully, Hosannah, praised be he who is arrived! Let the arrogant and shameless Goliath bring his mortal terrors from the limits of France to the confines of Russia! Peaceful religion, this sling of the Russian Da-

2 About fifteen leagues distant from Moscow.

vid, will soon destroy his sanguinary pride. This image of Saint Serge, ancient defender of our country's happiness, is offered to your imperial majesty's acceptance.

Astonished at a custom so different from ours, I asked whether it was really true, that the emperor Alexander had given this standard to his soldiers.

I am so certain of it that it would be sacrilegious to doubt it. Letters from Moscow have since informed us, that bishop Augustin, vicar of that capital, having assembled all the troops in the town,[3] chanted a *Te Deum* and presenting them with the image of Saint Serge, pronounced a discourse which dissolved the whole congregation in tears. We have seen these troops passing under the walls of our abbey, in their way to the battle of Moscow, and carrying with veneration that sacred standard. They marched to the combat like true christian soldiers, devoted to their religion, their country, and their prince. These sentiments were expressed in their countenances; a celestial joy beamed from their eyes at the thought of combating the enemy. Every warrior, even those who had just entered the service, glowed with the ardour of most experienced veterans, and showed that unlimited submission to his chiefs, and observed that strict discipline, which is the duty and the surest sign of a good soldier. The country people, who saw them pass, implored from the bottom of their hearts, the protection of heaven on these brave men who proceeded from the ancient capital of Russia, that city, which in former times, had, with her own forces, laid the insolent enemy in the dust, who presumptuously came to destroy it.

Filled with astonishment at the extraordinary things which this good old man had communicated to me, I felt the deepest respect for a nation so great even in its misfortunes; and I said to myself, 'That people must be invincible, who, firm to their principles, shrink not at the approach of danger, and stake their own preservation on that of their religion and their laws.'

Early on the following morning we quitted the abbey. As I retired from it, I looked behind, and saw the first rays of the rising sun, gilding the, summit of those lofty walls, which, after our departure, became a prey to undisciplined brigands. I ruminated on these painful ideas, and, taking a road parallel with the Moskwa, I observed that bridges had been erected before Zwenighorod, with the intention of opening a communication with the grand army, who marched towards Moscow on the opposite bank.

---

3   Saturday, August 17th, or, according to our calender, August 29th, which, as is well-known, anticipates the Russian calender by 12 days.

We followed the course of the Moskwa, when the cossacks again appeared, manoeuvring just in the same manner as they had done the night before. They attempted, for a moment, near Aksinino, to stop the Bavarian light horse; but some of their men being wounded, they fled in disorder, and retired beyond the Moskwa, which we crossed below the village of Spaskoë. The river was shallow at that point, and both men and horses easily effected a passage. The cossacks, who waited for us at the entrance of a wood dispersed when they saw that the barrier which separated them from us had been overstepped. Thence we pursued our march as far as Buzaïevo, where the post-house alone remained, and a castle, on a very steep eminence, surrounded by woods in which prince Eugene lodged.

The following morning, (September 14th), anxious to arrive at Moscow we commenced our march at an early hour, and passed through several deserted villages. On the banks of the Moskwa, towards our right, were some magnificent *chateaux*, which the cossacks had pillaged, to deprive us of every comfort which these places could afford. The corn, ready for harvest, had either been trodden down, or eaten by the horses. The hay-stacks. which covered the country, were given to the flames, and spread all around an impenetrable smoke, When we at last reached the village of Tscherepkova, and our cavalry continued their march, the viceroy ascended an eminence on our right, and long examined whether Moscow, the object of all our wishes, could be seen; for we regarded it as the end of our fatigues and the termination of our expedition. Several hills yet concealing it from our view, we perceived nothing but clouds of dust, which, rising parallel with our march, indicated the route which the grand army had pursued. A few cannon-shots, fired at a distance, and with long intervals, disposed us to think that our troops were approaching Moscow, without experiencing much resistance.

As we descended from the eminence, we suddenly heard the most dreadful cries. A troop of cossacks, issuing from a neighbouring wood, had, in their accustomed manner, rushed upon our chasseurs, and endeavoured to stop the march of our van-guard. But our brave fellows, far from being intimidated by this unexpected attack, quickly repelled those vain efforts by which a powerless horde strove to impede our entrance into the capital. These were the last struggles of a desperate courage, and the Russians, beaten and dispersed, were obliged to fly, under the walls of the Kremlin, as they had before done on the banks of the Kologha.

We distinguished, at a distance, and amidst the dust, long columns of Russian cavalry, all marching towards Moscow, and all retiring behind the town, as soon as we approached it. While the fourth corps was constructing a bridge across the Moskwa, the staff, about two o'clock, established itself on a lofty hill, whence we perceived a thousand elegant and gilded steeples, which, glittering in the rays of the sun, appeared at the distance like so many flaming globes. One of these globes, placed on the summit of a pillar, or an obelisk, had the exact appearance of a balloon suspended in the air. Transported with delight at this beautiful spectacle, which was the more gratifying, from the remembrance of the melancholy objects which we had hitherto seen, we could not suppress our joy; but with one spontaneous movement, we all exclaimed, *Moscow! Moscow!* At the sound of this wished-for name, the soldiers ran up the hill in crowds, and each discovered new wonders every instant. One admired a noble *chateau* on our left, the elegant architecture of which displayed more than eastern magnificence; another directed his attention towards a palace or a temple; but all were struck with the superb picture this immense town afforded. It is situated in the midst of a fertile plain. The Moskwa is seen meandering through the richest meadows; and, after having fertilized the neighbouring country, takes its course through the middle of the town, separating an immense cluster of houses, built of wood, stone, bricks, constructed in a style which partakes of the gothic and modern architecture, in which, indeed, the architecture of every different nation is strangely mingled. The walls, variously painted, the domes covered with lead, or slates, or glittering with gold, offered the most pleasing variety - whilst the terraces before the palaces, the obelisks over the gates, and, above all, the steeples, really presented to our eyes one of those celebrated cities of Asia, which we had thought had only existed in the creative imagination of the Arabian poets.

We were still contemplating this noble spectacle, when we saw a well-dressed man coming towards us through a by-way from Moscow. Several of our soldiers immediately ran to meet him, and, viewing him with suspicion, were disposed to make him pay dearly for his imprudent curiosity. But the calmness with which he addressed us, and the fluency with which he spoke our language, and above all, our impatience to hear some tidings from Moscow, made us all listen to him with pleasure and interest.

I am not come here to observe your manoeuvres, nor to give you false information; I am an unfortunate merchant, ignorant of everything which relates to war and, notwithstanding being a victim, I have not inquired into the motives which have induced our sovereign to engage in this fatal contest. Your emperor today, about noon, entered Moscow, at the head of his invincible legions; but he found only a deserted town. Some wretches, who have escaped from prison, and some miserable prostitutes, were the only creatures who interrupted its solitude. Hasten, if possible, to stop their excesses. Liberty has only been granted them, with the hope, that all the crimes which they may commit will be attributed to the French army. Being aware of the misfortunes which threaten us, I came to find among you a man sufficiently generous to protect my family; for, in spite of the orders of our government, I cannot consent to abandon my house, and to lead a wandering, miserable life in the woods. I prefer applying to French generosity, and I trust that I shall find a protector among those who have been ever represented to us as our m cruel enemies. The great men of our empire, deceived by a savage and destructive policy, will doubtless attempt to irritate you, by causing the whole population to emigrate, and leaving nothing but a deserted city, if indeed, it is not already sacrificed to the flames.

Every one interrupted him, saying, that it was impossible any people would thus effect their own ruin, from the uncertain hope of involving their enemy in it.

It is but too true that such a resolution is taken, and, if you yet doubt it, know, that count Rastopchin, governor of Moscow, quitted it yesterday. Before he departed, he charged the very outcast of human beings to assist him in his revenge. How far he will proceed I know not; but I tremble when I recollect that he has often threatened to burn Moscow, if the French should approach it. Such barbarity must seem atrocious and even incredible to you, if you are not aware of the deadly hatred which your unheard of victories have inspired in the nobility. They know that the whole of Europe is under your domination, and, from a sentiment of pride, they would destroy their native country, rather than see it subjugated.

If the nobility, ashamed of their defeats, had not meditated the destruction of the capital, why should they have fled with all their property? Why have the merchants likewise been compelled to follow them, carrying with them their goods and their treasures? Why, lastly, have no magistrates remained in this desolated town, to implore the mercy of the conqueror? They have all fled, and thus seem determined to urge your soldiers to every excess; for the legal authorities, the only protection of the citizens, by abandoning their posts, have abandoned every thing.

This unfortunate Moscovite shed many bitter tears while he thus addressed us. To calm his grief we promised what he requested, and endeavoured to console him by dissipating those fears, too well founded, which the dangers of his unhappy country had excited. We questioned him as to the direction in which the Russians had retreated; what they had done since the battle of the Moskwa, and, lastly, what was become of the emperor Alexander and his brother Constantine? He answered all our questions in the most satisfactory manner, and confirmed the intelligence which had been already communicated to me by the friar in Zwenighorod. This unhappy man, becoming more composed, and being secretly flattered by the agreeable surprise which the sight of Moscow and its environs had caused, consented at my request to give us some account of a city, the conquest of which promised to crown all our hopes. He expressed himself as follows:

> Moscow, built in the Asiatic style, has five enclosures, one within another; the last comprising the town and its suburbs, is about thirty werstes[4] in circumference; but the fourth enclosure, which comprises the town only, and which is called *Semlaingorod,* is but twelve. The suburbs, or *slobodes,* are thirty in number. In winter, the population amounts to three hundred thousand souls; but on the approach of summer, every one retires to his countryhouse, and this number diminishes one third.
>
> The high towers and the embattled walls, which you see rising in the midst of the town, trace the first enclosure, called *Kremlin.* This fortress in the form of a perfect triangle, is celebrated in our annals, and has never been taken.[5] The plan of it was drawn, towards the fourteenth century, by some Italian architects.[6] The interior of the *Kremlin* is divided into two parts; the one called *Krepots,* or citadel, contains only the palace, and some churches, each of which is surmounted by five domes. From this place you may perfectly distinguish them, as much by their elevation as by the gilding of the steeples, and their fantastical architecture. In the second enclosure are some noble houses, commercial streets, and the place called *Bazar,* or *Khitaigorod,* a name given it by the Tartars, who were its founders.
>
> Foedor, the elder brother of Peter the Great, began to improve Moscow. He constructed several buildings of stone, but without any regular architecture. To him we owe the first stud of beautiful horses, and some useful embellishments.[7] Although Peter had a particular affection for Petersburg, nevertheless his genius, which embraced every thing, did not neglect Moscow. He caused it to be paved, adorned it with many superb edifices, and enriched it with valuable manufactures; and, lastly, under Elizabeth, a university was established.[8]
>
> The arsenal within the krepots, is remarkable for six culverins, mounted on fixed carriages, the largest of which is twenty-four feet in length. Near the principal gate, is likewise an enormous howitzer, at least three feet in diameter. Further on is the ancient palace of the Czars. It is the residence of our emperors. Yours has now established himself

---

4   Seven leagues.

5   The people of Moscow believe that the preservation of the empire depended on the towers of this ancient fortress. A false tradition persuaded them that it had never been taken. Thus, to express the idea of security, it was a common saying, 'as safe as within the Kremlin.'

6   Voltaire's Histoire de Russie, volume I, page 50, stereotype edition.

7   Voltaire's Histoire de Russie, vol. I, page 52.

8   *Idem.*

there. Behind is the palace of the senate near which is the cathedral of St. Iwan, and the foundation of an ancient tower, with the famous bell which was cast in Moscow, towards the middle of the sixteenth century, under the Czar Boris Godono. It is an astonishing production, and proves, that even at that remote period, the Russians had made great progress in civilization and the fine arts. This bell, justly admired for the beauty of the figures which surround it, surpasses in size the most famous in Europe.[9]

From the krepots you enjoy a delightful prospect. On the right and left are two bridges, across the Moskwa. Beyond the river are some magnificent palaces; and in the back-ground is a fine country, embellished with many noble mansions.

'But,' said I, interrupting the Moscovite, 'tell us what immense fabric is this with an infinite number of windows on each side, and which, by its enormous magnitude, seems to command the whole town?'

It is the hospital Sheremitow, built by the illustrious family of that name. One of their ancestors was the glorious companion in arms of Peter the Great; and the riches which he acquired, were always devoted to the prosperity and glory of the nation. In this building were educated the orphans and the children of those who have defended the country. But at present the children have been removed, and their fathers, to the number of twenty thousand who have been gloriously wounded at Mojaïsk, occupy their places. These unhappy men are abandoned, death is before their eyes; and if your generosity does not in this moment of calamity afford them assistance, they will be left to the in the most frightful torments.

From the gate of Petersburg to that of Kaluga, numerous palaces are seen, which, by their riches and magnificence, attract the attention of the traveller. All these palaces are newly constructed, and announce the prodigious wealth that Russia has accumulated within these few years. But the most astonishing of all, is the palace of Orlow. It belongs to the only heiress of this name, whose income exceeds six millions of rubles.[10] The extent of this palace is immense, and the beauty of the interior corresponds with the spacious courts and enchanting gardens which surround it.

You will find in my country a great number of edifices, justly celebrated as the most beautiful in Europe. It is useless to describe them to you, since you will soon see them yourselves. I wish that you may long admire them, but a fatal presentiment convinces me, that this great and superb town, justly considered as the market of Europe and of Asia, will, ere long, astonish the world by the most dreadful catastrophe.

9   Voltaire's Histoire de Russie, tom.i, page 51.
10 One million sterling.

As he uttered these words the unfortunate man seemed suffocated with grief. I pitied him; but I could not leave him without asking the name of that great building of red and white brick, which was seen to the north of the town, on the road to Petersburg. He informed me, that it was the famous *chateau* of Peterskoë, where the sovereigns of Russia used to reside previous to their coronation.

Although the bridge over the Moskwa was not yet finished, the viceroy ordered the troops of his corps to cross the river. The cavalry had already passed it, and had taken post before the village of Khorchévo. We were here officially informed of the entry of our troops into Moscow. The fourth corps received orders to halt at this place till the following day, when an hour would be appointed for us to enter the capital of the Russian empire.

On the 15th of September our corps left the village, where it had encamped, at an early hour, and marched to Moscow. As we approached the city, we saw that it had no walls, and that a simple parapet of earth was the only work which constituted the outer enclosure. Nothing indicated that the town was inhabited; and the road by which we arrived was so deserted, that we saw neither Russian or even French soldiers. No cry, no noise was heard, in the midst of this awful solitude. We pursued our march a prey to the utmost anxiety, and that anxiety was redoubled when we perceived a thick smoke, which arose in the form of a column, from the centre of the town. It was at first believed that the Russians, agreeably to their custom, had, in retreating, set fire to some magazines. Recollecting, however, the recital of the inhabitant of Moscow, we feared that his prediction was about to be fulfilled. Eager to know the cause of this conflagration, we in vain endeavored to find some one who might satisfy our irrepressible curiosity, and the impossibility of satisfying it, increased our impatience, and augmented our alarm.

We did not enter at the first barrier that presented itself, but, moving to the left, we continued to march round the town. At length, according to the orders of the viceroy, I placed the troops of the fourth corps in a position, to guard the high road towards Petersburgh. The thirteenth and fifteenth divisions, encamped around the *chateau* of Peterskoë, the fourteenth established itself in the village between Moscow and this *chateau*, and the Bavarian light cavalry was a league in front of the village.

When these positions were taken, the viceroy entered Moscow, and fixed his headquarters in the palace of prince Momonoff, in the beautiful street of St. Petersburg. The quarter assigned to our corps was one of the finest in the town. It was composed entirely of superb edifices, and of houses, which, although of wood, had an appearance of surprising grandeur and magnificence. The magistrates having abandoned the town, every one established himself at his pleasure in these sumptuous palaces; even the subaltern officer was lodged in vast apartments richly decorated, and of which he could easily fancy himself to be the proprietor, since no one appeared but a humble and submissive porter, who, with a trembling hand, delivered to him the keys of the mansion.

Although Moscow had been entered by some of our troops the preceding day, so extensive and so deserted was the town that no soldier had yet penetrated into the quarter which we were to occupy. The most intrepid minds were affected by this loneliness. The streets were so long that our cavalry could not recognize each other from the opposite extremities. They were seen advancing with caution: then, struck with fear, they suddenly fled from each other, though they were all enlisted under the same banners. In proportion as a new quarter was occupied, reconnoitring parties were sent forward to examine the palaces and the churches. In the former were found only old men, children, or Russian officers, who had been wounded in the preceding engagements: in the latter, the altars were decorated as if for a festival; a thousand lighted tapers burning in honour of the patron saint of the country, attested that the pious Moscovites had not ceased to invoke him till the moment of their departure. This solemn and religions spectacle, rendered the people whom we had conquered, powerful and respectable in our estimation, and filled us with that consternation which is the offspring of injustice. With cautious steps we advanced through this awful solitude; often stopping and looking fearfully behind us; then, struck with sudden terror, we eagerly listened to every sound; for the imagination, frightened at the very magnitude of our conquest, inside us apprehensive of treachery in every place. At the least noise we fancied that we heard the clashing of arms, and the cries of the wounded.

Approaching however, towards the centre of the town, and especially in the neighborhood of the Bazar, we began to see some inhabitants assembled around the Kremlin. These deluded beings, deceived by a national tradition, had believed that this citadel was impregnable, and had attempted the preceding day to defend it for an instant against our valiant legions. Dismayed by their defeat, they contemplated with tears, those lofty towers which they had hitherto regarded as the *palladium* of their city. Proceeding further on, we saw a crowd of soldiers, who exposed to public sale a vast quantity of articles which they had pillaged; for it was only at the grand magazines of provisions that the imperial guards had placed sentinels. Continuing our progress, the number of soldiers multiplied; they were seen in troops, carrying on their backs pieces of cloth, loaves of sugar, and whole bales of merchandise. We knew not how to account for this shocking disorder, when at length some fusileers of the guards informed us that the smoke which we had seen on entering the town proceeded from a vast building, full of goods, called the exchange, and which the Russians had set on fire in their retreat. 'Yesterday,' said these soldiers, 'we entered the city about twelve o'clock, and towards five, the fire began to appear. We endeavored at first to extinguish it, but we soon learned that the governor had sent away all the engines. It is also believed,' added they, 'that this fire which cannot be subdued, has been kindled by the nobility, with an intention of exciting us to plunder, and destroying our discipline; and likewise with the determination to ruin those merchants who opposed the abandonment of Moscow.'

A natural curiosity made me proceed. As I advanced towards the fire the avenues were still more obstructed by soldiers and beggars carrying off goods of every kind. The less precious articles were despised, and soon thrown away, and the streets were covered with merchandise of every description. I penetrated at length into the interior of the exchange; but, alas! it was no more the building so renowned for its magnificence; it was rather a vast furnace, from every side of which the burning rafters were continually falling, and threatening us with instant destruction. I could still, however, proceed with some degree of safety under the piazzas. These were filled with numerous warehouses, which the soldiers had broken open; every chest was rifled, and the spoil exceeded all their expectations. No cry, no tumult was heard in this scene of horror. Every one found abundantly sufficient to satisfy his thirst for plunder. Nothing was heard but the crackling of the flames, and the noise of the doors that were broken open; and occasionally a dreadful crash, caused by the falling in of some vault. Cottons, muslins, and in short, all the most costly productions of Europe and of Asia, were a prey to the flames. The cellars were filled with sugar, oil, and vitriol; these burning all at once in the subterraneous warehouses, sent forth torrents of flame through thick iron grates, and presented a striking image of the mouth of hell.

It was a spectacle both terrible and affecting. Even the most hardened minds were struck with a conviction that so great a calamity would on some future day, call forth the vengeance of the Almighty upon the authors of such crimes.

The information which I endeavoured to obtain, with regard to the causes of this fire, were very unsatisfactory; but, returning in the evening to the palace where our staff was quartered, I met a Frenchman there, who had been tutor to the children of prince ———. This gentleman possessed much general knowledge, and a sound judgement in politics. His conversation was the more interesting, as he had long lived among the Russian nobility, and was perfectly acquainted with their character and views. Moreover, the events which happened in Moscow since the battle of the Moskwa had passed under his observation, and although a Frenchman, he formed one of the small number of those, who, by their talents and their prudence had always been on a footing of intimacy with count Rastopchin. This meeting was extremely fortunate, as it gave me an opportunity of learning what I was so desirous to know; particularly the true character of the governor, who, notwithstanding the blackest calumnies, will always be revered by his fellow citizens, and will be cited by future generations as a model of courage and patriotism.

Although the French advanced towards Moscow in three columns [said the tutor] so much prudence was employed by count Rastopchin, in concealing the truth from the people, that none but the nobility, and the persons attached to the government were acquainted with the terrible disasters with which the city was threatened. This, it is true, contributed to prolong our illusions; but when we saw the Russian army return within these walls, preceded by thirty thousand wounded, and dragging after them the whole population of the country, the citizens renounced their peaceable occupations, and abandoned themselves with the utmost agitation. All societies were dissolved, and the public institutions deserted. Even the mechanics, renouncing the work that supplied their families with bread, shut up their shops, and sharing in the consternation, which was become universal, mixed with the immense crowd which was running to the governor's house, to know they were to fly or remain.

In this painful and critical situation, the count Rastopchin, surrounded by the most illustrious of the nobility, and by the richest and most esteemed among the merchants, reminded his fellow-citizens of the solemn promises which they had made to their emperor. He recalled to their minds that memorable scene, when the sovereign, the father of his country, received from his children the homage of their fortunes and their lives. At this recollection, the governor overpowered by the sentiments which agitated him, was almost suffocated by excess of feeling, and lost the faculty of speech. This silent scene lasted several minutes, and produced more tears than the most eloquent harangue would have done. But the interest of the state, conquering a sensibility so natural, and so affecting, a nobleman in the assembly, who, from his diplomatic office, was well acquainted with the cause that had produced this disastrous war, addressed them in the following words:

'Inhabitants of Moscow! If you knew how the paternal heart of our monarch has suffered, and the means he has employed to ensure the repose and happiness of his empire - if you knew even how much his love of peace, and his desire to maintain even a disadvantageous alliance, have made him neglect the interests of his glory - you could then alone form an adequate idea of that excellent prince, who told us six weeks ago,

I have neglected nothing to ensure the peace of my country; but the more sacrifices I made, the more were demanded by our enemy. For our justification in the eyes of posterity, we must avow that we have taken up arms, only in the utmost extremity; and at the moment when our glorious empire was compelled to choose between the chances of war, or the infamy of having its laurels blasted. But, since injustice forces us to the combat, why should we fear it. For more than a century, war has always been to us favorable and glorious. The north was formerly the terror of the south; and now, when the north approaches to civilization, and wishes for universal peace, the south, blinded by an ungovernable and fatal ambition, abandons its rich provinces, to overrun our frozen regions. Is it then necessary always to be the oppressor, in order not to be oppressed; and must my pacific sentiments be now the misfortune of my reign? In vain this scourge of mankind alleges, that he wages a war of policy, and that this is the struggle of civilization against barbarism! a clumsy artifice, which can deceive those only who are unacquainted with our manners and principles. This civilization, so highly vaunted, what has it to fear from us, who exhaust our treasures, who traverse the seas, and explore both hemispheres, to cultivate and to naturalize it in our climate? And those to whom for instruction, and who enrich themselves by selling us the productions of their industry, these very people dare to call us barbarians? No, no, this is not the motive of the war which the ungrateful Napoleon makes upon us. He fears our rapid progress more than our barbarism. In fact, what nation is virtuous enough, not to be jealous of the miraculous protection which Providence grants to our empire. It is scarcely a century, since Peter, of illustrious memory, placed it in the rank of great nations; and since that time, how many countries have been subdued! - how many cities have been captured! – how many provinces reduced to submission! Yet, let us rather consider as the noblest trophies, the towns that have been founded, the districts, that have been civilized; the universities, colleges, and institutions which have been established; and you will find, that, in a short space of time, we have effaced the line which separated the civilized from barbarised Europe. It is our spirit of civilization, so closely resembling that of which the French are vain, which now attracts their hatred. They reproach us for our conquests over the Persians and Turks, pretending not to know that it is owing to the terror with which we have inspired the Musselmen, that Europe has ceased to be invaded by these infidels. Hungary owes to us its safety, and Italy its preservation: far different, in this respect, from our enemies whose conquests are only a new subject of dissention and war with their neighbours.'

This is the substance of the memorable speech which the emperor Alexander pronounced in the assembly of the nobles; and which the orator most judiciously repeated, as best calculated to rouse the courage of those who had not been present. Count Rastopchin, who hitherto had listened with silent attention, seeing that the inhabitants of Moscow, were sufficiently prepared, rose immediately from his seat, and running to the balcony, which opened on the great square, he thus addressed the people there assembled:

'Brave Moscovites!

'Our enemy advances; and you already hear the roar of the cannon, not far from our suburbs. This bad man wishes to overwhelm a throne, the splendour of which eclipses his own. We have yielded ground, but we are not conquered. You know that our emperor, in imitation of his ancestors, resides in the camp. Our armies are almost untouched, and are reinforced every day by new levies; but those of our perfidious enemy, arrive exhausted, annihilated. Insensible man! he thought that his victorious eagle, after having wandered from the banks of the Tagus to the sources of the Volga, could subdue one, which, reared in the midst of the Kremlin, proudly hovers over our heads, extending one wing towards the pole, and reaching with the other beyond the Bosphorus.

'Let us persevere, and I venture to predict that our country will reappear from the midst of its ruins, greater and more majestic than before. But, to attain an end so desirable consider, my friends, that the greatest sacrifices must be made, and the dearest affections renounced. It behoves you now to prove yourselves worthy descendants of the Pojarskies, the Palitsires, and of the Minines, who, in the most unhappy times, established, by their courage, the belief that the Kremlin is inviolable. Cherish this pious tradition, and maintain it, by arming yourselves against our dangerous enemy, who wishes to annihilate our empire, and to pillage our altars. Sacrifice every thing to obtain a victory, or be content to lose your honour, your fortunes, and your independence. But if God, in the dispensations of his wisdom, should allow vice to triumph for a moment, remember that it will be your sacred duty to fly into the deserts, and to forsake a country which will no longer be yours, when the presence of your oppressors has polluted it. The inhabitants of Saragossa, still recollecting the immortal courage of their ancestors, who to escape the yoke of the Romans kindled a funeral pile, and immolated their families and themselves, have, like them, chosen rather to perish under the ruins of their town, than submit to injustice. The same tyranny now threatens to crush us. Let us show to the whole universe, that the glorious example of the Spaniards has not been lost upon the Russians.'

After this speech the most violent agitation succeeded and an ungovernable populace, running through the principal streets, cried aloud that it was better to perish than to outlive their country and their religion. Those on whom nature had not bestowed the most ardent courage, ran to their homes to save their families from the impending danger. Some fled with haste from the city. Others on the contrary, vowed to defend it, whilst the rest of the population seizing their arms, either took refuge in the Kremlin, or, with torches in their hands, set fire to the exchange, which contained, as you know, immense riches, and where the French army might have found means of subsistence during the winter.

This was the account which the worthy tutor gave me of all that had happened at Moscow, previous to our arrival there. We both lamented these calamitous events; but, the day being calm, we hoped that the fire would not extend beyond the exchange. But what was our regret and our terror, when on the following morning, at the dawn of day (September 16), we saw the conflagration raging on every side, and perceived that the wind, blowing with violence, spread the flames in all directions.

The most heart-rending scene which my imagination had ever conceived, far surpassing the most afflicting accounts in ancient or modern history, now presented itself before our eyes. A great part of the population of Moscow, frightened at our arrival, had concealed themselves in cellars or secret recesses their houses. As the fire spread around, we saw them rushing in despair from their various asylums. They uttered no imprecation, they breathed no complaint, but, carrying with them their most precious effects, fled before the flames. Others, of greater sensibility, and actuated by the genuine feelings of nature, saved only their children, who were closely clasped in their arms. Many old people, borne down by grief rather than by age, had not sufficient strength to follow their families, and expired near the houses in which they were born. The streets, the public places, and particularly the churches, were filled with these unhappy people, who, lying on the remains of their property, suffered even without a murmur. No contention or noise was heard. Both the conqueror and the conquered were equally hardened: the one from excess of fortune - the other from excess of misery.

The fire, whose ravages could not be restrained, soon reached the finest parts of the city. Those palaces which we had admired for the beauty of their architecture, and the elegance of their furniture, were enveloped in the flames. Their magnificent fronts, ornamented with bas-reliefs and statues, fell with a dreadful crash on the fragments of the pillars which had supported them. The churches, though covered with iron and lead, were likewise destroyed, and with them those beautiful steeples, which we had seen the night before, resplendent with gold and silver. The hospitals, too, which contained more than twenty thousand wounded, soon began to burn. This offered a harrowing and dreadful spectacle; almost all these poor wretches perished. A few who still lingered, were seen crawling, half burnt, amongst the smoking ruins; and others, groaning under heaps of dead bodies, endeavoured in vain to extricate themselves from the horrible destruction which surrounded them.

How shall I describe the confusion and tumult when permission was granted to pillage this immense city! Soldiers, sutlers, galley-slaves, and prostitutes, eagerly ran through the streets, penetrating into the deserted palaces, and carrying away every thing which could gratify their avarice. Some covered themselves with stuffs, richly worked with gold; some were enveloped in beautiful and costly furs; while others dressed themselves in women's and children's pelisses, and even the gallery slaves concealed their rags under the most splendid court dresses; the rest crowded into the cellars, and forcing open the doors, drank the most luscious wines, and carried off an immense booty.

This horrible pillage was not confined to the deserted houses alone, but extended to those which were inhabited, and soon the eagerness and wantonness of the plunderers, caused devastations which almost equalled those occasioned by the conflagration. Every asylum was soon violated by the licentious troops. The inhabitants who had officers in their houses, for a little while flattered themselves that they should escape the general calamity. Vain illusion! the fire, progressively increasing, soon destroyed all their hopes.

Towards evening, when Napoleon no longer thought himself safe in a city, the ruin of which seemed inevitable, he left the Kremlin, and established himself, with his suite, in the castle of Peterskoë. When I saw him pass by, I could not, without abhorrence behold the chief of a barbarous expedition, who evidently endeavoured to escape the decided testimony of public indignation, by seeking the darkest road. He sought it, however, in vain. On every side the flames seemed to pursue him, and their horrible and mournful glare, flashing on his guilty head, reminded me of the torches of the Eumenides, pursuing the destined victims of the furies!

The generals likewise received orders to quit Moscow. Licentiousness then became unbounded, The soldiers no longer restrained by the presence of their chiefs, committed every kind of excess. No retreat was now safe, no place sufficiently sacred to afford any protection against their rapacity. Nothing more forcibly excited their avarice than the church of St. Michael, the sepulchre of the Russian emperors. An erroneous tradition had propagated the belief that it contained immense riches. Some grenadiers presently entered it, and descended with torches into the vast subterranean vaults, to disturb the peace and silence of the tomb. But instead of treasures, they found only stone coffins, covered with pink velvet, with thin silver plates, on which were engraved the names of the czars, and the date of their birth and decease. Mortified at this disappointment, they again searched every part of the building, and at length perceived, at the end of a dark gallery, a lamp, the half extinguished light of which fell on a small altar. They immediately proceeded towards it, and the first object which presented itself to their notice, was a young female, elegantly dressed, and in the attitude of devotion. At the noise of the soldiers, the unhappy girl screamed violently, and fell into a swoon. In that situation she was carried before one of our generals.

As long as I have life I shall retain the impression which the appearance of that young lady, pale, and almost dying, produced on my mind. Her countenance, in which grief and despair were equally legible, was irresistibly interesting. As her recollection returned, she seemed to deprecate the care which was employed in recalling her to life. While we gazed on her lovely form, every bosom was inspired with pity, and we all were anxious to become acquainted with her history. The general, in particular, but from very different motives, seemed eager to hear it; and, sending most of those who were present away, he begged her to relate to him her misfortunes.

Of what use [said she] would it be to mention to you the wealth of a house, which will soon be annihilated? Suffice it, that the name of my father is celebrated in the history of our empire; and that he is now serving with distinction in the army, which is gloriously fighting in defence of our country. My name is Paulowna. On the day preceding your entrance into Moscow, I was to be united to one of the young warriors, who had distinguished himself at the battle of Mojaisk. But amidst the nuptial solemnities, my father was informed that the French were at the gates of the city, and, suspending our marriage, and taking my husband with him, they hastened to join the army. Early on the following morning, being with my afflicted family, we heard the roar of the cannon; and, the noise evidently approaching nearer, we no longer doubted that we must quit Moscow. In the midst of this dreadful tumult, I fled with my relations; but, when we arrived near the Kremlin, an immense crowd met us, and, rushing hastily by, parted me from my mother and sisters. I endeavoured, in vain, to recall them by my cries. The noise of arms, and the cries of an infuriated populace, overpowered my feeble voice, and in an instant I was rendered truly miserable. The French, meanwhile, penetrated into the town, and, driving all before them, advanced towards the Kremlin. To find a shelter against their excesses, I, with many others, ran into the citadel, which was considered a place of security. As I could not mix with the combatants, I retired to the church of St. Michael seeking refuge among the graves of the czars. Kneeling near their sepulchres, I invoked the manes of those illustrious founders of our country, when, on a sudden, some wicked soldiers broke in upon my retreat, and dragged me away from an inviolable and sacred asylum.

When the unhappy girl had finished her history, she shed a torrent of tears; and, throwing herself at the general's feet, implored him to respect her virtue, and restore her to her relations. He was more interested by her beauty than by her tears; but, pretending to pity her misfortunes, he pledged himself to relieve them. He offered her his house as a protection; and, to retain her there, he promised to use his utmost endeavours to discover her father and her destined husband. But, as I knew the disposition of the man, I clearly perceived, that this apparent generosity was only a snare to deceive the innocent Paulowna. There wanted nothing more to complete the horrors of that day, when he resolved to outrage virtue and seduce innocence; and we afterwards found that neither noble blood, nor the candour of youth, nor even the tears of beauty, were respected.

Penetrated by so many calamities, I hoped that the shades of night would cast a veil over the dreadful scene; but they contributed, on the contrary, to render the conflagration more visible. The violence of the flames which extended from north to south, and were strangely agitated by the wind, produced the most awful appearance, on a sky which was darkened by the thickest smoke. Nothing could equal the anguish which absorbed every feeling heart, and which was increased in the dead of the night, by the cries of the miserable victims who were savagely murdered, or by the screams of the young females, who fled for protection to their weeping mothers, and whose ineffectual struggles tended only to inflame the passions of their violators. To these dreadful groans and heart-rending cries, which every moment broke upon the ear, were added, the howlings of the dogs, which, chained to the doors of the palaces, according to the custom at Moscow, could not escape from the fire which surrounded them.

I flattered myself that sleep would for a while release me from these revolting scenes; but the most frightful recollections crowded upon me, and all the horrors of the evening again passed in review. My wearied senses seemed at last sinking into repose when the light of a near and dreadful conflagration, piercing into my room, suddenly awoke me. I thought that my room was a prey to the flames. It was no idle dream, for when I approached the window, I saw that our quarters were on fire, and that the house in which I lodged, was in the utmost danger. Sparks were thickly falling in our yard, and on the wooden roof of our stables. I ran quickly to my landlord and his family. Perceiving their danger, they had already quitted their habitation, and had retired to a subterranean vault, which afforded them more security. I found them with their servants all assembled there, nor could I prevail on them to leave it, for they dreaded our soldiers more than the fire. The father was sitting on the threshold of the door, and appeared desirous of appeasing, by the sacrifice of his own life, the ferocity of those barbarians, who advanced to insult his family. Two of his daughters, pale, with dishevelled hair, and whose tears. added to their beauty, disputed with him the honour of the martyrdom. I at length succeeded in snatching them by violence from the asylum, under which they would otherwise soon have been buried. These unhappy creatures when they again saw the light, contemplated with indifference the loss of all their property, and were only astonished that they were still alive. Notwithstanding they were convinced that they would be protected from all personal injury, they did not exhibit any tokens of gratitude; but, like those wretches, who, having been ordered to execution, are quite bewildered, when a reprieve unexpectedly arrives, and the agonies of death render them insensible to the gift of life.

Desirous of terminating the recital of this horrible catastrophe, for which history wants expressions, and poetry has no colours, I shall pass over, in silence, many circumstances revolting to humanity, and merely describe the dreadful confusion which arose in our army, when the fire had reached every part of Moscow, and the whole city was become one immense flame.

A long row of carriages were perceived through the thick smoke, loaded with booty. Being too heavily laden for the exhausted cattle to draw them along, they were obliged to halt at every step, when we heard the execration of their drivers, who, terrified at the surrounding flames, endeavored to push forward with dreadful outcries. The soldiers, still armed, were diligently employed in forcing open every door. They seemed to fear lest they should leave one house untouched. Some, when their carriages were laden almost to breaking down, bore the rest of their booty on their backs. The fire, however obstructing the passage of the principal streets, often obliged them to retrace their steps. Thus wandering from to place, through an immense town, the avenues of which they did not know, they sought, in van, extricate themselves from this labyrinth of fire. Many wandered further from the gates by which they might have escaped, instead of approaching them, and thus became the victims of their own rapacity. In spite, however, of the extreme peril which threatened them, the love of plunder induced our soldiers to brave every danger. Stimulated by an irresistible desire of pillage, they precipitated themselves into the midst of the flames. They waded in blood, treading upon the dead bodies without remorse, while the ruins of the houses, mixed with burning coals, fell thick on their murderous hands. They would probably all have perished, if the insupportable heat had not forced them at length to withdraw into the camp.

The fourth corps having received orders to leave Moscow, we proceeded (September 17th), towards Peterskoë, where our divisions were encamped. At that moment about the dawn of day, I witnessed the most dreadful and the most affecting scenes which it is possible to conceive;

namely, the unhappy inhabitants drawing upon some mean vehicles all that they had been able to save from the conflagration. The soldiers, having robbed them of their horses, the men and women were slowly and painfully dragging along these little carts, some of which contained an infirm mother, others a paralytic old man, and others the miserable wrecks of half-consumed furniture; children, half naked, followed these interesting groups. Affliction, to which their age is commonly a stranger, was impressed even on their features, and, when the soldiers approached them, they ran crying into the arms of their mothers. Alas! what habitation could we have offered the them which would not constantly recall the object of their terror? Without a shelter and without food, these unfortunate beings wandered in the fields, and fled into the woods; but wherever they bent their steps, they met the conquerors of Moscow, who frequently ill-treated them, and sold before their eyes, the goods which had been stolen from their own deserted habitations.

Part II

Book VI

Malo-Jaroslavitz

The arrival of a victorious French army in the ancient capital of the czars, in the richest and most central city of Russia, which a religious belief had hitherto considered as sacred, was one of the most extraordinary occurrences of modern history.

Our former conquests had, for some years accustomed Europe to behold our vast and most astonishing plans crowned with complete success. But, of all our expeditions, none had, like this, an appearance of imposing grandeur, calculated to seduce those who were fond of the marvellous; while the difficulty of the enterprise equalled every romantic tale that the Persians, the Greeks, or the Romans, had conceived. The distance from Paris to Moscow, nearly equal to that which separated, the capital of Alexander from the residence of Darius; the nature of the country and rigour of the climate, which had been hitherto supposed inaccessible to the armies of Europe; the recollection of Charles XII, who, wishing to attempt a similar project, did not dare to pass Smolensko; the terror of the Asiatic nations, astonished to see the people who had fled before us, arrive amongst them; all, in short, concurred to give to the progress of the grand army, an air of wonder, which recalled to our recollection the most celebrated expeditions of antiquity.

Such was the aspect of our conquests, when taken in the most brilliant point of view; but, when sound reason had taught us to look into futurity, nothing presented itself but the darkest and most frightful images. The horrible extremity to which the inhabitants of Moscow bad been reduced, proved to us that we had no means of treating with the people determined to make such immense sacrifices; and that the vain-glory of signing a treaty of peace at Moscow, had kindled a fire, the ravages of which would spread through Europe, and would give to the war a character so sanguinary, that it could end only in the entire ruin of a generous people, or the fall of that evil genius, whom God, in his displeasure, seemed to have designed as a new exterminating angel to chastise mankind.

The wisest and most judicious witnessed, with terror, the destruction of a city, which, within five days, had become a prey to the flames, and the light of which illuminated our camp every night. 'There is no hope,' said they, 'of a speedy termination of the war, even should we still continue our conquests. Having completed the ruin of Moscow, who knows whether we shall not attempt that of Petersburg? And even when we have subdued all Russia, may we not anticipate an expedition to the Euphrates or the Ganges? Alas! when a sovereign possesses only a rash valour, which is not tempered by wisdom, the brilliant lustre of his arms renders him like those dangerous meteors which occasionally appear on the earth, and excite the most serious alarm.'

Although the ruin of Moscow was a great loss to the Russians, it was still more sensibly felt by us, and it ensured to our enemies all the advantages which they had promised themselves from the rigour of their climate. In vain did we represent to the inhabitants that the burning of their capital was useless, and that the French army ought to rejoice at being relieved from an immense population, whose natural ardour and fanaticism might have caused dangerous seditions. After much reflection, I am convinced that the Russian government had reasons to fear, from the crafty and treacherous character of our chief, that this population, instead of revolting against us, might have become instrumental to our projects, and that many of the noblesse, led away by an example so dangerous, or seduced by brilliant, but deceitful promises, might have abandoned the interest of their country.

It was, doubtless, to prevent this calamity, that count Rastopchin sacrificed the whole of his fortune in burning Moscow, thinking that this great example would be the only means of rousing the energies of the nobility, and, by rendering us the objects of their execration, would excite in the minds of the people the most violent hatred against us. Besides, the city being provisioned for eight months, the French army by occupying it, would have been able to wait the return of spring, and then renew the campaign, with the armies of reserve which were encamped at Smolensko, and on the Niemen; while by burning Moscow, they would compel us to a precipitate retreat, in the most rigorous seasons of the year.

Their hopes founded on this calculation, could not be disappointed; for our formidable army, though it arrived in the fine seasons, had lost a third of its numbers merely by the rapidity of our march; and the enemy had no reason to fear that we could maintain any position, since our want of discipline had made a desert of all our conquests, and our improvident chief had formed no plan to facilitate our retreat.

In short, to finish this picture of our distresses, in the midst of our apparent victory, the whole army was discouraged and worn out with fatigue. The cavalry was nearly ruined, and the artillery-horses, exhausted by want of food, could no longer draw the guns.

Although we were the deplorable victims of the conflagration of Moscow, we must do justice to the inhabitants of that city. It is impossible not to admire their generous devotedness to their country, and we must acknowledge that they have, like the Spaniards, raised themselves, by their courage and their perseverance, to that high degree of true glory which constitutes the greatness of a nation.

When we recollect the sufferings that we had endured, and the losses[1] we had experienced by fatigue alone, previous to our arrival at Moscow, and that at a time when the earth, covered with its choicest productions, offered us abundant resources, one can scarcely conceive how Napoleon could be so blind and obstinate as not immediately to abandon Russia; particularly when he saw that winter approached, and that the capital, on which he had so much depended, no longer existed. It seems as if divine Providence, to punish him for his pride, had deprived him of reason, since he presumed to think that they who had sufficient courage to lay waste and destroy their country, would afterwards be weak enough to accept his hard proposals, and sign a treaty of peace on the smoking ruins of their city. They who possessed the smallest foresight, predicted our misfortunes, and imagined that they read on the walls of the Kremlin, those prophetic words which an invisible hand traced before Belshazzar, in the midst of his greatest prosperity:

> God hath numbered this kingdom and finished it; thou art weighed in the balance and found wanting; thy kingdom is divided, and given to other hands.

During the four days (17, 18, 19, and 20, September) that we remained near Peterskoë,[2] Moscow did not cease to burn. In the meantime the rain fell in torrents; and the houses near the *chateau*, being too few in number to contain the numerous troops who were encamped there, it was almost impossible to obtain shelter: men, horses, and carriages, bivouacked in the middle of the fields. The staff-officers, placed around the *chateau* where their generals resided, were established in the English gardens, and quartered under grottoes, Chinese pavilions, or greenhouses, whilst the horses, tied under acacias, or linden-trees, were separated from each other by hedges or beds of flowers. This camp, truly picturesque, was rendered still more extraordinary by the new costume adopted by the soldiers; most of whom to shelter themselves from the inclemency of

---

1   The fourth corps, when we set out from Glogau, consisted of about forty-eight thousand men, but when we left Moscow, there were only twenty thousand infantry, and two thousand cavalry. The fifteenth division, consisting of thirteen thousand men at the commencement of the campaign, was then reduced to four thousand.

2   This imperial *chateau*, of which we have already spoken is but a quarter of a league from Moscow.

the weather, had put on the same clothing which used to be seen at Moscow, and which formed the most pleasing and amusing variety on the public walks of that city. Thus we saw, walking in our camp, soldiers dressed *à la Tartare, à la cosaque, à la Chinoise*; one wore the Polish cap, another the high bonnet of the Persians, the Baskirs, or the Kalmouks. In short, our army presented the image of a carnival; and from what followed, it was justly said that our retreat commenced with a masquerade, and ended with a funeral.

But the abundance which the soldiers then enjoyed, made them forget their fatigues; with the rain pouring on their heads, and their feet immersed in the mud, they consoled themselves with good cheer, and the advantages which they derived from trafficking in the plunder of Moscow. Although it was forbidden to go into the city, the soldiers, allured by the hope of gain, violated the order, and always returned loaded with provisions and merchandise. Under the pretence of going on marauding parties, they returned near the Kremlin, and dug amongst the ruins, where they discovered entire magazines, whence they drew a profusion of articles of every description. Thus our camp no longer resembled an army, but a great fair, at which each soldier, metamorphosed into a merchant, sold the most valuable articles, at an inconsiderable price; and although encamped in the fields, and exposed to the inclemency of the weather, he, by a singular contrast, ate off China plates, drank out of silver vases, and possessed almost every elegant and expensive article which luxury could invent.

The neighbourhood of Peterskoë, and its gardens, at length became as unhealthy as it was inconvenient. Napoleon returned to establish himself at the Kremlin which had not been burnt, and the guards and staff-officers received orders to re-enter the city (the 20th and 21st of September.) According to the calculations of the engineers, the tenth part of the houses still remained. They were divided between the different corps of the grand army. We possessed the faubourg of St. Petersburg, which we had at our first entry into the city. On re-entering the city, we experienced the most heart-rending sensations, at perceiving that no vestige remained of those noble hotels at which we had formerly been established. They were entirely demolished, and their ruins still smoking, were scattered in such confusion, that we could no longer distinguish even the outline of the streets. The stone palaces were the only buildings which preserved any traces of their former magnificence. Standing alone amidst piles of ruins, and blackened by smoke, this wreck of a city, so newly built, resembled some of the venerable remains of antiquity.

Each one endeavoured to find quarters for himself, but rarely could we meet with houses which joined together; and, to shelter some companies, we were obliged to occupy a vast tract of land, which only offered a few habitations scattered here and there. Some of the churches composed of less combustible materials than the other buildings, had their roofs entire, and were transformed into barracks and stables. Thus the hymns and holy melodies, which had once resounded within these sacred walls, now gave place to the neighing of horses, and the horrible blasphemies of the soldiers.

Curious to know in what state I should find the house at which I had lodged, I long sought for it in vain, until a neighbouring church, which had survived the general destruction, enabled me to ascertain it. I could scarcely believe that it was the same. The interior was entirely consumed, and the four walls alone remained, which were full of chinks, owing to the fierceness of the fire. I was reflecting on the terrible effects of this destructive element, when the unfortunate servants of the house made their appearance from the bottom of a vault. Emaciated by famine and distress, I should doubtless have found their features much altered, if the ashes and smoke had not rendered them totally unknown to me. They resembled spectres more than human beings. But what were my sensations when I recognized my former host amongst these miserable wretches. He was concealed under the rags which he had borrowed from his domestics. They now lived all together, for misfortune had equalized every condition! On seeing me, he burst, into tears, particularly when he presented to me his children, half naked and dying with hunger. Although his grief was silent, it made a deep impression on my heart. He told me by signs that the soldiers, after having plundered his dwelling while it was burning, had also robbed him of the very clothes which he wore. This distressing picture touched me to the soul. I wished to alleviate his sufferings, though I feared I had only barren consolation to offer. The same man who a few days before had given me a splendid repast, accepted with gratitude a morsel of bread.

Although the population of Moscow had entirely disappeared, there still remained many of those unfortunate beings whom misery had accustomed to look on all occurrences with indifference. Most of them took shelter in cabins which they had themselves constructed in the gardens or public walks, with planks half burnt, which they had collected from the ruins. There were also a number of unfortunate girls, and these alone derived any advantage from the plunder of Moscow. The soldiers eagerly associated with them, and when they were once introduced into our quarters, they soon became absolute mistresses of them, and squandered away all that the flames had spared. A small number, however, really merited our regard by their education, and above all, by their misfortunes; for horrible to relate, famine and misery had compelled their mothers to come and offer them to us. This immorality, under such circumstances, recoiled on those who had not sufficient virtue to resist the temptation, and who regarded with an eye of passion the forms which hunger had emaciated, and disease had rendered dangerous and loathsome.

Of all these victims, the most to be lamented, and the most worthy of pity, was the unfortunate Paulowna, whose history I have already related, and who, deceived by an apparent generosity, had been weak enough to place unlimited confidence in the general who had received her. This man well knew how to deceive his innocent captive, by his assiduities and false pity; and, by feigning sentiments which he never knew, and taking advantage of the impossibility of discovering her parents or her lover, he persuaded her that she would find in him a friend and a protector. On the faith of repeated promises, this innocent female, after having spent several days in unavailing tears, become a victim to the artifices of her ungenerous lover. Alas! the general was already married, and she, who had expected to become his wife, found herself only a dishonoured slave.

There yet remained at Moscow a class of men, the most contemptible of all, since they escaped the punishment due to their former crimes by consenting to commit still greater: these were the galley-slaves. During the whole time of the conflagration at Moscow they signalized themselves by the audacity with which they executed the orders they had received. Provided with phosphorus, they lighted the fire anew, wherever it appeared to be extinguished, and even crept by stealth into the houses which were inhabited, to involve them in the general ruin.

Several of these abject wretches were arrested with torches in their hands; but their punishment, too prompt and summary, produced little effect (24th September.) The people, who always detested their conquerors, regarded these executions merely as the effect of policy. In short these victims were too obscure for the expiation of such a crime; and, above all, their trial wanting publicity and legal form, threw no light on the cause of this dreadful calamity, and, could not justify us clearly in the estimation of the inhabitants.

When we entered Moscow, the Russian troops fell back on the grand road of Wladimir; but the greater part of their army having descended the Moskwa to go to Kolomna, took up their position along the river. It is said that this very army, followed by the whole population, in tears, passed, a few days after our arrival, under the walls of Moscow, while the city was still burning. The march of the troops was illuminated by the light of the fire; and the wind, blowing with violence, even carried into the ranks some of the ashes of their capital. Notwithstanding such accumulated misfortunes, the troops observed the greatest order, and maintained a profound silence. Such resignation, at the sight of a spectacle so melancholy, gave to this march a solemn and religious air.

When the main body of the Russian army had taken its different positions, the proprietors of the country in the neighbourhood of Moscow, perceiving that the disasters of the war had highly exasperated the people against us, availed themselves of the popular feeling to excite a general insurrection against the common enemy. Many raised levies at their own expense, and put themselves at the head of their insurgent peasants. These forces, united to the cossacks, intercepted our convoys on the great roads. But the principal aim of these military preparations was to harass our foragers, and above all, to deprive them of the resources which they were still able to procure from the neighbouring villages.

In digging under the ruins of Moscow, the soldiers often found magazines of sugar, of wine, or of brandy. These discoveries, although they would have been valuable in happier times, afforded no great relief to an army which had consumed all the grain of the country, and which would soon have neither bread nor meat to eat.

Our cattle perished for want of forage, and, to procure others, it was each day necessary to engage in combats, always disadvantageous to us; for, at so great a distance from our native country, the smallest loss was sensibly felt.

Our real misery was disguised by an apparent abundance. We had neither bread not meat, yet our tables were covered with sweet-meats, syrups, and dainties. Coffee, and all sorts of wines, served in china or crystal vases, convinced us that luxury might be nearly allied to poverty. The extent and the nature of our wants rendered money of little value to us, and this gave rise to an exchange rather than sale of commodities. They who had cloth, offered it for wine; and he who had a pelisse could procure plenty of sugar and coffee.

Napoleon buoyed himself up with the ridiculous hope of reclaiming, by mild proclamations, those who, to free themselves from his yoke, had made their capital an immense funeral pile. In order to seduce them, and inspire them with confidence, he had divided the remains of the town into districts, appointed governors for each, and instituted magistrates, to render to the few citizens who still remained, the justice which was their due. The consul-general Lesseps, appointed governor of Moscow, published a proclamation, to announce to the inhabitants the paternal intentions of Napoleon. The kind and generous promises, however, never reached the Moscovites; and even if they had, the rigorous circumstances under which they were placed, would have made them regard the proclamation as insulting irony. Besides, the greater part had fled behind the Volga, and the others, who had taken refuge in the midst of the Russian army, animated by a deadly hatred, breathed only sentiments of vengeance!

In the meantime prince Kutusoff, having conveyed the greater part of his forces to Lectaskova, between Moscow and Kaluga, to cover the southern provinces, so narrowly confined Napoleon, that in spite of his different manoeuvres, he could not disengage himself from his painful position, but was always constrained to fall back on his own lines. It was impossible to advance towards Petersburgh without leaving the Russian army on our rear, and endangering our safety, by abandoning all communications with Poland.

He could not march towards Jaroslaw and Wladimir; since every undertaking in that direction would only divide his troops and remove him further from his resources. Consequently nothing could be more critical than the situation of the French army, now encamped on the roads of Twer, of Wladimir, of Razan, and of Kaluga.

Our headquarters continued at Moscow, the neighbourhood of which was become highly infectious. It was indeed totally deserted, except by the peasants and the cossacks, who, overrunning the country, plundered our convoys, intercepted our couriers, massacred our foragers, and caused us irreparable evils. From that time our position became more and more painful. Our poverty and the discontent of the soldiers, augmented every day; and, to complete our misfortunes, there appeared no probability of a peace.

It would be curious to relate the extravagant projects which, under these circumstances, were discussed in the army. Some spoke of going to the Ukraine - others of marching on Petersburg. But those who were wise, maintained, that we ought, ere long to return to Wilna. Napoleon, always most obstinate when surrounded with difficulties, and passionately fond of extraordinary exploits, persisted in maintaining himself in an absolute desert, and thought to frighten the enemy, by feigning to pass the winter there. To give some colour to this ridiculous stratagem, he formed the plan of arming the Kremlin, and even of making a citadel of the large prison which was situated in the quarter of Petersburg, and vulgarly called the *Square House*; and, to complete the folly and absurdity of the whole, when every magazine was exhausted, and we had nothing to eat, he ordered us to make provisions for two months. While we were occupied in meditating all these chimeras, and particularly on provisioning Moscow, without any resource, the report of peace, believed by those alone who so ardently desired it, filled our hearts with joy, and flattered us with the hope that we should not be compelled to attempt the execution of projects absolutely impracticable. This news acquired much credit from the armistice which had been concluded between the cossacks and the advanced posts of the king of Naples. Such a convention seemed to augur that there might be hope of a reconciliation between the two emperors: especially as we knew that general Lauriston been sent to the head-quarters of prince Kutusoff, and that in consequence of his interview with this commander, a courier had been despatched to St. Petersburgh, to decide on peace or war.

In the mean time Napoleon, with his usual activity, daily reviewed his troops, and, by the severest proclamations obliged the colonels to maintain the strictest discipline throughout their regiments. The weather, to our astonishment, continued remarkably fine, and contributed much to the brilliancy of these reviews. A circumstance so rare, in this season, was regarded as a phenomenon by the Moscovites, who, accustomed to see it snow from the mouth of October, beheld with surprise the beautiful days which we enjoyed. The people, naturally superstitious, and who had long and anxiously expected the winter, as their certain avenger, impatiently despaired of. The assistance of Providence, and began to consider this prodigy as the effect of the manifest protection which the Almighty had afforded to Napoleon. But this apparent protection was precisely the cause of his ruin, as it rendered him so infatuated as to believe that the climate of Moscow resembled that of Paris. His foolish and impious vanity made him hope to command the seasons as he had commanded men; and, abusing his good fortune, he believed that the sun of Austerlitz would enlighten him even unto the pole, and that, like another Joshua, he would be able, by his voice, to arrest this luminary in its course, and compel it to protect him in his ambitious career.

While we were deluded by the protracted negotiation, preparations were made to recommence the war, but nothing was done to guard against the rigours of winter. Meanwhile our prospects became more alarming. The longer our stay at Moscow was continued, the more inconvenient and uncomfortable it became. In proportion as we exhausted the neighbouring villages, we were compelled to go to places more remote. Their distance rendered our excursions as perilous as they were fatiguing. Setting out at break of day, rarely did our foragers return before night. These excursions, daily repeated, harassed our men, and destroyed our cavalry, particular the artillery-horses; and, to complete our wretchedness, the audacity of the cossacks redoubled in proportion as our weakness rendered us defenceless.

As a proof of it, they intercepted, in the environs of Moscow, a convoy of artillery coming from Viazma, and conducted by two majors. Napoleon believed that these officers were culpable, and instituted an enquiry respecting their conduct. One of them destroyed himself, more from the disgrace of having lost his cannon, than the fear of being found guilty. To prevent similar losses, Broussier's division and the light cavalry, commanded by count Ornano, received orders to establish themselves in the environs of the *chateau* of Galitzin, situated between Mojaïsk and Moscow. These troops delivered the neighbouring country from the cossacks, who always avoided meeting them. But the smallest spot unoccupied by our troops, was immediately taken possession of by these hordes of Tartars, who profited by the advantages which their knowledge country afforded them, to attempt the boldest enterprises.

They made another attack on a convoy of artillery, coming from Italy, under the orders of major Vivés. It was reported that the escort, having taken to flight, surrendered to the cossacks, almost without opposition, the artillery which had been intrusted to it. The enemy carried off the field pieces and the horses, when count Ornano, informed of this attack, pursued the cossacks, and overtook them in the middle of the woods. At the sight of our cavalry they fled, and abandoned all the fruits of their victory, without resistance. Major Vivés would have been brought to trial; but our departure, and the disasters which ensued, forced Napoleon to relax from his accustomed severity.

While the fourteenth division guarded the road from Viazma, the thirteenth was on that of Twer. This last division occupied some excellent cantonments, when we were informed that count Saltikof, the favourite of the emperor Alexander, and proprietor of the village of Marfino, in the neighbourhood of Dimitrow, had armed all his peasants, and that, having entered into combination with several other lords, he was forming in his *chateau* a grand scheme of insurrection. To prevent the consequences of so dangerous an example, orders were given to a brigade of the thirteenth division to repair to the *chateau* de Marfino. The general who commanded it made strict enquiries to convince himself that these meetings had really taken place. The result was unsatisfactory and fruitless; nevertheless, obliged to conform to the orders which he had received, he committed to the flames a palace which had been justly celebrated as one of the finest in Russia. This pretended meeting caused a suspicion that Napoleon had only wished to revenge himself on count Saltikof, to whom he was an enemy, because that nobleman had continued faithful to his sovereign.

The various manoeuvres which the different corps of the army were obliged to make, confirmed us in the opinion that we should not long be able to maintain our position. Every thing presaged our approaching departure, and suspicion was changed into certainty on perceiving that the cavalry of the Italian guards quitted their good cantonments in the environs of Dimitrow, to return to Moscow; an proceeded thence to occupy the position of Charapovo, (15th October) a little village, situated on the road from Borovsk, about six leagues from Moscow. At the same time the viceroy ordered the thirteenth division to return, the fourteenth to advance, and the cavalry of general Ornano to march towards Fominskoë, whither it appeared that the whole of the fourth corps was about to direct its course. The cossacks, informed of this movement, availed themselves of the opportunity, when the baggage of our light cavalry was feebly escorted, to attack the convoy in the neighbourhood of Osighovo; but seeing general Broussier's division, they abandoned a part of their booty, and sheltered by the woods, escaped the pursuit of our soldiers.

We waited with the utmost anxiety the return of the courier which had been despatched to Petersburg. Persuaded that the answer would be favourable, our army neglected the necessary precautions, and imagined itself in the most perfect security. The enemy, profiting by this indiscretion, attacked on the 18th of October, the cavalry of the King of Naples, in the vicinity of Taroutina, and surprised a park of twenty-six pieces of cannon, which the carried off. This attack, made at the moment when the cavalry was foraging, was fatal to that division, which had been already been much reduced. The few who remained, still continued to face the enemy; and, supported by some Polish regiments, who were less fatigued than ours, succeeded in recovering the pieces which the enemy had captured. General Bagawout, who commanded the fourth Russian corps, was killed in the action and general Bennigsen was wounded. We lost nearly two thousand men; and we particularly regretted the death of general Dery, aid-de-camp of the king of Naples, who had on every occasion given proof of the greatest courage, and the highest talents.

The emperor was at the Kremlin, occupied in reviewing his troops, when he received this unexpected news. He immediately became furious, and in the transports of his rage, exclaimed, that it was treacherous and infamous; that they had attacked the king of Naples in contempt of all the laws of war, and that none but barbarians would have thus violated a solemn convention. The parade was immediately dissolved, all hopes of peace vanished, and the order for our departure was given that very evening. All the corps were to quit Moscow, and take the grand road to Kaluga. We then hoped that we should go to the Ukraine, to seek, under a milder sky, countries less savage and more fertile. But those who were best informed, assured us that our movement on Kaluga was only a false manoeuvre, to conceal from the enemy our design of retreating on Smolensko and Witepsk.

Those who did not witness the departure of the French army from Moscow, can form but a faint idea of what the Greek and Roman armies were, when they abandoned the ruins of Troy or of Carthage. But they who observed the appearance of our army at this moment, acknowledged the accuracy of those interesting scenes which are so admirably described in the writings of Virgil and Livy. The long files of carriages, in three or four ranks, extended for several leagues, loaded with the immense booty, which the soldiers had snatched from the flames, and the Moscovite peasants, who were now become our servants resembled the slaves which the ancients dragged in their train. Others carrying with them their wives and children, or the prostitutes whom they had found at Moscow, represented the warriors amongst whom the captives had been divided. Afterwards came numerous wagons filled with trophies, among which were Turkish or Persian standards, torn from the vaulted roofs of the palaces of the czars, and, last of all, the celebrated cross of Saint Iwan gloriously closed the rear of an army which, but for the imprudence of its chief, would have been enabled to boast that it had extended its conquests to the very limits of Europe, and astonished the people of Asia with the sound of the same cannon with which the pillars of Hercules had re-echoed.

As we set out very late, we were obliged to encamp at a miserable village, only one league from Moscow. The cavalry of the Italian guards, which still remained at Charopovo, marched on the following day (19th October) and joined us at Patoutinka, not far from the *chateau* of Troitskoë, where Napoleon had established his head-quarters. Nearly the whole army was reunited at this point, with the exception of the cavalry which was in advance, and the young guards who remained at Moscow to bring up the rear. We experienced much difficulty in procuring the means of subsistence, but we still continued to bivouac; and the carriages which every officer brought with him furnished us with some provisions.

On the following day, the cavalry of the royal guards were to have directed their course towards Charapovo, as well as the whole of the fourth corps; but at the moment when they were commencing their march, they were recalled, and the prince ordered these troops to pursue the same route which we had followed the preceding evening. We crossed the Pakra near Gorki. This beautiful village no longer existed but in name; and the river, choked up with the ruins of the houses which had been a prey to the flames, flowed in a black and muddy stream. Above was the beautiful *chateau* of Krasnoë, which had been entirely pillaged;

but the elegance of the building still formed a striking contrast with the rustic hills on which it was built. Arrived on this point, we halted, and an hour afterwards left the high road to seek on our right a path which would conduct us to Fomiuskoë, where general Broussier and our cavalry had been for four or five days in view of the enemy. Our march by this unfrequented road was very tedious and painful, but it procured us the advantage of finding some villages which, although they were deserted, had not been so completely plundered as those on the great road. We passed the night at Inatowo, where we discovered a *chateau*, situated on an eminence which overlooked the country by which we had arrived.

We afterwards continued our march, with an intention to regain the road to Charopovo, which we at length reached, near the village of Bouïkasovo. These geographic details, on which I dwell so much will not appear tedious, when it is recollected that they are absolutely necessary, in order to point out the difficulties which we had to encounter in our operations. Having only incorrect maps, and marching without guides, we could not even pronounce the names of the villages described on our charts; but having at length discovered a peasant, we seized him and kept him for two days, but he was so stupid that he only knew the name of his own village. This march was, however, very important the emperor, who followed us with the main body of the army; the prince, therefore made me every day draw out a plan of the road, to send to the major-general.

Having surmounted every obstacle, we regained the old road of Kaluga. In one hour afterwards we arrived at Fominskoë. Broussier's division was encamped in the environs of this village, and the cavalry placed in advance, were led on by the viceroy, who, without delay, proceeded to reconnoitre the height which the cossacks occupied; but at his appearance they immediately retired, leaving his highness at liberty to encamp peaceably on the ground for which we had expected to fight.

According to the military report, the position of Forminskoë would have been advantageous for the Russians, if they had resolved to defend it. Through the middle of the village, overlooked by a hill, ran the river Nara, which, towards this point, owing to the contraction of the valley, formed a little lake surrounded by marshes. The whole army had to pass this defile, and to cross a single bridge. This, however, was reserved for the carriages, and another constructed for the infantry.

In order to execute this operation, and to permit a part of the army to pass over before us, they allowed us a day of repose (22d October.) During this time, the Poles, commanded by prince Poniatowski, marched on Vereïa, where the Hetman Platoff was with his cossacks. Napoleon soon followed us with his accustomed suite, and in an instant the village was filled with carriages, horses, and men. But owing to the skilful precautions which had been adopted, all this passed without, confusion; a circumstance which excited not a little astonishment, for the *cohorts of Xerxes*[3] had not more baggage than we.

The same day captain Evrard, who had been despatched to Charopovo, announced to us that he heard a tremendous report in the direction of Moscow. We afterwards learned that it had been produced by the blowing up of the Kremlin. The destruction of this noble citadel, and of the magnificent buildings which it contained, was accomplished by the young imperial guards, who, on quitting Moscow, were ordered to destroy every thing that the flames had spared. Thus perished this celebrated city, founded by the Tartars, and destroyed by the French! Enriched with every gift of fortune, and situated in the centre of the continent, she experienced from the passions of an obscure and remote islander the most lamentable of human vicissitudes. The historian will not fail to remark, that the same man who affected to sacrifice us to promote the progress of civilization, boasted in his own bulletins, that he had caused Russia to retrograde, at least a hundred years.[4]

A part of the army having crossed the Nara, the fourth corps followed them about five o'clock in the morning (23d October) and proceeded towards Borovsk. The enemy appeared no more during this day's march. The cossacks had fled before us, doubtless to announce to the general-in-chief, that we had deceived his vigilance by leaving the new road to through Taroutina, and taking the old one which passes by Borovsk.

The enemy, informed of our march, immediately abandoned his intrenched camp at Lectaskova, but left us in doubt whether he would take the road by Borovsk, or by Malo-Jaroslavitz. Napoleon occupied the former city, situated on an eminence which ran the Protra in a deep and inaccessible channel.

The viceroy, who had encamped half a league beyond Borovsk, in a little village on the right of the road, ordered Delzon's division to march on Malo-Jaroslavitz, and occupy that position before the Russians could seize on it. This general having found it without defence, took possession of it, with only two battalions, leaving the rest of his troops in the rear on the plain. We consequently imagined that this position was secure, when on the following morning (24th October) at day-break, we heard a heavy cannonade in our front. The viceroy, suspecting the cause of it, immediately mounted his horse, and accompanied by his staff, galloped towards Malo-Jaroslavitz. On approaching this city, the noise of the cannon re-

3   An expression which Napoleon made use of in the bulletins of the campaign of 1809, when speaking of the Austrian armies.
4   See the bulletin of the campaign in Russia.

doubled; we heard the sharpshooters on both sides, and at last we distinctly perceived the Russian columns, who were advancing by the new road of Kaluga, to force the position which we occupied.

On arriving below the heights of Malo-Jaroslavitz, general Delzons came towards us, and, approaching the viceroy, said to him, 'Yesterday evening, on my arrival, I took possession of this place, and no one then appeared to dispute it with me, but, about four o'clock in the morning, I was attacked by a large body of infantry. Immediately the two battalions flew to arms, but, overpowered by a much superior force, they have been compelled to descend from the heights, and abandon Malo-Jaroslavitz.' The viceroy, feeling the importance of this loss, and wishing immediately to repair it, gave orders to general Delzons to march, with his whole division. An obstinate engagement now commenced, and fresh troops having arrived to the assistance of the Russians, our soldiers, for a moment, gave way. General Delzons thinking they were about to fly, rushed into the thickest of the battle, in order to reanimate them, but, at the moment when he was defending with obstinacy the barriers of the city, the enemy's sharp-shooters, intrenched behind the wall of a cemetery, fired upon him, and a ball entering his forehead, he fell, and immediately expired. The viceroy, on being informed of this sad event, appeared to be much affected at the loss of a general so worthy his esteem: and after having paid a just tribute to his memory, sent general Guilleminot to replace him. He also ordered the fourteenth division to advance, and relieve those who had been so long engaged. Our soldiers now resumed the offensive, when several fresh columns of Russians coming from Lectaskova, forced them to retreat. We saw them descending the hill with precipitation, and making towards the bridge, as if they wished to repass the river Louja, which ran at the foot of the eminence. But shortly afterwards our brave men, rallied by colonel Forestier, and seeing themselves supported by the chasseurs and grenadiers of the royal guards, resumed their accustomed courage, and once, more ascended the heights. In the meantime, a great number of wounded who had abandoned the field of battle, and, above all, the difficulty with which we maintained ourselves in Malo-Jaroslavitz, convinced the viceroy of the necessity of sending other troops against the continual reinforcements of the enemy. Pino's division, which, during the whole of the campaign, had sought for every opportunity of distinguishing itself, obeyed, with transport, the orders of the prince. They rapidly ascended the heights, with their bayonets fixed, and uttering shouts of joy, succeeded in establishing themselves in all the positions whence the enemy had driven us. This success, however, was dearly purchased. A great number of brave Italians were the victims of their emulation of French valour; nor was it without sincere regret that we heard of the death of general Levié, whom fate permitted to enjoy his new rank only eight days. We were equally afflicted, on beholding general Pino returning covered with blood; who, though he suffered much from the pain of his wound, felt still more sensibly the death of a brother who had fallen by his side. During this time the enemy's cannon raged with fury, and his balls, carried destruction into the ranks of the royal light troops, placed in reserve, and even amongst the staff of his highness. It was at this moment that general Gifflenge, a man of great merit, and extraordinary courage, received a ball in his throat, which obliged him to quit the field of battle.

The success of the day was decided, and we occupied the town, and all the heights, when the fifth division of the first corps joined us, and took up position on our left. The third division of the same corps arrived also after the battle, and occupied a wood on our right. Until nine o'clock in the evening, our batteries and foot soldiers did not cease their firing, at a very short distance from the enemy; but, at, length, night and excessive weariness put an end to this sanguinary combat. It was, however, nearly ten o'clock before the viceroy and the staff were able to take the repose which was necessary after so many fatigues. We encamped beneath Malo-Jaroslavitz, between the town and the river Louja; but the troops bivouacked through the whole extent of the positions which they had so gloriously carried.

The next day we were convinced that the obstinacy with which the Russians had disputed our possession of Malo-Jaroslavitz, was in consequence of their intention of effecting a movement on our right, in order to arrive at Viazma before us, well persuaded that our march on Kaluga was only a manoeuvre, with the design of concealing our retreat. About four o'clock in the morning, the viceroy mounted his horse. We ascended the eminence on which the-battle had been fought, when we saw the plain covered with cossacks, whose light artillery was firing on our troops: we also observed on our left three grand redoubts. On the preceding evening each of them had mounted fifteen or twenty pieces of cannon, with which they defended the right flank of Kutusoff, supposing that we should have attempted to turn his position on that side. About ten o'clock the firing abated, and at twelve it entirely ceased.

The interior of Malo-Jaroslavitz presented the most horrid spectacle. On entering the town, we beheld with grief the spot where general Delzons had perished, and regretted that a premature death had terminated his glorious career. We did equal justice to the memory of his brother, who received a mortal wound, while endeavouring to rescue him from the hands of the enemy. A little further on they showed us the place where general Fontane had been wounded, and at the foot of the hill, we saw the grenadiers of the thirty-fifth regiment of the line, who were bestowing funeral honours on their brave colonel.

The town where we had fought no longer remained. We could not even distinguish the lines of the streets, on account of the numerous dead bodies with which they were heaped. On every side we saw a multitude of scattered limbs, and human heads, crushed by the wheels of the artillery. The houses formed a pile of ruins, and under their burning ashes appeared many skeletons half consumed. Many of the sick and wounded had, on quitting the field of battle, taken refuge in these houses. The small number of them who had escaped the flames, now presented themselves before us, with their faces blackened, and their clothes and hair dreadfully burnt. In the most piteous tone, they besought us to afford them some relief, or kindly to terminate their sufferings by death. The most ferocious were affected at this sad spectacle, and, turning hastily away, could not refrain from shedding tears. This distressing scene made every one shudder at the evils to which despotism exposes humanity, and we almost fancied that those barbarous times were returned, when we could only appease the gods, by offering human victims on their sanguinary altars.

Towards the afternoon, Napoleon, having arrived with a numerous suite, coolly surveyed the field of battle, and heard, without emotion, the heart-rending cries of the unhappy wounded, who eagerly demanded assistance. But this man although accustomed for twenty years to the calamities of war, could not, on entering the town, repress his astonishment at the desperation with which both parties must have fought. Even had he intended to continue his march on Tula and Kaluga, the experience of this battle would have deterred him. On this occasion, even his insensibility was forced to render justice to those whom it was due. He gave a convincing proof of it by praising the valour of the fourth corps, and saying to the viceroy, 'The honour of this glorious day belongs entirely to you.'

While we were disputing with the enemy the position of Malo-Jaroslavitz, more than six thousand cossacks unexpectedly rushed on the head-quarters of the emperor, established at Ghorodnia, and carried off six pieces of cannon, which were posted not far from the village. The duke of Istria immediately galloped after them with all the cavalry of the guards, and succeeded in retaking the artillery. The cossacks, cut to pieces and dispersed, effected their retreat; but in their flight, one of their numerous detachments attacked the baggage of the fourth corps, and would have captured it if the cavalry of the Italian guards had not received them with the same intrepidity as the imperial guards. The coolness of Joubert, who, commanded the escort, was much praised in this affair. Seated in his carriage, he had the resolution not to stir from it, but drew his sword on the cossacks, who surrounded him, and defended himself till he could obtain assistance.

From the commencement of the campaign, the son of the Hetman Platoff, mounted on a superb white horse, from the Ukraine, was the faithful companion in arms of his brave father, and always at the head of the cossacks. He was often remarked by our advanced guards, on account of his courage and intrepidity. This fine young man was the idol of his father, and the hope of the warlike nation which expected hereafter to obey him. But Destiny had pronounced his doom, and the fatal hour was at hand. In a desperate charge of cavalry, which took place near Vereïa, between prince Poniatowski and the Hetman Platoff, the Poles and Russians, animated by a mutual hatred, fought with fury. Excited by the ardour of the combat, they gave no quarter, and on both sides fell numerous brave men, who had returned in safety from former battles. Platoff, who saw his best soldiers falling around him, forgot his own danger, and with an anxious eye, looked round for his favourite son. But the moment approached when the unfortunate father was destined to feel that life is sometimes almost insupportable. The unhappy youth had returned from the heat of the battle, and was preparing to renew the attack, when he received a mortal wound from a Hulan Pole.

At this moment his father appeared, and flying to his assistance, threw himself upon him. On seeing his beloved parent the son heaved a deep sigh, and would have expressed, for the last time, his affection and his duty; but, as he attempted to speak, his strength failed him, and he breathed his last. In the meantime, Platoff, who could not restrain his tears, retired to his tent, to give vent to his feelings. In the first burst of agony be considered life a burden, and could no longer endure the light. The following morning, at day-break, the chiefs of the cossacks came to express their grief, and earnestly to request that they might be permitted to render funeral honours to the son of their Hetman. Every one, on seeing this brave young man stretched on a bear-skin, knelt spontaneously, and respectfully kissed the hand of a youth, who, but for a premature death, would have equalled the greatest heroes, by his valour and by his virtues. After having, according to their ritual, offered fervent prayers for the repose of his soul, they removed him from the presence of his father, and carried him in solemn procession to a neighbouring eminence covered with cypress, where he was to be interned.

The cossacks, standing around, all arranged in order of battle, observed a religious silence, and bowed their heads in profound respect, while grief was painted in every countenance. At the moment when the earth was for ever to separate them from the son of their prince, they fired a volley over the grave. Afterwards holding their horses in their hands, they slowly and solemnly marched round the tomb, with their lances pointed towards the earth.

Book VII

Doroghoboui

The victory of Malo-Jaroslavitz discovered two melancholy truths: first, that the Russians, far from being weakened, had been reinforced by numerous battalions, and that they all fought with an obstinacy which made us despair of gaining new victories. 'But two battles more like, this,' said the soldiers, 'and Napoleon will be without an army.' It likewise discovered that we could no longer effect an easy retreat, since the enemy, having at the close of the engagement outflanked us, prevented our columns from retiring by the route of Medouin, Jouknov, and Elnïa, and reduced us to the unhappy necessity of retreating precipitately by the great road of Smolensko, or in other words, by the desert which we ourselves had made. Besides these apprehensions, too well founded, we also knew that the Russians had despatched before us the army of Moldavia, on the very route which we were to pursue, and that the corps of Wittgenstein was advancing to join that army.

After this sanguinary combat, those who judged only from appearances and popular report, supposed that we should march on Kaluga and Tula; but when they saw that a strong advanced guard of the enemy, instead of taking that direction, had outflanked our right by defiling on Medouin, all who were experienced in warlike manoeuvres perceived that the Russians had penetrated the designs of Napoleon, and that it was necessary for us to make a rapid march on Viazma, to arrive there before them. There was no longer any question of Kaluga or the Ukraine, but how to effect a safe retreat on the route of Borovsk. As soon as our retreat was decided, the fourth corps began its retrograde march, leaving all the first corps, and the cavalry of general Chastel, at Jaroslavitz. These troops were to form the rear-guard, at the distance of a day's march from us.

(October 26th.) We saw on our route to what the unfortunate and memorable victory of Jaroslavitz had reduced us. At every step were wagons abandoned for want of horses to draw them, and the fragments of innumerable military carriages burned for the same reason. With such misfortunes at the very commencement of our retreat, we formed sad and mournful presages of the future. Those who carried with them the spoils of Moscow, trembled for their riches. We were principally disquieted at seeing the deplorable state of the feeble remains of our cavalry, and we listened with melancholy foreboding to the frequent explosions of our ammunition-wagons, which sounded from afar like distant thunder.

It was night when we arrived at Ouvarooskoë. Surprised at seeing the place in flames, we were informed that orders had been issued to destroy every thing in our route. Near this village was a *chateau*, which, although in the centre of a wood, possessed a grandeur and magnificence equal to the noblest palaces of Italy. The richness of the furniture corresponded with the beauty of the architecture. We saw there many exquisite paintings, chandeliers of the greatest value, and numerous lustres of rock-crystal, which gave to these apartments, when lighted up, an appearance truly enchanting. Even these were not spared; and we learned on the morrow, that our artillery-men, finding the progress of the flames too slow, had hastened and completed the destruction, by placing several barrels, filled with gunpowder, on the ground floor.

The villages, which a few days before had afforded us shelter, were now level with the ground. Under their ashes, yet warm, and which the wind drove towards us, were the bodies of hundreds of soldiers , and peasants. Many an infant was to be seen cruelly butchered, and many a female savagely massacred on the spot which had witnessed her violation.

We left the village of Borovsk, which had been equally a prey to the flames, on our right, to reascend the Protva, and find a ford for our artillery. Having discovered one, half a league from the village, it would have been attempted by all our corps, but many of the wagons, sticking fast in the middle of the river, so much encumbered the only spot at which a passage there was practicable, that it was necessary to search for another ford. On reconnoitring the bridge of Borovsk, I found that it still remained, and that it offered great facility for carrying over the baggage. Immediately the prince caused the third division to fall back, and thus, by means of the bridge, opened to our corps a better and a shorter route. The only danger which we had to fear, was the passage of the wagons laden with ammunition, through a town completely in flames.

The corps filed across this vast conflagration without a single accident, and after having passed through many frightful defiles, the night found us at the execrable village of Alféréva (Oct. 27th), where the generals of division with difficulty found a barn to shelter them. That of the viceroy was so ruinous, that we pitied those who were destined to inhabit it. In addition to all these evils, the want of provision aggravated our sufferings. That which we had brought from Moscow, was almost consumed and every one, covetous of the little that remained to him, retired to eat in secret the morsel of bread which his industry had procured. Our horses fared yet worse. A little thatch torn from the roof of the houses, was their only food. Many of them died of fatigue and hunger, obliging the artillery to abandon all that was not absolutely necessary; and every day redoubled, in a frightful manner, the explosion of the wagons, which were blown up and destroyed. (October 28th.)

On the following day we recrossed the Protva a little below Vereïa. This town was burning at the moment of our passage; and the devouring flames rising in whirlwinds on every side, soon reduced it to ashes. Vereïa was the more unfortunate, since, lying at a distance from the great road, she had flattered herself that she might escape the calamities by which she was surrounded. In truth, with the exception of the engagement between the Russians and the Poles, she had hitherto experienced little of the horrors of war. Her fields had not been ravaged, and her well-cultivated gardens were now covered with vegetables of every kind, which our famished soldiers devoured in an instant. At night we slept at a wretched village, of which we could not learn the name. We supposed that it was Mitïaéva, because we were only a league from Ghorodok-Borisov. This place was yet more miserable than the hamlet at which we had halted the night before. The greater part of the officers passed the night in the open air, which was the more unpleasant, as the nights began to be extremely cold, and little wood could be procured. Even the huts which the generals had hastily erected, were demolished by the soldiers to supply a few scanty fires. and many who went to sleep in comfortable cabins, on waking in the middle of the night, found that the sky was their only covering.

Napoleon who preceded us one day's march, had already passed Mojaïsk, burning and destroying every thing which he found on his route. His soldiers were so intent on this devastation, that they set fire even to the places where we should have halted. This exposed us to great and unnecessary suffering; but our corps, in its turn, burned the few houses that the others had left, and deprived the army of the prince of Eckmuhl, which formed the rear-guard, of all power to shelter itself from the inclemency of the night. That corps had likewise to contend with an exasperated enemy, which, learning our retreat, hastened on every side to avenge itself. The cannon which we heard every day, and at distances continually diminishing, sufficiently announced to us the fatigues, the sufferings, and the dangers, of that division of the army.

At length, having passed through Ghorodok-Borisov (October 29th), in the midst of almost impenetrable clouds of smoke, we entered, an hour afterwards, on a plain which appeared to have been long since devastated. We saw at a distance the dead bodies of men and horses: but the numerous intrenchments, half destroyed, the aspect of the ruined town recalled to our memories the environs of Mojaïsk through which we had passed as conquerors, fifty-one days before. The Poles encamped upon the ruins, and at their departure burnt the few houses which had escaped the first conflagration; but the destruction had been already so complete that we could scarcely see the light of the flames. The only thing which struck us was the newly erected tower, rising amid the ruins, and, by its whiteness, forming a melancholy contrast with the black clouds which enveloped it. It remained entire, and the clock yet tolled the hours, though the city was no more.

Our corps not pass through Mojaïsk, but, turning to the left, we arrived (October 29th), at the site of the village of Krasnoë where we had slept at the day after the battle of the Moskwa. I say the site of the village, for the houses existed no longer, and the *chateau* alone had been preserved for the use of Napoleon. We encamped round the *chateau*, and, as long as I live, I shall recollect how pierced with the cold, we crowded together, and slept with comfort on the yet warm ashes of the houses that had been burned the day before.

(October 30th.) The nearer we approached to Mojaïsk, the more desolate the country appeared. The fields, trampled down by thousands of horses, seemed as though they had never been cultivated. The forests, cleared by the long continuance of the troops, partook likewise of the general desolation. But most horrible was the multitude of dead bodies, which, deprived of burial fifty-two days scarcely retained the human form. On arriving at Borodino, my consternation was inexpressible, at finding the twenty thousand men, who had perished there, yet lying exposed. The whole plain was entirely covered with them. None of the bodies were more than half buried. In one place were to be seen garments yet red with blood, and bones gnawed by dogs and birds of prey; in another were broken arms, drums, helmets, and swords. Fragments of standards lay scattered thick around, and, from the emblems with which they were adorned, it was easy to judge how much the Russian eagle had suffered on that bloody day.

On one side we saw the remains of the cottage at which Kutusoff had encamped; and more to the left the famous redoubt. It yet frowned threateningly over the plain. It elevated itself like a pyramid in the midst of a desert. When I mused on what it had been, and what it then was, I thought that I saw Vesuvius in repose. Perceiving a soldier on the summit, at the remote distance his immovable figure had the effect of a statue. 'Ah!' I exclaimed, 'if ever a statue is consecrated to the demon of war it should be placed on this pedestal.'

As we traversed the field of battle, we heard, at a distance, a feeble voice appealing to us for succour. Touched by his plaintive cries, some soldiers, approached the spot, and, to their astonishment, saw, stretched on the ground, a French soldier with both his legs fractured. 'I was wounded,' said he, 'on the day of the great battle. I fainted from the agony which I endured, and, on recovering my senses, I found myself in a desolate place, where no one could hear my cries, or afford me relief. For two months, I daily dragged myself to the brink of a rivulet, where I fed on the grass and roots, and some morsels of bread, which I found among the dead bodies. At night I laid myself down under the shelter of some dead horses. To day, seeing you at a distance, I summoned all my strength, and happily crawled sufficiently near your route to make myself heard.' While the surrounding soldiers were expressing their surprise, the general, who was informed of an occurrence so singular and so touching, placed the unfortunate wretch in his own carriage.

My history would far exceed the bounds prescribed, were I to recount all the calamities which that atrocious war produced. I will relate one circumstance alone, from which my readers may judge of the rest. Three thousand prisoners were brought from Moscow. Having nothing to give them during their march, they were at night driven into a narrow fold like so many beasts. Without fire, and without food, they lay on the bare ice, and to assuage the hunger which tortured them, those who had not the courage to die, nightly fed on the flesh of their companions, whom fatigue, misery, and famine had destroyed.

But I turn from a picture so shocking, and pursue the course of my narrative. I shall soon have horrors enough to describe, which fell to the lot of my friends and my companions in arms.

We repassed the Kologha, with as much precipitation as we had formerly crossed it under the auspices of victory. The steps which conducted to the river were so steep, and the frozen earth so slippery, that men arid horses continually fell over each other. Happy would it have been for us, if the passage of other rivers, so often multiplied upon us, had not been even more dangerous than this.

We saw again the abbey of Kolotskoi. Despoiled of its former splendour, and surrounded by ruins, it resembled more an hospital than a convent. It was the only house which had been spared since our retreat from Moscow. It was given to the sick and wounded, who wished to breathe their last in its peaceful asylum.

The fourth division, forming always the advanced-guard, halted at a miserable village, situated half a league to the right of the road, between the abbey of Kolotskoi, and Prokofévo. Of all the places of repose at which we had hitherto stopped, this was the most intolerable. Nothing remained but some wretched sheds, and the thatch had been torn from the roofs to give to the half-famished horses. Here, however, the prince and his staff were constrained to pass the night.

On the morrow (October 31st) we commenced our march at an early hour, and being arrived at the heights of Prokofévo, we heard the sound of cannon so near us, that the viceroy, fearing the prince of Eckmuhl was pushed by the enemy, halted on one of the heights, and drew up his troops in order of battle to succour him. For some days, many persons had complained of the slowness with which the first division marched. They had blamed the system of retreat by echelons, adopted by the commander-in-chief, saying that it had lost three days' march, and thus had enabled the advanced-guard of Miloradowitch easily to overtake us. Finally, they alleged that he ought to pass rapidly over a country which did not afford the means of subsistence. He might have replied in his own justification, that too rapid a retreat would have redoubled the audacity of the enemy, who, strong in light cavalry, could at all times overtake us, and cut in pieces our rear-guard, if it had refused the combat. He could have added this maxim of war - The more precipitate a retreat, the more fatal it becomes, because the fear which it occasions in the minds of the soldiers, is more to be dreaded than any physical evils.

The viceroy had made these dispositions on the heights of Prokofévo, to succour the prince of Eckmuhl, but soon understanding that that marshal was only harassed by the cossacks, he continued his march towards Ghiatz, always taking care that his divisions marched in the greatest order, and halting, whenever it was possible that the prince of Eckmuhl could want his support. It is impossible to give too much praise to prince Eugene, for his conduct in these critical circumstances. He was always the last of his column, and he now bivouacked a league on this side of Ghiatz, that he might, be ready the more promptly to repel the attack of the enemy.

The night which the prince and his staff passed here was the severest to which they had been exposed. They halted on a little hill, near the place where formerly stood the village of Ivachkova. Not one house remained; the whole hamlet had been long since destroyed. To complete their sufferings, a violent and piercing wind arose. Not a tree afforded them shelter, and nature, in depriving that situation of wood, had refused the only resource which could mitigate the severity of the climate of Russia.

Although our own sufferings were thus great, we were not insensible to those which our enemies endured. On approaching Ghiatz in the morning, we felt the sincerest regret when we perceived that the whole town had disappeared. We should have searched for it in vain, had it not been for the ruins of a few houses of stone, which showed that this had once been a place of human habitation, and that we were not wandering amid the remains of a forest consumed by fire. Never were cruelty and revenge pushed so far. Ghiatz, constructed entirely of wood, disappeared in a day, and left its former inhabitants, and even its enemies, to regret the fall of its industry, and the destruction of its prosperity. It was the most commercial and flourishing town in Russia. It contained many excellent manufactories of cloth and leather, and furnished the Russian navy with considerable quantities of tar, cordage, and machine stores.

The weather, which was piercingly cold in the night, was beautiful during the day; and the troops, though almost worn out by their sufferings, and exposed to privations of every kind, were full of courage, and eager to meet the enemy. All seemed to feel that their only safety consisted in manfully struggling with the difficulties by which they were surrounded. They had, for many days, been reduced to subsist on horse-flesh; even the generals had begun to share the same food. The mortality of these animals was there regarded as a fortunate circumstance; and without this resource, the soldier would have much more severely experienced the horrors of famine.

(November 1st.) The cossacks, whose approach we had dreaded, no longer delayed to realise our fears. Hitherto, while they had not been seen, the soldier marched with his accustomed confidence, and the baggage-wagons feebly escorted, were so numerous they formed many distinct convoys, at considerable distances from each other. Near the ruined village of Czarevo-Saïmiché was a causeway, about five hundred feet long, where the great road formerly passed. The passage of the artillery had so worn it, that it was no longer practicable, and to continue the route, it was necessary to descend into a marshy meadow, cut by a large river. The wagons, which went first, easily passed over the ice; but this, at length, being broken by the multitude which thronged over, it became necessary, either to expose themselves to the greatest danger in attempting to ford the river, or to wait whilst some wretched bridges were constructed in haste. In the meantime, the head of the column being thus arrested, fresh carriages continually arrived. Artillery, baggage-wagons, and sutlers' carts, all crowded one on another, and the drivers, according to their custom, profited by the momentary delay to light their fires and to chafe their limbs benumbed with cold. While all was in this imagined security and complete confusion, on a sudden, the cossacks, uttering the most frightful cries, rushed from a thick wood on our left, and precipitated themselves, on these poor wretches. All were panic struck at their sight, and almost unconscious of what they did. Some ran to the woods; others fled to their carriages, and, lashing their feeble horses, galloped in confusion over the plain. These were most to be pitied. The rivulets, the marshes, the slipperiness, or the breaking of the ice, soon arrested their progress and left them an easy prey to their pursuers. They were most fortunate who, taking advantage of the numerous carriages, intrenched themselves behind them, and awaited that deliverance which was not slow in arriving; for as soon as the cossacks perceived the infantry advancing upon them, they retreated, after having wounded a few of the drivers, and pillaged some of the ammunition wagons.

The soldiers, to whom the care of escorting or conducting the baggage was entrusted, profited by the disorder which the presence of the cossacks excited to pillage and destroy what they had sworn to defend. From that time dishonesty and theft spread themselves so rapidly and so universally through the army, that we were scarcely more secure amongst our own soldiers, than we should have been in the midst of the enemy. Whatever the soldiers took a fancy to, they availed themselves of some opportunity to purloin; and encouraged by the impunity with which they set all discipline at defiance, they procured more frequent opportunities to pillage, by industriously spreading false alarms.

The royal guard was clearing the defile of Czarevo-Seïmiché when the baggage was attacked. It immediately received orders to halt, and while it rested on its arms, we saw the cossacks on our left, not two hundred paces from us, reconnoitring our situation. It was even said, that profiting by the intervals which subsisted between some of our divisions, they frequently crossed our route. But their bravadoes, exercised with success on the followers of our camp, had no effect when attempted against the regular troops. When the royal guard saw the cossacks thus hovering on their flanks, they no longer continued their march, but halted by a wood not far from Vélitschevo. The other divisions, encamped near the viceroy, who remained constantly in the rear, since the Russians appeared so determined to harass our retreat.

(November 2d.) On the morrow, three hours before day, we abandoned this position. Our nocturnal march was truly terrifying. The night was fearfully dark, and, afraid of running one against another, we were compelled to grope along our way with a slowness which gave us full leisure to indulge in the most melancholy reflections. In spite of our precaution, we often fell into the ditches on each side of the road, and were precipitated into the deep ravines by which it was intersected. At length our impatience for the dawn became insupportable. We hoped that its cheering light would render our march less painful, and would protect us from the ambushes of an enemy, whose accurate knowledge of the country gave it a fatal advantage in all its manoeuvres.

We were assured, indeed, that we should soon be attacked. Those who were acquainted with the country, feared the position of Viazma, because they knew that, near that city, the road from Medouin, which part of the Russian army had taken after the battle of Malo-Jaroslavitz, and which was shorter than ours, joined the great road. They also regarded the cossacks, who had appeared on the preceding evening, as the advanced-guard of the numerous cavalry of Platoff, and the two divisions of general Miloradowitch, which would suddenly burst upon us near Viazma.

Our pioneers, and the equipage of the viceroy were only a league from that city, and nothing yet betokened the presence of the enemy. In the meantime, that prince being in the rear-guard with the first corps, and perceiving that the distance between the two extremities of his column hazarded the safety of the army, ordered the troops which were in advance to halt. In that interval, colonel Labedoyère, aid-de-camp to his highness, arrived from Viazma. On hearing the dangers to which that officer had been exposed, we doubted not that on the morrow we should be compelled to force our way with the point of the bayonet.

The viceroy halted at Foedorovskoé, although he was expected at Viazma. The divisions of the army encamped around him. At his right, facing the enemy, were the Poles, a little in front of the first corps, which, though it was the rear guard, yet having been sharply pressed, was but a short distance from us. Prince Eugene had indeed slackened his march to form a junction with them.

(November 3d.) Our divisions were on the march at six o'clock on the following morning. As we approached Viazma, and our baggage was already in that city, the cossacks showed that they were indeed near us, by commencing a sudden and violent attack. The wagons however drew up round a little church, until the arrival of our troops put the enemy to flight. But when these troops attempted to continue their march, the first brigade of the thirteenth division, commanded by general Nagle, which formed the rear-guard of our part of the army, was attacked on its flank, a league and a half from Viazma. Numerous squadrons of Russian horse issued from the road which we had dreaded, and threw themselves into the space which separated the fourth corps from the first. The viceroy perceiving the danger of his situation, suddenly halted his divisions, and his artillery, that the well directed fire of the batteries might check an enemy, all whose manoeuvres tended effectually to cut off our retreat by possessing themselves of Viazma.

While these divisions executed divers evolutions to frustrate the plans of the Russians, they were followed by the first corps, and we remarked, with regret that these troops, worn out, no doubt, by unheard-of sufferings, and incessant combat, had lost that due subordination, and undaunted courage, which we had so often admired. The soldiers were regardless of discipline, and most of them being wounded, or sinking under fatigue, increased the crowd of mere camp-followers.

The fourth corps was thus left for a considerable time, to sustain alone, not only the charge of a numerous cavalry, but also the reiterated attacks of a body of Russian infantry, consisting of more than twelve thousand men. The first corps, however, having filed off behind us, to the right of the road, at length took a position on the left of the same road, between Viazma and the point of attack, and thus relieved the troops of the fourth corps, which the viceroy had caused to advance, at the beginning of the action. These were now enabled to occupy some advantageous positions, which they found at of the right of the road, and thus, conjointly with the first corps, were ready to receive the attack, which the Russians again threatened.

Our fourteenth division, which had been in front of the thirteenth, suffered that division now to pass it, and relieved it by becoming the rearguard. The fifteenth which had followed the fourteenth, remained with the royal guard, near Viazma, as a reserve. The order of battle being thus arranged, the enemy's infantry advanced, and the engagement commenced with considerable warmth, but with a decided superiority in artillery on the part of the Russians. The miserable state of our horses would not permit us manoeuvre our pieces with much celerity. It was in this engagement that colonel Banco, aid-de-camp to the viceroy, and commandant of the second regiment of Italian horse-chasseurs, had his head carried off by a cannon-ball.

Our troops, notwithstanding their inferiority, maintained their positions long enough for the baggage to pass through Viazma, in the greatest order. A party of the enemy's cavalry then attempted to break through our two wings. That which, during our retreat, had advanced on our right, was repulsed by a body of infantry furnished with cannon. The other, on our left, was equally repulsed by the Bavarian horse, which were opposed to it, and by some battalions of sharpshooters concealed in the bushes, with which the field of battle was covered.

This manoeuvre of the Russians, however, spread the greatest consternation among those whom either disease of body or want of courage had caused to quit their ranks, and to mingle with the followers of the camp. This description of persons was, unhappily, very numerous, principally among the cavalry which was almost entirely dismounted. They were, in truth, become more than useless to us. In the perilous situation in which we then found ourselves, they constituted our greatest danger. They not only impeded all our manoeuvres, but they spread alarms and disorder on all sides, by flying with precipitation before an enemy with which their cowardice would not permit them to fight. The cossacks, likewise, seeing this feeble and unarmed multitude flying before them, acquired fresh courage, and attacked us with redoubled ardour, believing that these columns of fugitives were the only troops with which they had to contend.

Although we repulsed every attack, our situation was becoming exceedingly critical, until, happily, the grand ravine, situated at the left of our route, and above all, the excellent position which the duke of Elchingen occupied, arrested the progress of the Russians. That marshal, being left the day before in a position near Viazma to await the passage of the first corps, and to take its place as rearguard, had the glory of extricating us from the greatest danger, to which we had hitherto been exposed. During the whole action he assisted in person, and he continued to march with the viceroy and the prince of Eckmuhl, that he might confer with them on the measures which it was necessary to adopt.

It was nearly four hours after mid-day, when our division passed through Viazma. Leaving the city, we saw the third division encamped on a little hill on our left. We owed much gratitude to that corps for having so well defended that important situation. The bravery with which those troops maintained their ground, rendered the fierce and reiterated attacks of an enemy, superior in numbers, completely ineffectual, and contributed much to save the first and fourth corps from absolute destruction. That last division was thus enabled to accomplish its retreat behind the river of Viazma, where the prince endeavoured to repair the disasters of this battle so unfortunate, and sustained under circumstances in which the most skilful combinations could scarcely promise a favourable issue.

Traversing the forest at the foot of the hill of Viazma, we overtook a convoy of the sick and wounded, which had left Moscow before us. These unfortunate beings, after having been many days deprived of medical assistance, and almost of food, encamped in this forest, which served them for an hospital and a grave. The horses had perished of fatigue and hunger, and their guards had forsaken these unhappy wretches, and abandoned them to their fate. We encamped near them, and, at the approach of night, kindled an enormous fire, at the back of a little hill covered with brushwood. The royal guard was round the tent of the prince, the thirteenth and fourteenth divisions were placed on our flanks, while the fifteenth division, though considerably weakened, formed our rear-guard.

From this position the whole horizon appeared on fire. It was occasioned by the destruction of those houses at Viazma, which had escaped the first conflagration. The third corps, which always preserved its position to protect our retreat, although it was separated from the Russians by a river, and by deep ravines, seemed to be frequently attacked. Often in the silence of the night, we were startled by the report of cannon, which, passing over the thick forests, sounded in a peculiarly mournful and horrible manner. This unexpected sound repeated by the echoes of the valley, was lengthened into dismal reverberations; and often, when our harassed powers were sinking into calm and refreshing repose, suddenly roused us, while we hastily and fearfully ran to arms, expecting that the enemy, which we knew to be at hand, was advancing to surprise us.

(November 4th.) At one o'clock in the morning the viceroy deemed it prudent, to profit by the obscurity of the night, to effect his retreat, and gain some hour's march on the Russians with whom he could not fight, since famine would not permit us to remain one unnecessary day in a country completely depopulated and laid waste. We marched along the great road, groping our way in the dark. The route was entirely covered with the fragments of carriages and artillery. Men and horses, worn out with fatigue, could scarcely drag themselves along, and, as soon as the last fell exhausted, the soldiers eagerly divided the carcass among them, and hastened to broil on the coals that food, which during many days, had constituted their only nourishment. Suffering yet more from the cold than from hunger, they abandoned their ranks, to warm themselves by a fire hastily kindled; but, when they would rise to depart their frost-bitten limbs refused their office, a partial insensibility crept over them, and they preferred to fall into the hands of the enemy, rather than make a feeble effort to continue their journey.

Day had broken some time when we arrived at the village of Polianovo near which ran the little river Osma. The bridge was very narrow and bad. The crowd which had to pass it was immense. As every one eagerly rushed on to clear this narrow defile, the viceroy was compelled to order the officers of his staff to interpose their authority, and to maintain some little order in so dangerous a place. He even condescended to stay himself, and to use every necessary precaution to facilitate the passage of the artillery, in the midst of a crowd of carriages which pressed on towards the bridge.

Beneath the town of Semlevo ran another branch of the river Osma, more considerable than the first. The march of the troops was not, however, delayed. They profited by a bridge both large and solid, to extricate themselves from a situation, from which the enemy might have derived the greatest advantages, had they been able to gain possession of it. Semlevo, built on a steep bill, commands the road by which we arrived. At its foot is the Osma, which, almost surrounding it, would have rendered it impossible for us to have forced that position.

Towards the close of the day, we found shelter for the prince, in a little chapel situated near this river, which making a considerable circuit to the right from Semlevo, returns again, and passes the road, at the spot at which we now were. We had scarcely established ourselves round the chapel, when the camp-followers, having gone to forage, were attacked by the cossacks, and fled back with precipitation. Some had lost their horses, others their clothes, and many were covered with wounds from the sabre and the lance. It was necessary then to think of retreating, and while the baggage of the viceroy evacuated the position, we saw the troops of the enemy advancing to the banks of that branch of the Osma, which we were about to pass. In these circumstances, we were convinced how necessary it was in a retreat to secure well the passage of every river. This, though small, was scarcely fordable, and had no bridge. To cross it, men, horses, and wagons, precipitated themselves into the water. Our, situation was the more deplorable, as the Russians, profiting by our distress, began to harass the rear of the column, and to spread consternation among the immense crowd, which, remaining on the other side, saw itself compelled to cross a deep and half frozen river, whose banks were extremely boggy. During this time we heard the balls of the enemy whistling over our heads, and threatening every moment to destroy us. With this exception the passage of the river presented nothing unfortunate. Night approached, and the cossacks discontinued their attacks. Our loss merely consisted of a few carriages, which we were compelled to leave in the middle of the water.

This obstacle being surmounted, we entered on a forest, at the extremity of which, towards the left, was a *chateau*, long ago pillaged. We established ourselves there for the night, near the village of Rouibki. We had only horse flesh to eat, except a little flour that had been brought from Moscow, which remained in one of the wagons. A very small quantity of this was given to each officer to make his *bouillié*. It was carefully measured out to every one with a spoon. As for our horses, we were well content if we could give them the straw, which in our former passage had served them for litter.

(November 5th.) Early in the morning we pursued our retreat, and, without any fatal rencontre with the enemy, arrived at a large village, of which some houses had been spared. We particularly remarked a large house built of stone, and we designated that village by the name of the Stone-House.[1] We could rarely ascertain the names of the places through which we passed, and we described them in our journals by something characteristic, whether it referred to their situation, or

---

1   This village appears, from the map, to have been Jolkou Postoïa Door.

form, or any peculiar hardships which we there endured. One was called the 'Hurrah,' from the dreadful cry of the cossacks. Another, 'That near which we were beaten.' We spoke not of those at which we had suffered from hunger, for that was common to every village through which we passed.

Hitherto we had endured our misfortunes with calmness and resignation, buoyed up by the flattering hope that they would soon cease. When we departed from Moscow, we had regarded Smolensko as the limit of our retreat. There we trusted that we should rejoin the divisions left on the Nieper and the Dwina, and, taking these two rivers as the boundary of our territories, should have the beautiful country of Lithuania for our winter quarters. We likewise pleased ourselves with the thought, that Smolensko abounded in provisions of every kind; and that, to relieve us from the labours under which we were rapidly sinking, we should find the ninth division, composed of twenty-five thousand fresh troops. This city was therefore the object of our fondest and our most pleasing dreams. Every one was anxious to arrive thither, persuaded that within its walls the dreadful calamities which now environed us would forever cease. The name of Smolensko passed from mouth to mouth, and each pronounced it with confidence to those who were sinking under their sufferings, as their truest, their only consolation. There was magic in the name. It carried with it a happy oblivion of all our past miseries. and inspired us with courage to support the fatigues which we were yet to encounter.

(November 6th.) We marched towards Smolensko, with an ardour which redoubled our strength; and approaching Doroghobouï, distant from that city only twenty leagues, the thought that in three days we should reach the end of all our misfortunes filled us with the most intoxicating joy; when suddenly the atmosphere, which had hitherto brilliant, was clouded by cold and dense vapours. The sun, enveloped by the thickest mists, disappeared from sight, and the snow falling in large flakes, in an instant obscured the day, and confounded the earth with the sky. The wind, furiously blowing, howled dreadfully through the forests, and overwhelmed the firs, already bent down with the ice; while the country around, as far as the eye could reach, presented, unbroken, one white and savage appearance.

The soldiers, vainly struggling with the snow and the wind, which rushed upon them with the violence of a whirlwind, could no longer distinguish the road; and falling into the ditches which bordered it, there found a grave. Others pressed on towards the end of their journey, scarcely able to drag themselves along, badly mounted, badly clothed, with nothing to eat, nothing to drink, shivering with the cold, and groaning with pain. Becoming selfish through despair, they afforded neither succour, nor even one glance of pity, to those who, exhausted by fatigue and disease, expired around them. How many unfortunate beings, on that dreadful day, dying of cold and famine, struggled hard with the agonies of death. We heard some of them faintly bidding their last adieu to their friends and comrades. Others, as they drew their last breath, pronounced the name of their mothers, their wives, their native country, which they were never more to see. The rigour of the frost soon seized on their benumbed limbs and penetrated through the whole frame. Stretched on the road, we could distinguish only the heaps of snow which covered them, and which, at almost every step formed little undulations, like so many graves. At the same time vast flights of ravens, abandoning the plain to take refuge in the neighbouring forests, croaked mournfully as they passed over our heads and troops of dogs which had followed us from Moscow, and lived solely on our mangled remains, howled around us, as if they would hasten the period when we were to become their prey.

From that day the army lost its courage and its military attitude. The soldier no longer obeyed his officer. The officer separated himself from his general. The regiments disbanded, marched in disorder. Searching for food, they spread themselves over the plain, burning and pillaging whatever fell in their way. The horses fell by thousands.[2] The cannon and the wagons which had been abandoned, served only to obstruct the way. No sooner had the soldiers separated from the ranks, than we were assailed by a population eager to avenge the horrors of which it had been the victim. The cossacks came to the succour of the peasants, and drove back to the great road, already filled with the dying and the dead, those of the followers who escaped from the carnage made among them.

Such was the situation of the army, when we arrived at Doroghoboüi. This little town would have given new life to our unfortunate troops, if Napoleon had not been so far blinded by rage, as to forget that his soldiers would be the first to suffer by the devastation which he caused to be made. Doroghoboüi had been burnt, its magazines pillaged, and the brandy with which they were filled, had been poured into the streets, while the rest of the army was perishing for want of it. The few houses which remained, were occupied exclusively by a small number of generals and staff-officers. The few soldiers which yet dared to face the enemy, were exposed to all the rigours of the season; while the others, who had wandered from their proper corps, were now repulsed on every side, and found no shelter in any part of the camp. How deplorable was

2   See the twenty-ninth bulletin.

then the situation of these poor wretches! Tormented by hunger, we saw them run after every horse the moment it fell. They devoured it raw, like dogs, and fought among themselves for the mangled limbs. Worn out by want of sleep and long marches, they saw nothing around them but the snow; not one spot appeared on which they could sit or lie. Penetrated with the cold, they wandered on every side to find wood, but the snow had caused it entirely to disappear. If, fortunately, they found a little, they knew not where to light it. Did they discover a spot less exposed than others, it afforded them but a momentary shelter, for scarcely had their fire kindled, when the violence of the wind, and the moisture of the atmosphere, suddenly extinguished it, and deprived them of the only consolation which remained, in their extreme distress. In one place we saw a multitude of them, huddled together like beasts, at the root of a beech, or pine or under a wagon. Others were employed in tearing down huge branches from the trees, or pulling down by main force, and burning the houses, at which the officers lodged. Although they were exhausted by fatigue, they stood erect. They wandered like spectres through the livelong night, or stood immovable around some enormous fire.

The unfortunate Paulowna, whom the reader will recollect, when he calls to mind the pillage of Moscow, had hitherto accompanied us, and shared in all our misfortunes and privations. She endured them with the courage which her virtue inspired. Believing that she carried in her bosom a pledge of love, which she imagined to be legitimate, she was eager to become a mother, and proud to follow her husband. But he, who had pledged himself to her by the most solemn promises, having been informed in the morning, that we were not to take up our winter-quarters at Smolensko, determined to break a connection, which he had regarded as merely temporary. Inaccessible to pity, he approached this innocent creature, and, under some specious pretext, announced to her that they must part. At this intelligence she uttered a cry of surprise and horror, and frantically declared, that having sacrificed her family, and even her reputation for him, whom she regarded as her husband, it was her duty to follow him; and that neither fatigues nor dangers should turn her from a resolution, in which her love and her honour were equally interested. The general little sensible of the value of an attachment so rare, coldly repeated, that they must part, since circumstances would no longer permit the women to remain with the troops ; that he was already married, and that by returning speedily to Moscow, she might find the husband for whom her parents had destined her. At these cruel words, his interesting victim felt almost annihilated. Paler than when she rushed from the tombs of the Kremlin, she uttered not a word. She sighed, she wept, and suffocated by her grief, fell into a state of insensibility. Her perfidious seducer took advantage of this to withdraw from her presence, not because he was overpowered by his sensibility; he, alas! was a stranger to every tender and generous feeling; but to fly from the Russians, whose cries of vengeance he already fancied that he heard.

Book VIII

Krasnoe

When Napoleon quitted Moscow, he intended to reunite his troops between Witepsk and Smolensko, and make the Nieper and the Dwina the grand line of his operations. The 6th and 7th of November, having destroyed the third part of his army, he, on his arrival at Smolensko, alleged that destruction, and the inclemency of the winter, as the reasons of his abandoning his former design. But the true and only motive which induced him to change his plan, was the news which he received at Smolensko (10th November) that Wittgenstein had forced the Dwina, that Witepsk had been taken with its garrison, and that the army of Moldavia, united to that of Volhynia, having driven before it the corps of prince Schwartzenberg, was taking a position on the Beresina with the design of joining Wittgenstein,, and effectually cutting off the retreat of the French army. This manoeuvre of the enemy was so well known, and appeared so natural, that a report soon spread among the troops, that it was the intention of the Russians to take Napoleon alive, and to put his whole army to the sword; wishing, by this severe chastisement, to give Europe an example of the punishment which they deserved who disturbed the world with unjust wars.

In truth, it was not the severity of a premature winter which rendered the plans of Napoleon abortive, because if he could have maintained himself between Smolensko and Witepsk, he would easily have repaired the losses which he had hitherto suffered. The principal, and the only cause of his ruin, was his determination to proceed to Moscow, without considering the forces which he left in his rear, and to effect, at the price of our blood, that which the most headstrong and imprudent monarch[1] had not dared to attempt.

The desire of pillaging that capital, and the ambition of dictating his laws there, made him sacrifice every thing. He rushed on, eager to destroy the ancient palace of the czars, forgetful of the winter, and all its horrors; forgetful that Wittgenstein had never abandoned the Dwina; and that Tschikakoff, returned from Moldavia, would attack him on his return from his foolish expedition.

Napoleon, ignorant as yet of the progress which the enemy had made on the Dwina, determined that the fourth corps should pass the

---

1   Charles XII of Sweden

Nieper, and march on Witepsk, to effect a junction with the garrison of that town, commanded by general Pouget. After reconnoitring whether the approach of winter had still left this route practicable, general Samson, with some engineers which he commanded, was ordered to traverse the country, and examine particularly the banks of the Wop. These officers had scarcely passed the Dnieper, when they fell into the hands of a party of cossacks, by whom all these rivers were infested.

(November 7th.) While the fourth corps proceeded in the direction of Witepsk, we left Doroghoboüï, and passed the Borysthenes on a bridge of rafts, opposite that village. The horses found the greatest difficulty in climbing the opposite bank. The road was become as slippery as glass, and these animals, already exhausted, were no longer able to draw. Twelve or sixteen horses harnessed to one cannon had scarcely strength to drag it over the smallest hill. It was intended to proceed the first day as far as Zazélé; but the road was so execrably bad, that even on the following morning, the wagons had scarcely reached the sixth league. Many cannon and horses were of necessity abandoned; and it was on that cruel night that the soldiery, no longer under control, began to pillage the baggage. The ground was covered with portmanteaus, boxes, and papers; and many articles stolen from Moscow, which some remains of shame had hitherto concealed, once more saw the light.

The beautiful *chateau* of Zazélé presented us, during the night, with a repetition of the scenes of yesterday. With the exception of those whom the pillage of the wagons had reanimated, we saw nothing on every side but men dying of hunger and of thirst; and horses tormented by thirst, endeavouring to break the ice with their feet, to find that water which we were unable to give them.

(November 8th.) Our baggage was so considerable, that the losses which it had sustained were yet scarcely felt. We marched all day, and with much alacrity, for we thought that, having quitted the great road of Smolensko, and pursued one which had experienced less of the calamities of war, we might find some villages to shelter us from the inclemency of the night, where our famished troops might obtain refreshment, and especially where we might procure some forage for our meagre horses. But this flattering hope was soon destroyed. The village of Sloboda, at which we were to sleep, presented us with new horrors. Every thing was destroyed; and the cossacks, hovering on our flanks, seized, and pillaged or massacred, every one who urged by necessity, wandered but a little way from the ranks to seek for food. In these dreadful circumstances, general Danthouard, whose talents had before proved so useful, appeared to multiply himself, and to be present wherever danger threatened. He caused our artillery to act with effect, on every point where it could be brought to bear, when, as he was passing our lines, a cannon ball fractured his right thigh, after having killed the orderly soldier by his side.

The viceroy, knowing that we ought to cross the Wop on the following day, had sent general Poitevin forward in the right, with some engineers, to construct a bridge for our passage. We arrived on the banks of the river at an early hour on the morrow, when, to the our great grief of the prince, and our utmost despair, we saw the whole army and the baggage ranged along the Wop, without being able to pass it. The bridge had been begun, and nearly finished, but the waters had suddenly increased, during the night, and carried it away.

The cossacks, whom we had seen the night before, did not fail to advance upon us, when they were apprised of our critical situation. We already heard the fire of our sharpshooters, who endeavoured to keep them in check; but the noise of the firearms rapidly approaching, convinced us that the audacity of the enemy increased at the view of our dangers. In the meantime the viceroy, whose noble soul was always calm in the midst of the greatest dangers, maintained a presence of mind most important in circumstances so desperate. To reanimate the spirits of the soldiers, who were more terrified at the presence of the cossacks, than at the dangers of the Wop, he despatched some chosen troops, who, repulsing the Russians on our flanks, and on our rear, left us at liberty to attempt the passage of the river.

The prince, seeing that it was necessary for some officer of rank to set an example of courage, in crossing first, ordered colonel Delfanti to place himself at the head of the royal guard, and to pass the ford of the Wop. That brave officer, whose intrepidity cannot be too highly praised, embraced with ardour this opportunity of showing his devotion to the service; and in sight of all our corps, with the water reaching to his waist, made his way through the accumulated ice, at the head of the grenadiers, and surmounted every difficulty.

The viceroy immediately followed with his staff, and, having arrived at the other side, he issued the necessary orders to facilitate a passage so dangerous. The wagons now began to file off. The first passed happily over, and after them a few pieces of artillery. But as the channel was far below the level of the ground, and the banks steep, and glittering with ice, the only practicable point was where a gentle declivity had been dug to descend to the river. The cannon, all following in the same track, formed ruts so deep, that it was impossible to drag them out. Thus the only accessible ford was soon choked up, and rendered utterly impassable for the rest of the artillery and baggage.

In this situation every one yielded to despair; for, notwithstanding the efforts made by our rearguard to repulse the Russians, it was but too evident that they advanced. Our very fear doubled our danger. The river was half frozen, and as the wagons could not possibly cross it, it was necessary for those who had no horses, to determine to wade through the stream. Our situation was the more deplorable, as we were forced to abandon a hundred pieces of cannon, and a great number of ammunition and provision wagons, carts, and *drouschki*[2] which contained the little which remained of the provisions of Moscow. As soon as the necessity became thus apparent, every one abandoned his vehicle, and hastily loaded his horse, with his most valuable effects. But scarcely had any one resolved to leave his carriage, before a crowd of soldiers giving the owner no time to select what he thought proper, violently seized on it and in a moment pillaged it of every thing which it contained, principally searching for flour and brandy. The artillery-men abandoned their pieces, and on the report that the enemy rapidly approached, immediately spiked them, despairing to convey them across a river, every part of which was choked with wagons sticking fast in the clay, and the bodies of innumerable soldiers and horses, who had been carried away by the stream. The cries of those who were crossing the river, the consternation of others who were preparing to descend, and whom with their horses, we every moment saw overwhelmed by the current, the despair of the women, the shrieks of the children, and the terror even of the soldiers, rendered this passage a scene so horrible, that the very recollection of it yet terrifies those who witnessed it.

Although it is most painful to recall to memory the dreadful events of that day, I cannot prevail on myself to for-bear recounting one trait of maternal love, so touching, and so honourable to human nature, that the sight of it compensated for the affliction which those unfortunate beings occasioned me.

A female sutler of our corps, who had been with us during the whole campaign, returned from Moscow, carrying in a wagon five young children, and all the fruit of her industry. Arrived at the Wop, she regarded with horror the rapid stream, which compelled her to leave on its banks, all her little fortune, and the future subsistence of her children. For a long time she ran up and down, eagerly looking for a new passage, when, returning in despair from her fruitless search, she said to her husband, 'we must indeed abandon all; let us now try only how to save our children.' Saying this, she took the two youngest from the wagon, and placed them in her husband's arms. I saw the poor father closely hug the

2   An elegant little carriage much used at Moscow.

innocent creatures, and, with a trembling foot traverse the river, while his wife on her knees at the edge of the water, now gazed eagerly on him, and then raised her eyes to heaven; but as soon as she saw him safely landed, she lifted her hands in gratitude to Providence, and leaping on her feet, exclaimed with transport, 'they are saved, they are saved.' The anxious father, depositing his precious burden on the bank, hastened back, seized on two more of them, and again plunging into the waves, followed by his wife, who bore the fifth on one arm, and with the other hand clung fast to her husband, reached the shore in safety. The children who were first carried over, thinking themselves abandoned by their parents, had made the air resound with their cries, but their tears soon ceased to flow, when the affectionate family was again reunited.

Night approaching, we quitted this place of desolation, and encamped near a wretched village, half a league from the banks of the Wop, whence we often heard, in the middle of the night, the lamentable cries of those who were yet attempting their passage. We had left the fourteenth division on the other side, to hold the enemy in cheek, and to endeavour to save some part of the immense baggage which we had abandoned. I was sent on the morrow, to recall this division, and was thus enabled to perceive all the extent of our loss. For more than a league, nothing was to be seen on the road and the banks of the river, but ammunition wagons, pieces of artillery, and the most elegant carriages, brought from Moscow. The articles with which these wagons had been filled, and that were too heavy to be carried away, were heaped on every side. I saw many figures of antique bronze, chandeliers of the greatest value, original and exquisite paintings, and the richest and the most esteemed porcelain. I perceived among the rest, a cup of the most beautiful workmanship, on which was depicted the sublime composition of Marcus Sextus. I took it, and drank from it some of the water of the Wop, full of dirt and ice. After I had thus used it, I cast it from me with indifference, near the place where I had found it.

Our troops had scarcely quieted the other bank when clouds of cossacks, no longer finding any opposition, advanced to the river, where they found many unhappy wretches who, feeble and diseased, had been unable to pass the ford. Although our enemies were now surrounded and oppressed with plunder, they yet stripped their miserable prisoners, and left them naked on the snow. We could see, from the opposite bank, the cossacks sharing among themselves the bloody spoils. If their courage had equalled their love of pillage, the Wop would not have defended us from their attacks. But these cowardly assailants were always stopped by a few bayonets, or contented themselves with firing at us a few cannon shot, which often, indeed, reached our ranks.

The last night had been truly dreadful. To form some idea of it, the reader must picture to himself an army encamped on the bare snow, in the midst of the severest winter, closely pursued by the enemy, and having neither artillery nor cavalry to oppose to him. The soldiers without shoes, and almost without clothes, were enfeebled by fatigue and famine. Sitting on their knapsacks, they slept on their knees. From this benumbing posture they only rose to broil some slices of horse-flesh, or to melt a few morsels of ice. Often they had no wood, and to make fires, they destroyed the houses in which the generals lodged; sometimes, therefore, when we awoke in the morning, the village which we had seen the night before had disappeared, and towns, which today went untouched, would form on the morrow one vast conflagration. In the midst of these sufferings the viceroy, always at our head, never lost his calmness and serenity of mind. Enduring comparatively far greater privations than we, he was always cheerful, and preserved his presence of mind amidst the most urgent dangers, offering, at the same time, in his own example the most perfect model of military discipline.

The cossacks, perceiving that we had quitted our position, soon crossed the river and attacked our rear. The fifteenth division, which had preserved twelve pieces of cannon, formed the rear-guard, and repulsed the enemy. In the meantime the prince and his officers endeavoured to reduce to some order, and entice back to their ranks, those soldiers whom misery had forced to leave their colours to search for food. They attempted this, however, without success. The number of stragglers was so great, that it was impossible either to arrest or to check them. Even when some had returned to their duty, the desertion soon recommenced. Hunger, imperious hunger, seduced them again from their colours, and threw all our columns into confusion. The more enfeebled we became, the more enterprising were our adversaries. Their attacks on our rearguard were almost incessant, and we were frequently compelled to halt, and, contend against superior forces, which endeavoured to overwhelm us on every side.

The rear of our column was briskly pressed, when the royal guard, which formed its head, was stopped before Dukhovchtchina, by some squadrons of cossacks, which issuing from the town, deployed in the plain, as if they would surround us. Seeing that we were thus pressed on every side, our corps fell into such disorder, that it resembled one immense crowd, half of which were sick and disarmed. In the meantime the enemy maintained his ground on one side of us, and on the other attacked us with vigour. But the prince ever preserving his courage unbroken, formed the Italian guard, and the Bavarian dragoons and light horse, into a square, which, marching in platoons, drove back the cossacks, and permitted us to enter Dukhovchtchina. The thirteenth division was formed in column close to these troops, in spite of the multitude of stragglers, which, pressing round our battalions, impeded every manoeuvre. That he might accelerate the march of the army, the prince himself watched during the night, and superintended the repair of an old bridge which arrested our progress. To encourage the engineers, he even condescended to assist at the work, while every privation to which he exposed, himself, rendered him dearer to those whom he commanded.

The little town of Dukhovchtchina, through which our army had not before passed,[3] had escaped the general destruction. The inhabitants, flying at our approach, left us some provisions, which we eagerly collected, coarse as they were. But that which rendered them most precious was the opportunity of preparing them in some human habitation, and enjoying for a little while a shelter from the excessive cold of a piercing wind.

The viceroy despatched an officer towards Smolensko, to announce to Napoleon the disasters which we had experienced on the Wop. It was, doubtless, to await the reply of the emperor, and to know whether we were yet to continue our march upon Witepsk, that we were permitted to enjoy one day's rest at Dukhovchtchina. But, when that officer did not return, it was determined that we should recommence our march at two o'clock on the following morning. We had been undisturbed during the whole of the day, but at ten o'clock at night, while we were indulging in a sweet repose, to which we had been so long unaccustomed, the cossacks appeared before the town, and directed their artillery on the fires round which our soldiers were sleeping. Many picquets were surprised; those of the one hundred and sixth regiment, placed before a church, suffered considerable loss; but the presence of the viceroy soon repaired the disorder which so unexpected an attack had occasioned. The troops were immediately collected, and occupied every position which could be favourable to us in a nocturnal encounter. This attack was followed by nothing of consequence, for it was made by the cossacks, who took care to be far enough always when they perceived that we were taking measures to punish their temerity.

(November 12th.) The hour of departure being arrived, we set fire to Dukhovchtchina, whose houses had been so useful to us. Although sufficiently accustomed to all the effects of a conflagration, we could not restrain our astonishment at the horrible, yet superb spectacle, which it

---

3 Excepting the cavalry commanded by general Grouchy, and the division of Pino, when it returned from Porietsch.

now presented, amid the shades of a forest covered with snow, and strangely illumined by torrents of flames. The trees, covered with a sheet of ice, dazzled the sight and produced as with a prism, the most vivid and variegated colours. The branches of the birch, dropping to the ground like the weeping willow, appeared like beautiful chandeliers, while the icicles, melted by the frost, seemed to scatter around us a shower of brilliant and sparkling diamonds.

In the midst of a scene full of splendid horror, our troops reunited, and proceeded from the town on the road to Smolensko. Although the night was unusually dark, the flames that ascended from the neighbouring villages, which had been also destroyed, formed so many aurorae-boreales, and till the dawn of day, shed a frightful glare upon our march. Beyond Toporovo, the road of Pologhi, which we had followed when we came from Smolensko to Doroghoboüi, was on our left. The snow, that covered all the country, had nearly buried the villages, which formed from afar only a black spot on one boundless surface of white. The difficulty of approaching them saved many from the general desolation. When I compared these peaceful asylums with the torments to which we were a prey, I could not refrain from exclaiming, 'Happy people! exempt from ambition, you live tranquil and undisturbed, while we are fast sinking under the most frightful calamities. The winter preserves your existence, but it devotes us to death. When the sweet spring shall have accomplished your deliverance, you will see our carcasses bleaching on the plain, and you will be doubly happy in having suffered so little from our tyranny, and in having added nothing to the weight of our misfortunes.

The little river Khmost, was frozen when we crossed it, and the bridge, which was yet entire, enabled us to pass without delay or danger. Arriving at Wolodimerowa, the viceroy established himself in a *chateau* a little above the village, where he had lodged on our former march. Encamping around him, we were certain that the cossacks, who had flanked our route during the day, would halt on a height not far distant from us, and accordingly they soon drove in our foragers, who, urged by imperious necessity, had spread themselves through the neighbouring villages in search of food.

(November 13th.) We were now only one day's march from Smolensko, where abundance would succeed to want, and repose to fatigue. Impatient to enjoy a happiness so long desired, we left Wolodimerowa long before day, burning, as was our custom, the cottages which had afforded us an asylum. Arrived at the heights of Stabna, where the road of Dukhovchtchina joins with that of Witepsk, we experienced an almost insuperable difficulty in ascending the mountain.

Wherever we attempted to climb it, we found one solid mass of ice, bright, and slippery as glass. Men and horses rolled over one another; and happy were they who, after the utmost exertion, could extricate themselves from the dreadful pass.

Before we arrived at Smolensko, where all our misfortunes were to terminate, the most melancholy scenes presented themselves every instant, and increased our eagerness to reach that city, the object of our most ardent prayers. Among the sports of cruel fortune, none had more cause to complain than the French women, who, following us from Moscow to escape the vengeance of the Russians, hoped to find with us certain protection. Most of them on foot, with shoes of stuff, little calculated to defend them from the frozen snow, and clad in old robes of silk, or the thinnest muslin, were glad to cover themselves with tattered pieces of military cloaks, torn from the dead bodies of the soldiers. Their situation would have drawn tears from the hardest hearts, if dire necessity had not stifled, in every bosom, the feelings of humanity.

Of all the victims of the horrors of war, no one inspired warmer pity than the young and interesting Fanny. Beautiful, affectionate, amiable, and sprightly, speaking many different languages, and possessing every quality calculated to seduce the most insensible heart, she now begged for the most menial employment; and the morsel of bread which she obtained drew from her rapturous expressions of gratitude. Imploring succour from us all, she was compelled to submit to the vilest abuse; and though her soul loathed the prostitution, she every night belonged to him who would charge himself with her support. I saw her when we quitted Smolensko. She was no longer able to talk. She was clinging to the tail of a horse and was thus dragged along. At length her powers were quite exhausted. She fell on the snow, and there remained unburied, without exciting one emotion of compassion, or obtaining one look of pity; so debased were our souls now become, and our sensibility quite extinguished. But what need of more testimonies of the calamities which befell us; we were all fellow-sufferers.

It was horrible to see and to hear the enormous dogs, with shaggy hair, which, driven from the villages that we had burned, followed us along our march. Dying with hunger, they uttered one incessant and frightful howl, and often disputed with the soldiers the carcasses of the horses which fell on our route. In addition to this, the ravens, with which Russia abounds, attracted by the scent of the dead bodies, hovered over us in black and innumerable crowds, and by their cries of mournful presage, struck the stoutest hearts with terror.

Happily we were only two leagues from Smolensko, and the tower of its celebrated church, which we already saw at a distance, flattering us with the sweetest illusions, seemed the most lovely object in the whole perspective. An hour before we arrived, we left the fourteenth division, with the few Bavarian horse which remained, to observe and hold in check the cossacks, who, increasing in numbers every moment, seemed determined to follow us to the very walls of Smolensko. But what was our grief, when we learned, in the very suburbs of the city, that the sixth corps was gone, that it had not even halted at Smolensko, and that the provisions were all consumed! A thunderbolt falling at our feet would have confounded us less than did this news. Our senses were for a moment suspended. We would not believe the fact; but our eyes soon gave us sad confirmation of the truth, when we saw the garrison of Smolensko eagerly rushing out, and immediately devouring the horses which every moment dropped, exhausted with fatigue and hunger. We then no longer doubted that famine reigned in that city, which, till this moment, we had regarded as the abode of plenty.

As we were musing on the sadness of our lot, its rigour was somewhat alleviated by the promise of a little rice, flour, and biscuit, which yet remained in the magazines. The hope of this reanimated our drooping courage, when suddenly we were filled with new consternation. We had scarcely arrived within the gates of Smolensko, when crowds of stragglers covered with blood, rushed upon us, and announced that the cossacks were only two hundred paces distant. The next moment, captain Tresel, aid-de-camp to general Guilleminot, who had been left behind with the fourteenth division, came at full speed. He apprised us that that division had taken up a position in a *chateau*, in a wood which commanded the road; that the enemy had surrounded it, but that being perfectly intrenched round the *chateau*, and the approaches being defended by pallisades, the cossacks, despaired of attacking them with, success, and retired to fall upon the stragglers; that they had speedily overtaken these unhappy beings, had massacred some, and wounded a great number.

The road was covered with these miserable wretches, and presented a spectacle well calculated to excite our liveliest compassion. We saw them, moreover, at a distance, descending the mountain of Smolensko. The declivity was so rapid, and the frost rendered it so slippery, that numbers of these unfortunate beings, unable to support themselves, rolled down the declivity, and immediately perished.

Having left the royal guard on this height, to protect the division of Broussier, which formed the rear-guard, we descended towards the Nieper, and endeavoured to enter the city. Beyond the bridge was the junction of the road of Doroghoboüi, with that from Valentina, which all the other divisions had taken; and as these corps had not passed the Wop, they yet retained a great part of their artillery and baggage. The numerous carriages, which flocked in on every side, mingled with the foot soldiers and the cavalry; and all of them attempting to rush into Smolensko, where they had been promised some rations of bread, the greatest confusion ensued. The entrance was completely choked up, and more than three hours elapsed ere we could penetrate into the city.

(November 13.) The wind was tempestuous, and the cold excessive. We were assured that the thermometer was more than twenty-two degrees below the freezing point. Notwithstanding this, every one ran into the streets, hoping that he might be able to purchase provisions. Smolensko was built on the side of a mountain, and the ascent was so slippery, that it was necessary to crawl on our knees, and to hold by the rocks which projected above the snow, in order to gain the summit. We at length reached the top, where we found the great square, and those houses which had suffered least from the conflagration. Although the weather was insupportably severe, we sought rather for food than for lodging. Some soldiers of the garrison, to whom a little bread had been distributed, were compelled by force to sell it to us. Others immediately entreated those who had bought it, to spare it, and soldiers and officers mingled together, were ravenously devouring in the streets, every kind of provision which they could procure, however coarse or disgusting. In the meantime the cossacks arrived. We distinctly perceived them scouring the heights, and firing on the troops which defiled below the town. Our fourth division being actively engaged with them, the viceroy was eager to transport himself to that point. He was accompanied, along a difficult and perilous road, by general Gifflenge, and by his aids-de-camp, Tacher, Labedoyère and Mejean, and by Corner, officer of artillery, all indefatigable in misfortune, and always ready to brave the greatest dangers.

We had great difficulty in finding shelter, for the houses were few, and the crowd, which was to occupy them immense. At length, heaped one upon another in the great halls whose arches had defied the flames, we waited with impatience for the distribution of the bread. But the formalities necessary to be gone through were so long, that night came on ere any thing was delivered. It was now necessary to run anew into the streets, and with money in our hands, seek in the quarters of the imperial guard for something to support our existence. They, more favoured than the rest of the army, often rolled in abundance, when we were destitute of every comfort.

Thus, Smolensko, which we had thought would have been the termination of our misfortunes, cruelly deceived our dearest hopes, and became the witness of our greatest disgrace, and our most profound despair. The soldiers, who could not find a shelter, encamped in the middle of the streets, and some hours after, were found dead around the fires which they had kindled. The hospitals, the churches, and the other public buildings, were unable to contain the sick, who presented themselves by thousands. These, unhappy beings, exposed to all the rigours of a frosty night, lay uncovered on the wagons, or in the ammunition-carts, or perished in vainly searching for an asylum. In fine, when every thing had been promised us at Smolensko, nothing had been provided to enable us to maintain ourselves there; nothing had been prepared to relieve and comfort an army whose salvation depended on that place alone. Hence despair seized upon us. We thought only how to save our wretched existence. Honour and duty were forgotten, or rather, we were no longer disposed to submit to the commands of a rash sovereign, who troubled not himself to provide bread for those who had sacrificed their lives to gratify his ambition.

We saw those who were once the gayest, and the most intrepid, entirely lose that character. They predicted only disasters and dangers.[4] One thought occupied their minds - that country which they were never again to see. One object filled their view- that death which every moment threatened them. With a mournful presentiment, each inquired tremblingly, and with the most profound mystery, where were the armies to which we looked for deliverance? 'Where is the duke of Reggio?' one secretly asked his companion. 'He wished to have protected the Dwina, but he was forced to abandon Polotsk, and to fall back upon Lessel,' was the whispered reply. 'And where is the duke of Belluno?' – 'He could not leave Sienna,' – 'And where the Russian army of Wolhynia?' – 'It has repulsed prince Schwartzenberg; it has made itself master of Minsk, and it is advancing against us.' – 'Ah! if this news be true,' repeated the first to himself, 'our situation is truly desperate; and one great battle, on the borders of the Nieper or the Beresina, will complete our ruin.'

Reflections, if possible, yet more depressing occupied and tormented us, when a confused murmur spread the report that the whole of France was agitated; that the town of Nantes had been destroyed, and that Paris, where, during nearly twenty years, the fate of Europe had been decided, was also in a state of commotion, which made us tremble for the fate of our beloved country! We were informed that certain men, known for their love of democracy, had conceived the project of spreading a false report of the death of Napoleon, and the entire destruction of his army; and that profiting by the grief and consternation which this news would occasion it was their intention to overthrow the existing authorities, and

4   See the twenty-ninth bulletin.

to elect a government which would be subservient to their views. If this design had been conceived by honest and patriotic men, who, emulous to render themselves illustrious by the deliverance of their country, sought only to dethrone the emperor, that they might preserve the French people from the disgrace of hereafter owing their freedom to those whom they called their enemies, certainly such a project would have been truly heroic. But, instead of an enterprise so noble, we were told that the conspirators wished to deliver us from despotism, that they might plunge us into the horrors of anarchy. Far from wishing success to such a scheme, we rejoiced when we were afterwards informed, that our country was not again delivered over to the fury of the different factions, for the political perfidy of our oppressor had caused the fate of the people to depend solely on his safety. By his monstrous Machiavelism, France was at war with the whole human race, that the preservation of France might be connected with that of his own person.

As we lay under some wretched thatch, and indulged in many a melancholy reflection, we were suddenly roused by unexpected cries. 'Rise, rise; they pillage the magazines.' Springing immediately on our feet, and seizing a sack, a pannier, or a bottle, we exclaimed to each other, as we rushed out, 'I will go to the flour magazine, you go to the magazine of brandy; let the servants run to the place where the meat, the biscuit, the pease, are kept.' In an instant the room was empty. After a considerable interval, friends returned, and informed us, that the soldiers, dying with hunger, and no longer able to await the dilatory distribution of the provisions, had, in spite of the guard, forced the gates of the magazines, and begun to pillage them. Some came back with their clothes covered with flour, and even pierced with the bayonet, bearing on their shoulders sacks of flour which they had taken by force from the soldiers who were dividing it. Others entered, harassed with fatigue, and deposited on the table a great pannier of biscuit, or what was better, an enormous leg of beef. An hour after, the domestics followed them bringing rice, pease, and brandy. At the unexpected view of such abundance, our hearts once more expanded. One laughed with joy, as he kneaded his bread; another sung as he cooked his meat but most of them eagerly seizing the brandy, quickly caused the wildest gayety to succeed to the most distressing sadness.

Although the weather was beautifully clear, the air was so exceedingly piercing, that it froze us as we passed the streets. At every step were seen the dead bodies of the soldiers, stretched on the snow, who, harassed by fatigue, had perished of cold as they were searching for a place of repose. All these disasters, and especially our stay at Smolensko, remind me of the death of colonel Battaglia, commandant of the guard of honour of Italy. I have long reproached myself with not having interested the feelings of my readers, by recounting the misfortunes of that distinguished corps. The rapidity of my narration has hitherto prevented me from occupying myself with the calamities of individuals, while I was oppressed and overpowered by the recollection of those which were endured by the whole army. At this epoch, that corps was completely annihilated; and ere I quit the fatal walls of Smolensko, I will succinctly recount its history.

It was composed of young men selected from the first families in Italy, and whose parents allowed them a pension of twelve hundred francs, when they entered the corps. It was an honour to be admitted into the regiment, as its very name testified. It was not rare to find, among these young men, the most brilliant talents, united to the most affluent fortune. Many of them were the only sons of illustrious families. To the titles which they derived from their ancestors, they added a well-cultivated understanding, and every quality which promised ultimately to form the most distinguished military characters. In this school were educated the best informed and the most excellent officers of the Italian army. They acquired experience in submitting to the rules of their corps, which, while it gave them the rank of sublieutenants, obliged them to perform the service of private soldiers.

This corps conducted itself well on every occasion, and was remarkable for its fine appearance and strict discipline, but it suffered more than any other, by the privations attendant on this memorable campaign. The guards of honour, unused to shoe their horses, or to mend their garments or their boots, were obliged to submit to these degradations, when the artificers and domestics attached to their regiment were no more. Having lost all their horses, and wearing enormous and heavy boots, they were unable long to support the fatigue of our continual marches. Confounded with the stragglers, they remained in the rear, without food and without lodging. In this manner the descendants of the noblest families, born to the happiest destines, perished far more miserably than the common soldiers; for their education and their habits ill-disposed them to submit to the menial offices by which others gained a scanty morsel, and prolonged a wretched life. Some of them were seen wrapped in the tattered fragments of their cloaks; others, mounted on sorry cognias,[5] suddenly fainted from weakness and want, and fell to rise no more. Out of the three hundred and fifty, of which they were originally composed, all, except five, perished in the most deplorable manner. They had, however,

5   Cognia, in the Polish language, signifies a horse; and as the horses of Russia are very small, they distinguished ours by the name of Cognia.

this consolation, that they possessed the esteem of the prince, who formed them at first, and who now sighed over the calamities which the fatal circumstances of the campaign would not permit him to alleviate.

(November 14.) The emperor, who was at Smolensko when we arrived there, received every day disastrous news of his armies. That which most afflicted him, was the defeat of general Baraguey D'Hilliers, sent on the road of Kaluga, with general Augereau, to oppose count Orloff Denisoff, who threatened to cut off our retreat between Smolensko and Krasnoë. At a loss how to repair so many disgraces, Napoleon, on that day, and for the first time, held a grand council, at which all the generals of division and marshals of the empire assisted. As soon as the council was broken up, he burned part of his equipage, and immediately departed in his carriage, accompanied by his chasseurs, and by the Polish lancers of the guard. It was reported, at the close of the council, that we were to march tomorrow with the first corps, and that the third was to remain behind to blow up the fortifications of the town, and to form our rear-guard. The same day, the viceroy was long closeted with the chief of his staff, and we awaited with anxiety the result of all these conferences.

(November 15.) The order was given to continue our march, but at a very late hour, from the delay occasioned by the dilatory distribution of the whole contents of the magazines. The Russian women, whose sufferings only added to our misfortunes, were left at Smolensko. Dreadful situation! since these unfortunate beings well knew that the remains of the city would be sacked, the houses delivered to the flames, and the churches undermined. We soon, however, heard that the Hetman Platoff, entering unexpectedly, into the town, had prevented our rear-guard from executing the inhuman order.

Marching from Smolensko, a spectacle the most horrible was presented to our view. From that point till we arrived at a wretched ruined hamlet,[6] at the distance of about three leagues, the road was entirely covered with cannon and ammunition-wagons, which they had scarce time to spike, or to blow up. Horses in the agonies of death were seen at every step, and sometimes whole teams, sinking under their labours, fell together. All the defiles which the carriages could not pass, were filled with muskets, helmets, and breast plates. Trunks broken open, portmanteaus torn to pieces, and garments of every kind were scattered over the valley. At every little distance we met with trees, at the foot of which the soldiers had attempted to light a fire, but the poor wretches had perished ere they could accomplish their object. We saw them stretched by dozens around the green branches which they had vainly endeavoured to kindle; and so

6   On inspecting the map, this appears to be Loubna.

numerous were the bodies, that they would have obstructed the road had not the soldiers been often employed in throwing them into the ditches and the ruts.

These horrors, far from exciting our sensibility, only hardened our hearts. Our cruelty, which could no more be exercised on the enemy, was extended to our companions. The best friends no longer recognised each other. Whoever discovered the least sickness, if he had not good horses and faithful servants, was sure never to see his country again. Every one preferred to save the plunder of Moscow, rather than the life of his comrade. On all sides we heard the groans of the dying, and the lamentable cries of those whom we had abandoned. But every one was deaf to their supplications, or, if he approached those who were on the point of expiring, it was to plunder, not to assist them; it was to search whether they had any remains of food, and not to afford them relief.

Arrived at Loubna, we were able to save only two miserable barns from destruction - one for the viceroy, and the other for his staff. We had scarcely established ourselves there, when we heard a loud cannonade in our front. As the noise appeared to come from our right, some thought that it was an engagement with the ninth corps, which, not having been able to relieve Witepsk, was obliged to retreat before a superior force; but they who were best acquainted with the country, believed that it was the emperor and his guard, who had been attacked by prince Kutusoff, before his arrival at Krasnoë. That prince had marched from Elnïa, and passed our army while we halted at Smolensko.

We can scarcely imagine a picture more deplorable than the bivouac of the staff. Twenty-one officers, confounded with as many servants, had crept together round a little fire, under an execrable carthouse scarcely covered. Behind them were the horses, ranged in a circle, that they might be some defence against the violence of the wind, which blew with fury. The smoke was so thick that we could scarcely see the figures of those who were close to the fire, and they who were employed in blowing the coals on which they cooked their food. The rest wrapped in their pelisses or their cloaks, lay one upon another, as some protection from the cold; nor did they stir, except to abuse those who trod upon them as they passed, or to rail at the horses, which kicked whenever a spark fell on their coats.

(November 16.) We recommenced our march before the dawn of day, and the road was again covered with the wrecks of our baggage and artillery. The horses could no longer draw, and we were obliged to abandon our cannon at the foot of the slightest hill. The only duty which then remained to the artillery-men, was to scatter the powder of the cartridges, and to spike the pieces, lest the enemy should turn them against us. We were reduced to this extremity when, at the distance of two hours' march from Krasnoë, the generals Poitevin and Guyon, who were in the van-guard, saw a Russian officer coming towards them, followed by a trumpeter, who announced that a herald was advancing. Surprised at an appearance so unexpected, general Guyon halted and permitting the officer to approach, demanded whence he came, and what was the object of his mission. 'I come,' said he, 'from general Miloradowitch, to tell you, that yesterday we beat Napoleon, with the imperial guard; and that to-day the viceroy is surrounded by an army of twenty thousand men. He cannot escape us, and if he will surrender, we offer him honourable terms.' To this, general Guyon replied with indignation, 'Return quickly whence you came, and announce to those who sent you, that if you have twenty thousand men, we have here four times twenty thousand.' These words, uttered with a confident air, so confounded the herald, that he immediately returned to the camp of the enemy.

While this was going on, the viceroy arrived, and listened to the intelligence with mingled surprise and indignation. Although his corps was so dreadfully weakened, and he probably had some knowledge of the serious affair which had taken place on the day before, between the advanced guard of Kutusoff and the imperial guard, yet, reflecting on the boasting manner in which this had been related, he conceived the hope, that, by forcing a passage, he might in a short time rejoin the emperor. He was likewise fully determined to fall honourably in the field, rather than accept of conditions incompatible with his fame. He immediately ordered the fourteenth division to front the enemy, carrying with them the only two pieces of cannon which remained; then calling general Guilleminot, he conferred with him for a long time, and the result of their conference was, that it was absolutely necessary to force our way through the enemy. In the mean time our troops had marched on, and the Russians, permitting them to advance to the very foot of the hill on which they were encamped, suddenly unmasked their batteries, and directed them on their squares. Their cavalry soon after descending from their position, completed the destruction of our troops, and captured their cannon, of which they had made but few discharges, through want of ammunition.

General Ornano advanced across the fire of the enemy, with the remains of the thirteenth division, to succour the troops of the fourteenth, which were so cruelly beaten, when a cannon-ball passed so near him that he fell from his horse. The soldiers thought that he was dead, and ran forward to plunder him, when they perceived that he was only stunned by the violence of the fall. The prince then sent his aide-de-camp, colonel Delfanti, to endeavour to reanimate the troops.

That brave officer, rushing forward amidst a shower of balls and grape-shot, encouraged his soldiers by his exhortations and by his example, when receiving two dangerous wounds, he was compelled to retire from the ranks. A surgeon having applied a slight dressing, he returned with difficulty from the field of battle. On his way he met Monsieur de Villeblanche, who in the capacity of auditor of the council of state, had quitted the town of Smolensko, of which he was the intendant, with general Charpentier, who was the governor. Unfortunately he had obtained leave of the viceroy to accompany him. This generous young man, perceiving colonel Delfanti wounded, and leaning on an officer, listened to the dictates of his sensibility and offered him his arm also. As all three were slowly retiring from the field, a cannon ball struck the colonel between the shoulders, and carried off the head of the brave Villeblanche. Thus perished two young men, who, in different professions, had proved their talents and their courage. The first fell a victim to his bravery - the other to his humanity. The prince, deeply affected by this unhappy catastrophe, showed the regard which he felt for the memory of colonel Delfanti, by an act of benevolence towards the author of his being; and he would have afforded the same consolation to the father of Villeblanche, if the death of his only son had not shortly brought him to is grave.

Many officers of distinguished merit perished on that bloody day. We particularly regretted major d'Oreille, whose intrepidity was so well known, and the captain of engineers, Morlincourt, whose modesty was equal to his talents. The cannonade yet continued, and carried destruction through all our ranks. The field of battle was covered with the dead and the dying. Great numbers of the wounded, abandoning their regiments, took refuge in the rear, and increased the crowd of stragglers. The firing, which had proved fatal to our first ranks, extended its ravages to the rear of our army, where the dismounted officers were stationed. The captains Bordoni and Mastini perished there. They constituted a part of the small number of the Italian guards who yet survived.

The viceroy, seeing the obstinacy with which the enemy disputed our passage, feigned, by a skilful movement, to prolong the engagement on our left, by rallying and reuniting all that remained of the fourteenth division; and, while the enemy concentrated the greater part of his forces on this point, to surround and cut off these troops, the prince took advantage of the close of the day to file off to the right with the royal guard, which had not been engaged. Colonel Kliski gave a remarkable proof of presence of mind in that march. He was familiar with the Russian language, and marched, in the van-guard of the column. Suddenly he was stopped by a scout of the enemy, who cried in Russian, 'Who goes there!'

That intrepid officer, not at all embarrassed by a rencontre so unfortunate, advanced towards the sentinel, and said to him in his own language, 'Hold your tongue, scoundrel, don't you see that we belong to the corps of Ouwarow, and that we are going on a secret expedition!' At these words the soldier was silent, and suffered us to pass under the protection of the night, without giving the alarm.

The whole army thus escaped the vigilance of the enemy, with the exception of the fifteenth division, which, forming the rearguard, was placed under the command of general Triaire, with orders to march as soon as the prince had effected his manoeuvre. While this division rested on its arms, it beheld, with grief, the destruction which spread among the stragglers who were left in the rear. They likewise waited for night to continue their route; but, when harassed by fatigue, they found themselves warm and comfortable round a blazing fire, many of them would not proceed until the return of day. Thus they perished, the victims of their own apathy. The fifteenth division soon filed off in the utmost silence, regarding those whom they left behind as the destined prey of the cossacks.

It was necessary to pass the enemy during a night, which, instead of protecting us by its obscurity, suddenly presented a beautiful unclouded moon. The snow, covering the surface of the ground, rendered our march more conspicuous, and it was not without horror that we saw ourselves flanked by clouds of cossacks, who continually approached close to us, as if to reconnoitre, and then returned to the squadrons from which they had been detached. We often thought that they were about to charge us, but general Triaire, halting his column, presented a front so imposing, that they did not dare to attack us. At length in spite of the ravines, and the mountains of snow that obstructed our passage, we reached the great road, and half an hour afterwards, effected a junction with the young guard, which encamped near a river half a league from Krasnoë. There we found the emperor, and there consequently, our fears were dissipated.

Recounting to the soldiers of the guard the combat which we had sustained, they informed us, that they likewise had been obliged to cut their way through the enemy. Napoleon was exposed to the most imminent danger in this engagement, and was indebted for his safety to the bravery of his troops. We were told that the band of the guard, rejoining him, after having been separated from him in the heat of the battle, immediately struck up the air, 'Where can we be happier than in the bosom, of our family.' But as this might have a double meaning in the midst of frozen deserts, he understood it in the worst sense, and said to the musicians, in a rough tone of voice, 'You had much better play, "Let us awake and save the empire." '

The staff of the emperor, his guard, his cavalry, and the fourth corps, forming a junction in this little town, so completely filled it, that it was scarcely possible to move. The streets were thronged with soldiers lying round their fires, which they could only keep up by demolishing the houses that were built with wood, and burning the doors and window-frames of the others.

The viceroy was well received at the quarters of the emperor, in spite of the ill humour which he felt in consequence of the late disgraces, to which he had been unaccustomed. He highly approved of the stratagem that had been employed to deceive the enemy. The prince remaining all night in conference, his suite encamped in the streets, until Napoleon and the viceroy, placing themselves at the head of the guard, marched on the position which the Russians occupied, to succour the first and third corps, who were in the same perilous situation, in which we had been placed on the preceding evening.

A new engagement commenced. The action was obstinate and bloody, and it was only by the greatest sacrifices, that we were enabled to save the few soldiers who were on their march to join us. The third corps was entirely dispersed, and there remained with the duke of Elchingen, only two or three thousand men, who had escaped from the enemy by passing the Nieper. Twenty-five pieces of cannon, and many thousands of prisoners, were the fruits which the Russians reaped from four successive battles, in which we had nothing to oppose against a complete army, but some miserable soldiers, harassed by continual marches, and who during more than a month, had been without food, without ammunition, and without artillery.

To reward the bravery of the Russian imperial guard, who had distinguished themselves in these different engagements, prince Kutusoff permitted them to carry all the trophies of victory from the field of battle to their camp. Among these, was the baton of the marshal prince of Eckmuhl.[7] But that baton, used by our marshals on days of ceremony alone, added no glory to the enemy, for they found it, doubtless, in a baggage-wagon that had been abandoned.

The Russians have divided our retreat into three principal epochs, which, besides the constant increase of our misfortunes, have each a peculiar character. The first ended at the battle of Krasnoë, the second at the passage of the Beresina, and the third at the Niemen.

---

7   See the official report of our retreat, published by the Russians at Wilna, December 22, 1812.

At the conclusion of the first period, to which we are now arrived, they had already taken forty thousand men, twenty-seven generals, five hundred pieces of cannon, thirty-one standards, and, beside our own immense baggage, all the plunder of Moscow, that we had not destroyed. If, to all these disasters, we yet add forty thousand more, dead of fatigue or famine, or killed in the different battles, we shall find that out army was reduced to thirty thousand, including the imperial guard, of whom not more than eight thousand combatants survived. The twenty-five pieces of artillery, which the guards had preserved, could not be reckoned, since it was uncertain whether they would not be obliged to abandon them on the morrow. Our cavalry was almost extinct. This is the exact statement of the losses which we had sustained, at the end of one month's march. From this we formed mournful presages of what we were yet to endure, since we were scarcely half way to the Niemen, and had three rivers to cross, and two mountains to climb.

Book IX

The Beresina

The dreadful disasters which we had endured in our retreat from Moscow to Krasnoë, led us to conclude that our misfortunes must have reached their utmost height, and that happier events would succeed. In fact, the noble position of Orcha being guarded by general Jomini we were assured that we should pass the Nieper without opposition, and effect a junction with the corps of general Dombrowski, and the dukes of Reggio and Belluno; moreover we were approaching the line of our magazines, and we should soon enter on an inhabited and friendly country. In fine, prince Kutusoff, wishing to concert his plan of attack with the army of Moldavia which was ready to join him, ceased to harass us, and reserved for the Beresina, the great results which the battle of Krasnoë had promised him.

All these advantages, on which it was said that we might build the surest hopes, imposed on the soldiers only for a short time. They who were best acquainted with the state of affairs, soon dissipated our illusions, by circulating the report that admiral Tschikakoff, coming from the Danube, had repulsed near Varsovia, the troops that opposed his passage; that the Austrians had suffered him to take Minsk; and that by seizing the bridge of Borisov, on the Beresina, the admiral intended to form a junction with generals Wittgenstein and Stengel. These generals, in fact, being no longer held in check by the twelfth and sixteenth corps, since the battle of Polotsk, had gone, the one on Vileika, to attack the Bavarians, and the other towards Tschachniki, to place itself in communication with the army of Moldavia. On this junction depended the fate of the French army, and it was to prevent the most dreadful, and the most memorable of all defeats, that Napoleon advanced by forced marches on the Beresina.

(November 17th.) As soon as the prince of Eckmuhl had joined us, and the duke of Elchingen had thrown himself on the other side of the Nieper, we left Krasnoë, about eleven o'clock in the morning, and marched towards Liadouï. During the short repose that we had taken at Krasnoë, the cossacks had passed by that city, and now, ranged in columns, followed us, along the road. They did not venture to attack the armed soldiers; but perceiving that the small remains of our baggage was stopped, and in great disorder from the difficulty which the horses found in clearing the valley which separated the town from a little hill, they rushed upon them, and plundered them without resistance. We there lost the baggage-wagons of the staff, which contained the registers of correspondence, and all the plans, charts, and memoirs relative to the campaign. Night began to overtake us as we entered Liadouï. Above a little river, which we were to cross previous to our arrival at Liadouï, was a lofty hill, the side of which was so slippery as to render the descent not a little dangerous. The town offered a new aspect to us, for there we first saw inhabitants. Although they were Jews, we forgot the filthiness of that venal people, and by force of entreaty, or rather by force of money, we made them find considerable resources, in a town that at first appeared to be ruined. Thus that cupidity, the object of our supreme contempt in the Jews, was advantageous to us, because it made them brave every danger to procure us what we demanded.

Liadouï forming a part of Lithuania, we thought that it would have been respected, because it belonged to ancient Poland. We departed before daybreak on the following morning (November 19,) when to our great astonishment, we were, as usual, lighted by the fire of the houses. That conflagration produced one of the most horrible scenes of our whole retreat, and my pen would refuse to recount it, if the recital of our misfortunes had not for its object, and its moral, to render odious that fatal ambition, which forced the most civilised people to become, barbarians in war.

Amongst the buildings which were burning, were three vast barns, filled with soldiers, most of whom were wounded. They could not escape from the two which were behind, without passing through the one that was in front, and that was enveloped in flames. The most active saved themselves by leaping out of the windows, but the sick and the wounded unable to move, saw, with horrible consternation the flames rapidly advancing to devour them. Moved by the cries. with which these unhappy beings rent the air, some whose hearts were less hardened than others, attempted to save them. Vain effort! Before we could reach them, they were more than half buried under the burning rafters. Eagerly did they cry to their comrades through the whirlwinds of fire, to shorten their sufferings by immediately depriving them of life. It became the painful duty of humanity to comply with their entreaties. 'Fire upon us, fire upon us, at the head, at the heart; do not hesitate,' were the cries which proceeded from every part of the building, nor did they cease, till every wretched victim was consumed.

We quickly entered into Doubrowna. That town was in a better state of preservation than any through which we had passed in our journey from Moscow. It had a Polonese sub-prefect, and a commandant of the town. The inhabitants were principally Jews, who procured us a little flour, brandy, and metheglin. They also exchanged the paper money of the soldiers for cash. In fine, astonished at the confidence of these Israelites, and the honesty of our soldiers, who paid for every thing which they took, we thought plenty was about to revisit us, and that our misfortunes were near their close. Yet we were struggling under accumulated evils. 'Bread! bread!' was the incessant cry of the feeble remains of our once powerful army. The followers of the camp of every kind, greatly suffered: particularly the commissaries and store-keepers, who had been little more accustomed to privations. But none were more to be pitied than the physicians, and especially the surgeons, who, without hope of advancement, exposed themselves like the common soldiers, by dressing them on the field of battle. While we were at Doubrowna, I saw a young surgeon near a house which the soldiers surrounded in crowds, because it was reported that provisions were to be procured there. He was plunged in the profoundest grief, and with an eager and anxious countenance was violently endeavouring to force his way into the place. But when he was again and again driven back by the crowd, he exhibited the wildest despair. I ventured to inquire the cause. 'Ah, captain!' said he, 'I am a lost man. For two days I have had no food, and ascertaining that they sold bread in this house, I gave the sentinel six franks to suffer me to enter. But while the bread was yet in the oven, the Jew would not promise to supply me, unless I gave him a louis in advance. I consented, but when I came back the sentinel was changed, and I was cruelly repulsed from the door. Ah, sir!' continued he, 'I am indeed, unfortunate; I have lost all the money that I had in the world, and unable to procure a morsel of bread, though I have not tasted any far more than a month.'

At that moment, Napoleon passed by in a close chariot filled with furs. He wore, likewise, a pelisse and bonnet of sable-skin, which prevented him from feeling the severity of the weather. On the day when we arrived at Doubrowna, he had marched a great part of the way on foot, and, during that march he could easily conceive himself to what a miserable state his army was reduced, and how much he had been deceived by the false reports which some generals had made, who, knowing how dangerous it was to confess the truth, did not dare to acquaint him with the real state of things, lest they should incur his displeasure. As he had often experienced the wonderful effects of his discourse on the soldiers, he once more mingled among them, and addressing himself angrily to the officers, and familiarly and jestingly to the soldiers, he endeavoured to inspire the one with fear, and the others with courage. But the time of enthusiasm was passed, when one word from him would have produced miracles. His tyranny had oppressed and debased us, and stifling within us every generous feeling, had deprived him of the only means of reanimating our drooping spirits. Napoleon was most affected at seeing his old guard equally dispirited and despairing. Wounded to the very soul, he assembled a party of them before he quitted Doubrowna, and, placing himself in their centre, recommended the officer to maintain strict discipline, and reminded them that they had always been the pride of his army, and that to their bravery he had often been indebted for the most splendid victories. But sentiments like these were out of season, and the man, who destitute of virtue aspired to the character of a hero, now too plainly found, that the grandest projects were followed by no glory, when they had not some laudable object, and, when, their execution was beyond the scope of human ability.

(November 19th.) Half an hour after we quitted Doubrowna, we passed a very wide and deep ravine through which flowed a considerable river. The opposite bank completely commanded that at which we had arrived. On seeing this important position, we thanked heaven that the Russians had not seized upon it to oppose our passage, and this gave us reason to hope that the village of Orcha was not occupied by them. In fact, some troops lately arrived from France maintained themselves there, and we effected a junction with them at two o'clock in the afternoon, without being harassed by the cossacks. This was a new instance of good fortune, for in the disorder in which we then were, it would have been impossible for us to have forced either of these strong positions.

These troops had constructed two bridges over the Nieper, and as every one rushed on to pass first, the crowd was immense, yet fortunately no accident occurred. Napoleon arrived at Orcha soon after us, and in an instant every house was occupied. The Jews, as usual, immediately procured us trifling refreshments, but the number of purchasers was so great that all was soon consumed.

The more I examined the position of Orcha, the greater was my astonishment that the Russians had not taken possession of it. The town is built on the right bank of the Nieper, which rises considerably higher than the left. Many projections appear from the bank in the form of natural bastions, and perfectly command the passage. The river flows immediately beneath, and is about one thousand two hundred feet wide, and of immense depth. The most formidable army could not pass it without being exposed to entire ruin. While we halted upon these heights, we heard many discharges of musketry, and shortly afterwards, we saw those who had been left on the other side retiring with the greatest precipitation, and crying as they, approached us, 'The cossacks, the cossacks.' In fact they soon actually appeared, but in numbers so small, that we should have been indignant if those who fled before them had not been wretched stragglers, without arms, and mostly wounded.

(November 20th.) On the following day we were unmolested, except that we occasionally heard some discharges of musketry, directed against the cossacks; but accustomed to see them advance upon us, and immediately betake themselves to flight when faced by the regular troops, their presence gave us no uneasiness. We were thus permitted to taste undisturbed the sweets of one day's repose, and some provisions were distributed amongst us, which general Jomini, governor of Orcha, had preserved for the passage of the army. They proved the more acceptable to us, as we had received no rations of bread since our retreat from Smolensko, the magazines of Krasnoë having been pillaged by the cossacks before we arrived.[1]

If the day was tranquil, the night was much disturbed. The duke of Elchingen, who since the disastrous day of Krasnoë, had been obliged to abandon the road that we pursued, and seek a safer retreat on the other side of the Nieper, had been engaged with the enemy during three whole days. That march, in which he had recourse to every manoeuvre that the most extraordinary courage and talents could effect, completed his brilliant reputation. His valour was seconded by the generous movement of the prince Viceroy, who proceeded by forced marches to succour him, and whose assistance effected his deliverance.

(November 21st.) We marched from Orcha at the moment that they began to set it on fire. As we climbed the mountain to recover the grand road, we heard a considerable firing of musketry. It proceeded from the soldiers of the first corps, who had been left in the town to form the rear-guard, and who were already engaged with the cossacks.

During our stay at Orcha, Napoleon, foreseeing that he should soon be placed in a most critical situation, made every effort to rally his troops. He caused it to be proclaimed by sound of trumpet, and by three colonels, that every soldier who did not immediately rejoin his regiment should be punished with death; and that every officer or general, who abandoned his post should be dismissed. But when we regained the great road, we perceived what little effect this measure had produced. All was in the most frightful confusion, and in contempt of this severe proclamation, the soldiers, naked and without arms, continued to march in the same disorder.

We encamped at a sorry village on our right, where two or three habitations remained, at the distance of an hour's march from Kokanovo. The village of Kokanovo, which we passed on the following day, was en-

---

1   I ought to observe, that only the soldiers who were present at the roll call, received any distribution, and they did not form a fifth part of the army; and there were only three distributions in the space of two months, namely at Smolensko, at Orcha, and at Kowno.

tirely ruined; the post-house, which had been inhabited by the staff, alone remained. We continued our march along a road which the thaw had rendered horribly dirty, when we received orders not to push forward to Tolotschin, where Napoleon had fixed his quarters, but to halt at a great *chateau* half a league distant.

The road of Orcha, as far as Tolotschin, is undoubtedly one of the best in Europe. It forms a perfectly straight line, and is bordered on each side by a double row of birch trees, the branches of which, laden with snow and ice, hung down to the ground like the weeping willow. But these majestic avenues excited in us no admiration. They witnessed only our tears and our despair. On every side we heard only groans and lamentations. Some feeling that they could proceed no farther, laid themselves on the ground, and with tears in their eyes, gave us their papers and their money to be conveyed to their families. 'Ah! If more fortunate than we,' they exclaimed, 'you are permitted to re-visit our dear country, give our parents this last pledge of our love. Tell them that the hope of seeing them again alone sustained us till this day; and that at length, compelled to renounce this pleasing expectation, we died thinking of them, and blessing them. Adieu, God bless you! When on your return to our beloved France, you rejoice in your good fortune, think, sometimes of our unhappy fate.' A little further on we met others, who, holding in their arms their famished children or their wives, implored one morsel of bread to preserve their lives.

In the meantime, Napoleon was informed that the army of Wolhynia, joined to that of Moldavia, had marched on Minsk (Nov. 16th,) and that it had seized on the bridge of Borisov, to cut us off from the passage of the Beresina. He also knew, that the army of Wittgenstein, reinforced by the division of Stengel, sharply pressed the twelfth and sixteenth corps, that it might be enabled to march on the Borisov, and form a junction with admiral Tschikakoff and prince Kutusoff. To oppose the execution of a plan which would complete our ruin, Napoleon sent general Dombrowski against the army of Wolhynia, hoping also that he might anticipate it, in seizing the bridge of Borisov. This general did establish himself there, but he was forced to evacuate his position (Nov. 23d.) The enemy having then passed the Beresina, marched upon Bohr, and came to meet us. The twelfth corps commanded by the duke of Reggio, which was at Tschéréïa, received orders to proceed immediately to the succour of general Dombrowski, and to secure for the army the passage of the Beresina. On the following day (Nov. 24th) he met the division of the Russian general Lambert, four leagues on this side of Borisov. He attacked and beat it. At the same time general Berkheim made a brilliant charge with the fourth regiment of chasseurs, and forced the enemy to retreat to the other bank of the river, after having lost two thousand men, six cannon and a quantity of baggage.

The Russians having destroyed in their flight the great bridge of Borisov, defended all the right bank of the Beresina, and occupied, with four divisions, the principal points where we could possibly attempt to pass it. During the 25th, Napoleon manoeuvred to deceive the vigilance of the enemy, and, by stratagem, obtained possession of the village of Studzianca, placed on an eminence that commanded the river which we wished to pass. There, in the presence of the Russians, and notwithstanding their utmost opposition, he constructed two bridges, of which the duke of Reggio profited to cross the Beresina; and attacking the troops which opposed his passage, he put them to flight, and pursued them without intermission, to the head of the bridge of Borisov. General Legrand, an officer of distinguished merit, was wounded in this affair.

The duke of Belluno, who for some days had kept the corps of Wittgenstein in check, having received orders to follow the movements of the duke of Reggio, was pursued in his retreat by the Russian army of the Dwina, which had then formed a junction with prince Kutusoff, near Lochnitza. During all these operations, which took place between the 23d and 27th of November, we passed four dreadful days, traversing many villages, among which we could only learn the names of Bohr and Kraupki, where fatigue compelled us to halt. The days were so short, that although we made but little progress we were obliged to march during part of the night. It was from this cause that so many unhappy wretches wandered from their regiments, and were lost. Arriving very late at the encampments, where all the corps, were confounded together, they could not distinguish or learn the situation of the regiment to which they belonged. After having marched the whole day, they were often compelled to wander about all the night to find their officers, and rarely were they sufficiently fortunate to accomplish their object; they then laid themselves down to sleep, ignorant of the hour of march, and on awaking, found themselves in the power of the enemy.

As we passed the Borisov, we saw the division of Parthonneaux forming the rear-guard of the ninth corps. We then quitted the great road that led to the bridge occupied by the Russians, and turned to the right to proceed to Studzianca, where we found Napoleon. The other troops of the ninth corps, commanded by the duke of Belluno, arrived likewise by the same road.

The twelfth and ninth corps and the Poles, commanded by general Dombrowski, not having been at Moscow, had so much baggage, that from Borisov to Studzianca the road was covered with carriages and wagons. The reinforcements which these troops brought us were very acceptable, yet we almost doubted whether the junction of so many men, in the centre of a vast desert, might not increase our misfortunes. Always marching in the midst of a confused mass of stragglers, with the divisions of the ninth corps, we were two hours afterwards arrested in our progress by a great crowd, and unable to penetrate, we were compelled to march round it. In the midst of this multitude were some paltry barns, on the summit of a little hill. Seeing some chasseurs of the imperial guard encamped around it, we judged that Napoleon was there, and that we were approaching the borders of the Beresina. In fact, it was the very spot where Charles XII crossed that river, on his march to Moscow.[2]

What a frightful picture did this multitude of men present, overwhelmed with misfortunes of every kind, and hemmed in by a morass; that very multitude which, two months before, had exultingly spread itself over half the surface of a vast empire! Our soldiers, pale, emaciated, dying with hunger and cold, have nothing to defend them from the inclemency of the season, but tattered pelisses, and sheep-skins half burnt, and uttering the most mournful lamentations, crowded the banks of this unfortunate river. Germans, Polanders, Italians, Spaniards, Croats, Portuguese, and French, were all mingled together, disputing among themselves, and quarrelling with each other, in their different languages; finally, the officers, and even the generals, wrapped in pelisses covered with dirt and filth, confounded with the soldiers, and abusing those who pressed upon them, or braved their authority, formed a scene of strange confusion, of which no painter could trace the faintest resemblance.

They, whom fatigue, or ignorance of the impending danger, rendered less eager to cross the river, were endeavouring to kindle a fire, and repose their wearied limbs. We had, too frequently, occasion to observe, in these encampments, to what a degree of brutality, excess of misery would debase human nature. In one place we saw several of the soldiers fighting for a morsel of bread. If a stranger, pierced with the cold, endeavoured to approach a fire, those to whom it belonged inhumanly drove him away; or, if tormented with racing thirst, any one asked for a single drop of water from another who carried a full supply, the refusal was accompanied by the vilest abuse. We often heard those who had once been friends, and whose education had been liberal, bitterly disputing with each other for a little straw, or a piece of horse flesh, which they were attempting to divide. This campaign was therefore the more terrible, as it brutalised the character, and stained us with vices to which we had before been strangers. Even those who once were honest, humane, and generous, became selfish, avaricious, dishonest, and cruel.

2   June 25th, 1708.

Napoleon having, with the assistance of his guard, forced his way through this immense crowd, crossed the river (November 27) about three o'clock in the afternoon. The viceroy, who had passed the whole day with him, announced to his staff, that what remained of the fourth corps should pass the bridge at night o'clock at night. Although not a moment should have been lost in escaping from a place so dangerous, many could not prevail upon themselves to leave the fires round which they were sitting. 'It is much better,' said they, 'to pass the night on this side of the river than on the other, where there is nothing but marshes; besides, the bridge is as much encumbered as ever, and by waiting till to-morrow, the crowd will have lessened, and the passage will be easy.' This unfortunate advice prevailed on too many, and at the hour appointed, only the household of the prince, and a few of the officers of the staff crossed the river.

It was, indeed, necessary to know all the danger that would have attended our stay on the left side of the river, to induce us to pass to the other. The viceroy and his suite, arriving on the right bank, encamped on a marshy piece of ground, and endeavoured to find out the places which were most frozen, to pass the night on them and escape the bogs. The darkness was horrible and the wind tremendous, blowing a thick shower of ice and snow full in our faces. Many of the officers, pierced with the cold, did not cease running, and walking, and striking their feet, during the whole night, to preserve themselves from being completely frozen. To complete our misfortunes, wood was so scarce, that we could with difficulty supply one little fire for the viceroy; and to obtain some firebrands, we were obliged to appeal to the Bavarian soldiers, the daughter of whose king had been united in marriage to prince Eugene.

(November 28th.) Napoleon being gone towards Zembin, left behind him this immense crowd, which, standing on the other side of the Beresina, presented a lively, but frightful picture of the unhappy ghosts who are said to wander on the banks of the Styx, and press tumultuously towards the fatal barge. The snow fell with violence; the hills and forest presented only some white indistinct masses, scarcely visible through the fog. We could only see distinctly the fatal river, which, half frozen, forced its way through the ice that impeded its progress.

Although there were two bridges, one for the carriages, and the other for the foot-soldiers, yet the crowd was so great, and the approaches so dangerous, that near the Beresina, the passage was completely choked up, and it was absolutely impossible to move. About eight o'clock in the morning, the bridge for the carriages and the cavalry broke down; the baggage and artillery then advanced towards the other bridge, and attempted to force a passage. Now began a frightful contention between the foot-soldiers and the horsemen. Many perished by the hands of their comrades, but a great number were suffocated at the head of the brigade; and the dead bodies of men and horses, so choked every avenue, that it was necessary to climb over mountains of carcasses to arrive at the river. Some, who were buried in these horrible heaps, still breathed, and struggling with the agonies of death, caught hold of those who mounted over them; but these kicked them with violence, to disengage themselves, and, without remorse, trod them under foot. During this contention, the multitude which followed, like a furious wave, swept away, while it increased the number of victims.

The division of Parthonneaux, which formed the rearguard, having received orders to return, left a brigade to burn the bridge. That brigade, setting out two hours afterwards to rejoin the first, found it no more. Doubtless, it had hastened its retreat, for it has now been fully proved, that general Parthonneaux, who had been unjustly accused of abandoning his troops, received three or four orders in the course of the day, which rendered him uncertain how to act, and placed him in a very critical situation. Be this as it may, the second brigade lost its way, and wandered more than three leagues in a wrong direction. In the middle of a dismal night and pierced with cold, it mistook the fires of the enemy for ours, and ran to join us; when, seeing itself surrounded, and without the least hope of escape, it was compelled to surrender.

Borisov being evacuated, the three Russian armies effected their junction, and the same day (November 28th) about eight o'clock in the morning, the duke of Reggio was attacked on the right bank, and half an hour afterwards the duke of Belluno was engaged on the left. Every soldier, who had before been wandering in confusion, fell into the ranks. The battle was obstinately fought, and the duke of Reggio could only obtain the victory at the price of his own blood. He was wounded at the beginning of the action, and compelled to quit the field. The command then devolved on the duke of Elchingen.

In the mean time the enemy, notwithstanding the valour of our soldiers, and the exertions of their commanders, briskly pressed the ninth corps, which formed the rear-guard. We already heard the roar of the cannon, and the sound dismayed every heart. Insensibly it approached, and we soon saw the fire of the enemy's artillery on the summit of the neighbouring hills, and we no longer doubted that the engagement would soon extend to that spot which was covered with thousands of unarmed men, sick and wounded, and with all our women and children.

The duke of Elchingen, having rallied his troops, the battle recommenced with new fury. The division of cuirassiers, commanded by general Doumerc, made a very brilliant charge, and at the same moment the legion of the Vistula was engaged in the woods, endeavouring to force the enemy's centre. These brave cuirassiers, although enfeebled by fatigue and privations of every kind, performed prodigies of valour. They pierced the enemy's squares, took several pieces of cannon, and three or four thousand prisoners, which our weakness would not permit us to retain: for in our cruel situation we fought not for victory, but only for life, and the honour of our arms.

In the heat of the engagement many balls flew over the miserable crowd which was yet pressing across the bridge of the Beresina. Some shells burst in the midst of them. Terror and despair then took possession of every heart. The women and children, who had escaped so many disasters, seemed to have been preserved, only to suffer here a death still more deplorable. We saw them rushing from the baggage-wagons, and falling in agonies and tears at the feet of the first soldier they met, imploring his assistance to enable them to reach the other side. The sick and the wounded, sitting on the trunks of trees, or supported by their crutches, anxiously looked around for some friend to help them. But their cries were lost in the air. No one had leisure to attend to his dearest friend. His own preservation absorbed every thought.

Monsieur de Labarriere, the muster-master of the fourth corps, was a man of respectable character, and engaging manners. His advanced age, and more especially his feeble constitution, had long rendered him unable to march, and he was now lying with many others on an open sledge. He accidentally perceived an officer of his acquaintance, and although he was scarcely able to stand, he ran to him, threw himself in his arms, and implored his protection. The officer was severely wounded, but too generous to refuse his feeble help, he promised that he would not leave him. These two friends, closely embracing each other, slowly proceeded towards the bridge animated by the consoling thought, that at least they would be permitted to die together. They entered the crowd; but, feeble and helpless, they were unable to sustain the intolerable pressure, and were seen no more.

A woman was likewise marching with the equipage of Napoleon, whom her husband had left a little way behind, while he went forward to endeavour to find a place where they might safely pass. During that time a shell burst near the unfortunate female. The crowd that was around her, immediately took to flight. She alone remained. But the enemy soon advancing, caused the soldiers to rush back all at once to the bridge, and, in their confused march they hurried the poor woman with them, who strove in vain to return to the place where her husband had left her. Buffeted by the tumultuous waves, she saw herself driven from the spot, without the possibility of return. We heard her from afar, loudly calling to her husband, but her piercing voice was unattended to, amidst the noise of arms, and the cries of the soldiers. At length pale and speechless, she beat her breast in agony and fell lifeless at the feet of the soldiers, who, attentive to their own escape, neither saw nor heard her.

At length the Russians continually reinforced by fresh troops, advanced in a mass, and drove before them the Polonese corps of general Girard, which till then had held them in check. At the sight of the enemy, those who had not already passed, mingled with the Polanders, and rushed precipitately towards the bridge. The artillery, the baggage-wagons, the cavalry, and the foot-soldiers, all pressed on, contending which should pass the first. The strongest threw into the river those who were weaker, and hindered their passage, or unfeelingly trampled underfoot all the sick whom they found in their way. Many hundreds were crushed to death by the wheels of the cannon. Others, hoping to save themselves by swimming, were frozen in the middle of the river, or perished by placing themselves on pieces of ices, which sunk to the bottom. Thousands and thousands of victims, deprived of all hope, threw themselves headlong into the Beresina, and were lost in the waves.

The division of Girard made its way, by force of arms, through all the obstacles that retarded its march; and climbing over that mountain of dead bodies which obstructed the way, gained the other side. Thither the Russians would soon have followed if they had not hastened to burn the bridge. Then the unhappy beings who remained on the other side of the Beresina abandoned themselves to absolute despair. Some of them, however, yet attempted to pass the bridge, enveloped as it was in flames; but, arrested in the midst of their progress, they were compelled to throw themselves into the river, to escape a death yet more horrible. At length the Russians, being masters of the field of battle, our troops retired, the uproar ceased, and a mournful silence succeeded.

As we marched towards Zembin, we re-ascended the right bank of the Beresina, whence we could distinctly see all that passed on the other side. The cold was excessive; and the wind blew in loud and hollow gusts. The obscurity of the night was dissipated only by the numerous fires of the enemy, who occupied the heights. At the foot of these hills were our unfortunate companions. Their destitution was now inevitable, and, amidst all their former disasters never were they exposed to, nor can imagination conceive, horrors equal to those which encompassed them during that frightful night. The elements let loose, seemed to conspire to afflict universal nature, and to chastise the ambition and the crimes of man. The conquerors and the conquered, were alike overwhelmed with sufferings. Round the encampment of the Russians, however, we saw enormous masses of burning wood, but on the spot which held our devoted companions, there was neither light nor shelter. Lamentable cries and groans alone marked the place which contained these miserable victims.

More than twenty thousand sick and wounded fell into the power of the enemy. Two hundred pieces of cannon were abandoned. All the baggage of the two corps which had joined us was equally the prey of the conquerors; yet, when we contemplated the deplorable fate of the wretched beings who were left on the other side of the Beresina, the consciousness of our safety rendered us insensible to the loss of all our riches. They were for ever deprived of the hope of revisiting the land that gave them birth; and were doomed to pass the sad remnant of their days amidst the snows of Siberia, where they would water with their tears the black bread which would be the only wages of the most humiliating servitude.

(November 29th.) Setting out on the morrow for Zembin, and endeavouring to rejoin what remained of the fourth corps, we again commiserated the fate of the numerous friends who were no longer with us. We eagerly embraced those who had returned, whom we had feared we should never again have beheld, and congratulated each other on surviving a day more terrible than the bloodiest battle. We mutually recounted the dangers that we had run, and the difficulties with which we had struggled to escape with life. 'I have lost every thing,' said one, 'servants, horses, baggage; but I think not of it; I rather esteem myself most fortunate, that I have preserved my life, that I have escaped from the inclemency of the weather, the horrors of famine, and the arms of the enemy.' 'I have nothing but what I carry about me,' said a second, 'and all of that I had, I only wish for some shoes to defend my feet, and some bread to eat: these are the truest riches.' 'I have lost all,' exclaimed a third, 'but I do not regret it, since the sacrifice of my baggage has enabled me to save my wounded brother.' Such was the language which we heard, during several successive days; and those who were silent, deeply mused on the dangers which they had passed, and rendered their secret but fervent thanks to Providence, for a preservation almost miraculous.

Book X

The Niemen

The fatal passage of the Beresina having reduced our corps of reserve to the same condition as those who had been as far as Moscow, realised the fatal predictions, which had long been announced to us; and, with the exception of our chief (whose life Providence seems to have continued, only to deliver him to greater remorse and despair,) all was accomplished.

How dreadful was the punishment of this conqueror, to lose the provinces which he occupied with more rapidity than he had invaded them; to have the melancholy cypress, instead of the laurels of victory, and cities smoking with recent slaughter, instead of the incense of applause; and, finally, as the companions of his triumph, twenty thousand disarmed soldiers, without linen and without stockings, whose only shoes were contrived from their worn-out hats, whose shoulders were covered with pieces of sacking, and the skins of horses, newly flayed.

These were deplorable remains of five hundred thousand brave warriors, who, but for the ambition of a single man, would always have been the honour of France, and the terror of their enemies.

(November 29th.) We arrived very early at the village of Kamen, and were continuing our route to Plescenkovice, when Colaud, commander of the advanced-guard, returned, and announced to us that two thousand cossacks had entered the city, crying 'Hourra!' and were massacring every one whom they found in the streets, 'The duke of Reggio,' said he, 'being wounded last night, was scarcely able to reach the place; but, happily, many officers hastening to render him assistance, or to die at his side, excited a fear in the enemy that we were contriving some ambush. They retired to a neighbouring height, and cannonaded the marshal's house, to make it capitulate. As if a fatality pursued the duke of Reggio, a cannon-ball striking on a beam, broke off a splinter, by which he was again slightly wounded.' This officer likewise informed us, 'that general Pino had been in the same quarters, and that count Danthouard, on entering into Plescenkovice, had scarcely time to escape to his carriage.'

This news determined us to remain at Kamen. The next day (30th November) we set out before day break, and passing by Plescenkovice, the accounts which we had received on the preceding evening, were confirmed. We saw the house where the duke of Reggio had taken up his quarters, and were surprised that two thousand cossacks had not ventured to carry off by force, a marshal who was only defended by twenty wounded officers. Napoleon halted in this city, but the viceroy continuing his route, encamped in a deserted village, near Zavichino, which according to the map, was named Niestanovitsch.

(December 1st.) The, following day, about seven in the morning, the viceroy, accompanied by a few officers, placed himself at the head of some grenadiers of the royal guard, who yet remained faithful to their colours. After a very long march, for men exhausted with fatigue, we arrived at the town of Iliïa. The Jews, forming the majority of the population, had not quitted their houses, and the love of gain induced them to bring out some provisions, which they had intended to conceal. We paid them liberally, for in such a situation the poorest nourishment was preferable to gold. Without this assistance, we should have lost the brave and estimable colonel Durieu, whose health had much declined; less perhaps on account of deprivations to which he had been exposed, than the ardent zeal with which he fulfilled his important and laborious duties.

(December 2d.) The next day, when we marched upon Molodetschino, was still more fatiguing and oppressive. We marched for twelve hours without halting, through an immense forest. The cold was excessive, and the only thing which could afford us consolation, was the persuasion, that the cossacks would no longer harass our right. Captain Jouard, who had been sent to Vileika, to general Wrede, assured us that the Bavarians still maintained that important position.

We were in a pitiable situation when we arrived at Molodetschino. Happily the houses were good, and some of the proprietors, who still remained, procured us the means of subsistence. The next morning the equipages of Napoleon began to depart. They were scarcely out of the village, when a multitude of cossacks presented themselves, and would have taken them, if they had not hastily returned to place themselves under the protection of the troops, who yet retained their arms. The viceroy was preparing for his departure, when it was announced to him that we were to remain at Molodetschino, but that he must evacuate the *chateau* which he occupied, for the use of Napoleon, who would soon arrive..

This repose was the more precious as the ability to procure, some provisions, by dint of searching for them, enabled us to employ it profitably. Nevertheless, many soldiers expired in the streets. The same desolation extended to the houses where the officers lodged. Some were sick from excessive fatigue, and protested that they could go no further; others whose feet were frozen, and who had no horses, found themselves obliged, though full of courage, to remain in the hands of the Russians. The generals were exposed to the same calamities for many of them, having lost their servants and their carriages, were unable to replace them. In such circumstances if the slightest sickness attacked them, they expired for want of assistance. Such was our situation in Molodetschino, when Napoleon wrote in characters of blood, the fatal twenty-ninth bulletin, which made France and her allies, a large family of mourners.

(December 4th.) We quitted the village, but did not take the great road which leads through Zachkévitschi, directly to Smorghini. We kept to the left of this rock, when, indeed, promised little safely, and pursued a by-road, which conducted us by Lebioda to Markovo. We encamped in this village with some soldiers of the first corps, while the emperor and his guard were at Bienitsa, about half a league from us.

(December 6th.) Setting out for Smorghoni, we crossed some marshy country, which would have been absolutely impassable, had it not been for the rigour of the season. It was therefore evident to us that these regions are completely defended by their very nature, and that, independent of the rigour of winter, the marshes of Lithuania would have been our grave. When we arrived at this little town, we did not find the resources which we had been promised. All the houses were deserted, and the Jews, having taken flight, had deprived us of their assistance. We found however, in the magazines, some casks of biscuits, which were immediately devoured.

Napoleon, terrified by so many disasters, and still more so by the fear of losing his authority in France, conceived the idea of abandoning these miserable, remains of his army, for the purpose of demanding from his senate new levies; and, tortured by that just terror which always pursues the despot, he imagined that his allies were eager to dissolve the compact, which had placed them under his iron yoke.

Full of this resolution, he felt assured, when he arrived at Smorghoni, that the road was safe as far as the Niemen, and called together the chiefs of the army. Afterwards he had a private conference with the viceroy. This being finished, Napoleon issued from his cabinet, followed by the master of the horse, the marshal of the palace, and general Lefebre Desnouettes. Crossing one of the halls, he met the king of Naples, and said to him, with an indifferent air, *'Adieu, king of Naples!'* While pronouncing these words, he went out, accompanied by the three persons who were going with him. Being seated in his carriage, he placed at his side general Desnouettes. The master of the horse, and the marshal of the palace entered a second, which immediately followed on the route to Wilna. No address was made to the army, no proclamation to the Lithuanians, to reanimate their dejected spirits. The one was without a chief, the other abandoned by him who had promised them every thing.

The king of Naples took the command of the army, but they marched with so much disorder and precipitation, that it was only when they arrived at Vilna, that the soldiers were informed of a departure as discouraging as it was unexpected. 'What' said they among themselves, 'is it thus that he abandons those of whom he calls himself the father? Where then, is that genius, who, in the height of prosperity, exhorted us to bear our sufferings patiently? He who lavished our blood, is he afraid to die with us? Will he treat us like the army of Egypt, whom, after having served, him faithfully, he became indifferent, when, by a shameful flight, he found himself free from danger?' Such was the conversation of the soldiers, which they accompanied by the most violent execrations. Never was indignation more just, for never were a class of men so worthy of pity.

The presence of the emperor had kept the chiefs to their duty, but when they heard of his departure, the greater part of them followed his example, and shamefully abandoned the remains of the regiments with which they had been entrusted. Until then we had found, at, intervals, some few armed soldiers who, conducted by their officers, rallied round the standard which they had sworn never to forsake, but with life. But from the moment that they were deprived of their chiefs, and that unheard of calamities had reduced their numbers, those brave soldiers, who were intrusted with the immediate charge, were reduced to the painful necessity of hiding them in their knapsacks. Many of them, sensible that they were expiring, and knowing that the honour of a French soldier consisted in preserving his colours, with a weak hand dug up the ground. to save from the Russians those ensigns under which our arms had been raised to the pinnacle of glory.

The division of Loison, which had come before us from Koningsberg, and that of the Neapolitans, from Wilna, having been obliged to encamp in a cold of twenty-two degrees, were totally destroyed, and out of six thousand men, of which each was composed, we could only see, through a thick fog, some feeble battalions, who ran on the road like madmen. They beat the earth with their feet, to keep themselves from being benumbed by the frost, and if, unfortunately, they were urged by the wants of nature, losing the use of their hands, they fell on the ground, and rose again no more. They who could support the fatigue of marching, only prolonged their misery; and if, at length, weary of life, they wished to terminate their sufferings, it was necessary only to stand still.

The road which we followed, presented, at every step, brave officers, covered with rags, supported by branches of pine, their hair and beards stiffened by the ice. These warriors, who, a short time before, were the terror of our enemies, and the conquerors of Europe, having now lost their fine appearance, crawled slowly along, and could scarcely obtain a look of pity from the soldiers whom they had formerly commanded. Their situation became still more dreadful, because all who had not strength to march were abandoned and every one who was abandoned, by his comrades, in an hour afterwards inevitably perished. The next day every bivouac presented the image of a field of battle. Whenever a soldier, overcome with fatigue, chanced to fall, his next neighbour rushed eagerly upon him, and before he was dead, robbed him of all that he possessed, and even of his clothes. Every moment we heard some of these unhappy men crying out for assistance. 'My comrades' cried one, with a heart-rending voice, 'assist me to rise, lend me a hand to pursue my march.' Every one continued his march without regarding him. 'Ah!' he continued, 'I conjure you by every thing which is dear to you, do not abandon me to the enemy; in the name of humanity, grant the little assistance I ask; help me to rise.' But those who passed, far from being moved by this touching prayer, regarded him as already dead, and immediately began to strip him. We then heard him crying out, 'Oh, help! help! They murder me; they murder me! why do you trample upon me? Why do you snatch from me my money and my bread, and take from me even my clothes!' If some generous officer did not arrive in time to deliver them, many of these unfortunate beings would be assassinated by their own comrades.

(December 7.) We arrived at Joupranouï a little before night. Overcome with fatigue, we were obliged to stop there. The ruined houses afforded us no shelter from the rigour of the season. Lying on each other, suffering with hunger, and pierced with cold, we passed the night in groans.

We marched early in the morning, (8th December) and arrived at Ochmiana about eleven o'clock. The winter was so severe, that the soldiers burnt whole houses to avoid being frozen. We saw round the fires, the half-consumed bodies of many unfortunate men, who, having advanced too near in order to warm themselves, and being too weak to recede, had become a prey to the flames. Some miserable beings blackened with smoke, and besmeared with the blood of the horses which they had devoured, wandered like ghosts, round the burning house. They gazed on the dead bodies of their companions, and, too feeble to support themselves, fell down, and died like them.

We expected to have received some provisions in this town, but we were informed that the cossacks had pillaged the magazines, and that Napoleon had passed through half an hour after they were gone. We then continued our route, marching in the midst of the dead and the dying, and at length arrived at the wretched stone *chateau* of Rovno-Polé, where the prince and his staff passed a miserable night.

Misfortune having equalised all conditions, every thing was confounded. It was in vain that the officers endeavoured to assert their authority; it was insolently denied. The colonel, who had no food, was obliged to beg a piece of biscuit from the private soldier. The man who possessed provisions, although he were a servant, was surrounded by a crowd of courtiers, who, to obtain food, threw aside their rank and distinction, and condescended to caress him. In short, to form an adequate idea of the dreadful disorder to which famine and cold had reduced us, you must figure to yourself thirty thousand men of different ranks, marching together, without order and without discipline, ignorant of the road upon which they were going, and only stopping when weariness or caprice compelled them. The chiefs themselves, being accustomed to command, were the most unfortunate. They were shunned, to avoid rendering them assistance; for, in our situation, even to give a glass of water, or to raise a fellow-soldier from the ground, were offices of kindness which claimed the warmest gratitude.

The route was covered with soldiers who no longer retained the human form, and whom the enemy disdained to make prisoners. Every day these miserable men made us witnesses of scenes too dreadful to relate. Some had lost their hearing, others their speech, and many, by excessive cold and hunger, were reduced to a state of frantic stupidity, in which they roasted the dead bodies of their comrades for food, or even gnawed their own hands and arms.[1] Some were so weak, that, unable to lift a piece of wood, or roll a stone towards the fires which they had kindled, they sat upon the dead bodies of their comrades, and, with a haggard countenance, steadfastly gazed upon the burning coals. No sooner was the fire extinguished, than these living spectres, unable to rise, fell by the side of those on whom they had sat. We saw many who were absolutely insane. To warm their frozen feet, they plunged them naked into the middle of the fire. Some, with a convulsive laugh, threw themselves into the flames, and, perished in the most horrible convulsions, and uttering the most piercing cries; while others, equally insane, immediately followed them, and experienced the same fate.

Such was our situation when we arrived at the village of Roukoni, where some wretched barns alone remained filled with dead bodies. Being only three leagues from Wilna, many continued their march, that they might arrive first in that city where they hoped not only to find abundance of provisions, but to remain some days and enjoy that repose which they so much needed. The fourth corps, which could not muster

---

1   Official Report, published by the Russians at Wilna, 2d December, 1812.

more than two hundred men, who were yet faithful to their duty, halted in this wretched village.

At break of day we hastened to quit Roukoni, where the cold and the smoke had prevented us from closing our eyes. When we were commencing our march, the Bavarians, who formed the rearguard, hastily advanced, crying out that the enemy was pursuing them. The evening before, it was reported that they had obtained some advantages over the cossacks; but the disorder in which they now arrived, proved that this intelligence was false. However, we must do them the justice to say that they yet retained some pieces of cannon, but the horses were so weak that they could not drag them along.

Every day's march presented a repetition of the mournful scenes of which I have given a slight sketch. Our hearts were so hardened to these dreadful spectacles, that all sensibility was entirely lost. Self-preservation was the only motive which actuated us, in the state of barbarism to which we were reduced. Wilna occupied every thought, and the hope that that position would permit us to take some repose, inspired those who were able to continue their march, with such extreme joy, that they regarded with indifference the miserable beings who crowded the road, struggling with the agonies of death. Wilna, however, the object of our dearest hopes, and to which we were pressing on with such eagerness, was soon found to be another Smolensko.

At length we arrived at its suburbs, so ardently desired; but our happiness was sadly allayed when we saw the whole of this immense place obstructed by a crowd of carriages, horses, and men. This confusion recalled the Beresina to my mind; and such was our stupidity, that, being accustomed to follow our column, we were afraid of losing ourselves if we ventured a few steps from it; thus, while all were pressing against each other to enter at the same gate, there were, at the right and left, other avenues unobstructed.

When we arrived in the city, we found it in extreme disorder: the soldiers were running in every direction to ascertain the quarters assigned to their respective corps. Those of the fourth corps going to the municipality, saw written in large characters, that they were to quarter in the convent of St. Raphael on the other side of the Vilia. Before they went thither they ran as if they were almost famished from house to house demanding food. The eating houses and taverns, not being sufficient for the immense number of guests, were instantly shut up. But hunger determined us to find provisions; and we were compelled to break open the doors. Others, with money in their hands, pursued the Jews, who, in spite of our generosity, could not satisfy us to the extent of our wants.

At Wilna, we heard that Napoleon had passed through incognito, escorted by a feeble detachment of three regiments of Neapolitan cavalry, which had been sent before him to clear his route. These poor inhabitants of the south were half dead when they passed in review; scarcely had they departed from Wilna, when a third part of them fell into the rear, having their hands, feet, and noses, entirely frozen. The departure of Napoleon in this disguised manner, not only spread consternation among the Lithuanians, who were devoted to us, but sadly discouraged the French troops. The first were indignant at finding themselves exposed to the resentment of a master, whose yoke they had wished to shake off; the others were alarmed for their own preservation, for, in a situation so critical, every one thought that the absence of the chief, consummated our ruin. Many, however, who felt all the dangers to which we were exposed, yet jealous for the glory of our arms, thought his departure was fortunate. 'Napoleon,' said they, 'when at Paris, will reorganise a noble army; will secure the peace of France, and maintain the co-operation of the allies, whose defection would be so dangerous.' About three o'clock in the afternoon, the rear of our long column had scarcely entered the suburbs, when we heard that the cossacks had taken possession of the heights which commanded the city. In effect they soon began to fire upon us. At the report of the cannon, the new troops who were at Wilna, beat the drum and sounded the trumpet. In an instant the place was in arms. By one of those chances by which Providence confounds the proud, and punishes the indolent it happened that the colossal power of Napoleon was so completely reduced in this iron climate, as to have no other support than the remains of a Neapolitan division, formed from the garrisons of Tarentum and Capita. These troops being quickly dispersed, terror immediately spread through the city; and at the single word of the 'cossacks,' all the soldiers rushed from their quarters and betook themselves to flight. The king of Naples, forgetting his rank, suddenly abandoned his palace, and on foot, followed by his officers, pierced through the crowd, and escaped from the town to encamp on the road to Kowno.

While some of the soldiers took arms, others, as night advanced, profiting by the evacuation of the magazines, carried off the clothes and military equipments which had been collected there, but the greater part searching only for food, knocked at every door, and their redoubled blows seemed to be a dreadful presage of a universal pillage. The inhabitants, trembling in their houses, dreaded the impending desolation, as they heard on every side the noise of cannon, which thundered over their heads.

We gave up all hope of repose, and the feeble relics of our army not able to resist the attacks of the enemy, we determined to profit by the obscurity of the night, to quit so dangerous a position. It was decided that at eleven o'clock we should evacuate the town. The hour being arrived, we silently proceeded on our route, leaving the streets covered with soldiers, intoxicated, asleep, or dead. The courts, the galleries, the stairs of the various buildings, were filled with them, and not one would march, or even rise to obey the orders of the chief who called him. After leaving Wilna, with as much difficulty as we entered it, the prince and the staff went to the king of Naples, where all the officers remained till one o'clock in the morning.

In the middle of a dark night (10th December,) we marched on the road to Kowno, but the snow which covered the country, caused us to wander every moment, and left us for a long time uncertain of the road; for the Poles going to New-Troki, had left the traces of another route which was calculated to mislead us. Two hours afterwards we arrived at the foot of a mountain, inaccessible on account of its steepness, and the ice with which it was covered. All around were the remains of the equipages of Napoleon, the baggage left at Wilna, the treasures of the army, and the wagons containing the fatal trophies brought from Moscow, so that we no longer doubted that we were on the road to Kowno.

While we were groaning at the foot of this mountain, without the power to climb it, we distinctly heard the firing between the cossacks and our sharpshooters. Actuated by that unseasonable discontent and ill-humour which misfortune inspires, many exclaimed that it would have been better to have gone to New-Troki, and to have avoided this fatal mountain. All who were thus arrested here, and who were mostly sick or wounded, considered themselves as a certain prey to the enemy. Their grief was increased by the reflection that they must perish after having so nearly reached the wished for post, and having escaped the dangers of Krasnoë and the Beresina. Their grief was soon changed to despair, when we heard that the cossacks, having passed Wilna, had pursued our rear-guard and were advancing towards us. Dire necessity, however compelled us to wait till the dawn of day, that we might discover whether there were any means of going round the mountain, which our horses could not climb. In this interval we kindled a fire, and every one deeply sighing, impatiently waited the return of day.

We looked every where in vain; the mountain was so slippery, and the horses so fatigued, that we despaired of escape. The idea then occurred to us of compelling the soldiers of the escort to carry the money belonging to the military chest. It then contained about five millions, the greatest part of which was in crowns. We had little doubt, however, that the soldiers, whom it was impossible to watch, or to detect, would carry off, for their own use, that which was intrusted to their care. The standards taken from the enemy, respecting which these venal wretches were no longer interested, were cowardly abandoned at the foot of the mountain. Among these was the famous cross of St. Iwan, which would have made so glorious an addition to our trophies, if the Russians, whom we termed barbarians, had not given us a noble example of a moderation which rarely accompanies victory.

Those who followed augmented the number of plunderers, and it was truly curious to see those who were dying with hunger, laden with more riches than they could possibly carry. They saw the money distributed among them, with the most perfect indifference; and searched in preference for the coarsest food. Trunks and portmanteaus broken open and plundered, were seen in every direction. The most superb court-dresses, and the richest furs were worn by those whose countenances were hideous and disgusting. Returning from the pillage, many of them offered sixty francs for a louis, and some gave ten crowns, for a glass of brandy. One of the soldiers, in my presence, offered to sell a cask filled with silver, for a few pieces of gold : it was bought by a superior officer who placed it on his sledge. It is impossible to form an adequate idea of the confusion which our army now presented. Far from being re-animated by the presence of some battalions lately arrived from Prussia, they spread consternation among these new troops, who, not knowing whom to obey, likewise threw away their arms, and increased the crowd of stragglers. In short, all our soldiers, transformed into brokers, only sought to sell their stolen goods, while those who had pillaged the military chest were eager to buy, that they might, at least, retain something valuable. Every one spoke familiarly of ingots and jewels. Every soldier was laden with silver, but none with a musket. Ought we to be astonished at the fears which the cossacks inspired?

In this state of confusion, after five hours distressing march, we arrived at Evé, about ten leagues from Wilna. We had scarcely entered it when the count Mejean,[2] supported by his son and the valet de chambre of the prince, arrived. This unfortunate father, to whose generous devotion to the service I regret that the limits of my work will not permit me to do justice, had been obliged to travel on foot, from the mountain of Wilna, across a country covered with snow. But this nobleman, whose courage had often astonished us, and who, though not a soldier, had patiently endured the sufferings to which we were subjected, felt such great attachment to the prince, that he quite forgot the misfortunes of the day as soon as he found himself in the presence of his highness.

2 Counsellor of state of the kingdom of Italy, and secretary to the viceroy. He had been present during the whole campaign with his two sons, and heard at the Beresina, that his youngest son had been killed at the battle of Polotsk.

Similar miseries happened to others. The prince of Eckmuhl, weakened by a fever, could only travel in a carriage. The quarter-master-general Joubert, who had long been destitute of servants, had been left in this village, in a situation so miserable, that he excited the tears of all who saw him. We were equally anxious respecting the fate of many other officers who remained with the baggage of the prince. In the evening we ascertained, that owing to the skill and extraordinary activity of the adjutant of the palace Boutarel, these stragglers, had gone to New-Troki to avoid the mountain of Wilna, and that it was only the length of the journey which prevented them from arriving at Evé.

(December 11th.) Leaving this village, we were informed by those who had escaped from Wilna that the Russians had entered it at day-break. A crowd of generals, colonels, and officers, and more than twenty thousand soldiers, who were detained by weakness, fell into their hands. They added, that the officers had been well treated, but that every soldier or servant was immediately ordered to Moscow to he employed in rebuilding the city. These unfortunate men lying in the streets, or public places, without fire, without food, and most of them wounded or sick, presented a spectacle so afflicting, that the enemy endeavoured to mitigate their sufferings. The least to be pitied, were those who, having been plundered by the cossacks, died shortly after our departure. We now had a thousand proofs of human weakness! the same men who had dragged themselves along from Moscow to Wilna, wanted courage to pursue their course a few leagues more, when that little space would have ensured their existence. We heard also that the Jews had ill-treated many of our soldiers, particularly those of the imperial guard, thus wishing to take revenge for the losses which they had suffered; but the Russians, with that justice which always characterised them, hung many of these Israelites, as a lesson to the people that they should not mingle their passions with the quarrels of sovereigns.

The rear of our long column, which covered all the road with the dead and the dying, was continually followed by a cloud of cossacks, who pillaged our soldiers, and afterwards left them to the custody of the peasants, who carried them into the rear, after treating them with a thousand indignities. At length the Russians, weary of making prisoners, liberated all the soldiers belonging to the confederation of the Rhine, and contented themselves with detaining officers of distinction. But when they seized a Frenchman, miserable as he was, they stripped him, and treated him with the greatest ridicule. If he marched with them during the night, he was ordered to fetch water or wood. They afterwards brutally drove him from the fire which he had kindled. Such was the fatal lot of the soldiers, who, compelled to fight, are always the principal victims of the calamities which flow from the quarrels of kings.

A cossack officer, who spoke very good French, overtook one of our sutlers, who earnestly implored mercy, exclaiming that he was not a soldier. He then offered his purse to satisfy the cossacks. Not content with this prize, they began to search him, and found in his pockets boxes of gold, diamonds, and numerous rings enriched with precious stones, which he had, no doubt, taken at the pillage of Moscow. At the sight of this, the officer could not restrain his indignation, and said to the sutler, 'See to what your avarice has reduced you. In the hope of plunder, you have followed the armies, to share in their booty, without partaking of their dangers. In obtaining these much desired riches, you have been enfeebled by their weight, and could not escape my pursuit. I could easily send you captive to the city you have ravaged; but you are too miserable to re-build that which you have destroyed. Return if you can to France; and when you speak of our clemency, describe to your fellow citizens the miserable state, to which they expose themselves who trouble the peace of the world, by following the standards of an unjust aggressor.' At these words he left him to the cossacks, who, disdaining to make him prisoner, drove him before them, beating him with the handle of their lances.

Before we arrived at Zismori, we heard a cannonade at our rear, and at no great distance; we hence concluded that the few soldiers of the rear-guard which remained, were briskly pursued. Notwithstanding this, the fatigue of the troops was so great that many, preferring repose to safety, stopped at Zismori; but the viceroy went on to the village of Roumchichki.

(December 12th.) Exhausted by long and harassing marches, and dying with fatigue, we at length arrived at Kowno, where the wrecks of the different corps were re-united. They encamped as usual in the streets, and as we knew that our deplorable situation no longer permitted us to preserve any discipline, we gave up to pillage the magazines, which were amply stored. Immediately, clothes, corn, and rum, were every where seen in abundance. Our quarters were filled with broken casks, and the liquor which was spilled, formed a little sea, in the middle of the public square. The soldiers, having long been deprived of this beverage, drank to excess, and more than two thousand of them, completely intoxicated, slept upon the snow. Benumbed with cold, they all perished.

It was announced in the evening that the fourth corps would take the road to Tilsit; and as many of us, to avoid the strange confusion which generally prevailed, had been accustomed to sleep one or two leagues beyond the headquarters, a great number set out towards that town. In the middle of the night, the chief of the staff came to look for the fourth corps, which was literally shut up in a single room. He told us that the order had been revoked and that we were to proceed to Gumbinnen instead of Tilsit. This order and counter-order completed our ruin. From that time, the fourth corps consisted only of the household of the prince, and about eight or ten staff-officers.

(December 13th.) As we left Kowno on the morrow, we found the same tumult which we had experienced at the gate of Wilna. The crowd was pressing towards the bridge, although the Niemen was frozen hard enough to have borne the weight of artillery. In Kowno and its environs, we saw a great number of unfortunate soldiers lying on the snow, who had perished when they so nearly reached the end of this fatal expedition. We were particularly affected at seeing colonel Vidman among the dead. He was one of the small number of the Italian guards of honour, who had, till then, sustained the same fatigues as ourselves; but, unable to proceed further, he fell, as he was leaving Kowno to cross the bridge, and expired, without having the satisfaction of dying out of Russia.

The calamities of the army had extended to the imperial guard, and many of its soldiers died every day from hunger, cold and fatigue. Among these victims I saw one truly worthy of admiration. He was an old grenadier. As he lay on the bridge of Kowno, he was spared by the crowd, who, passing by him, had respected his uniform, his decorations, and above all, his three chevrons. This brave man seemed to await his death with the utmost firmness, and disdained to have recourse, like so many others, to useless supplications. By chance, some of his comrades passed by, and then he made a last effort to rise, but unable to accomplish it, and feeling himself dying, he summoned all his strength, and said to one of his companions, who approached to assist him, 'Cease my friend. Do not lavish on me superfluous assistance. I die with regret at being conquered by enemies with whom we could not fight. Famine and winter have alone reduced me to the state in which you now see me. This body, which has supported more than ten wounds, falls miserably to-day for want of a morsel of bread. Ah! if our enemies indeed triumph by means of the rigour of their climate, let them not profane the distinctions that I have gained in fighting against them. Carry to my captain this decoration, which was given to me on the field of Austerlitz; take him likewise my sabre; I used it in the battle of Friedland, and it would still be as fatal to the Russians, as it was at that period, if the approaching spring would permit us to go to Petersburgh, as we have been to Moscow.'

On the morning of the 13th of December, out of four hundred thousand warriors, who had crossed the Niemen, at the opening of the campaign, scarcely twenty thousand men repassed it, of whom at least two thirds had not seen the Kremlin. Arrived at the opposite bank, like ghosts returned from the infernal regions, we fearfully looked behind us, and beheld with horror the savage countries where we had suffered so much. No person would then easily believe, that we had once regarded these climates with envy, and thought those dishonoured who arrived at them last.

After crossing the bridge, we turned to the left to reach Gumbinnen. Many wished to go to the right; still thinking, after the order of the preceding evening, that they must march to Tilsit. We who followed the proper road, had not proceeded far, when we were obliged to climb a lofty mountain, prodigiously steep, and which would have been fatal to our equipages, if we had not long ago been deprived of them. Many carts and carriages which were in the depot of Kowno, and a superb park of artillery, lately arrived from Koningsberg, were left at the foot of the mountain.

Scarcely had we arrived in Poland, when our soldiers dispersed in different roads, and wandered like simple travellers, in the same country, which six months before, had been covered with our numerous armies. In the evening the king of Naples and the prince halted at Skrauda. The same morning (14th December,) when we departed from this village, the cossacks entered Kowno, passed the Niemen, which was frozen at every point, and spread themselves over the immense plains of Poland where they massacred, or made prisoners many of our scattered soldiers, who, not thinking that the Russians would pass the Niemen, thought that they were safe.

From Skrauda many took the direction of Thorn; but the viceroy still continued to follow the road of Gumbinnen, and arrived in this little town after having slept at Pillwizken, Virballen, and Darkehmen (14th, 15th, 16th, and 17th December.) Thence he sent general Gifflenge, his aid-de-camp, to Koningsberg, to order all those of the 4th corps who had taken the road of Tilsit, to proceed to Marienwerder.

Koningsberg being the first great city in the vicinity of our march, was soon filled with those who, having escaped from Moscow, hoped now to recover from the misfortunes which they had suffered. The coffee-houses, the restaurateurs, the furnished hotels, could not at any one price satisfy the extent of our wants. It was necessary to pierce through a crowd to enter any of them. The cold was terrible but the delicious sensation of knowing that we could now defend ourselves against it, and moreover the pleasure of obtaining whatever we desired, were still more heightened, since six months of continual hardships had deprived us of every thing in which the comforts of life consisted.

The king of Naples came to Koningsberg, where he was coldly received by the principal authorities of the town. The chiefs of each corps placed themselves in cantonments along the Vistula, and occupied the towns of Plock, Thorn, Marienberg, Marienwerder, and Elbing. During this time the viceroy, having quitted Gumbinnen, passed by Insterberg and Weblau, (18th, 19th December) to visit the fields of Friedland, Eylau, and Heilsberg (20th, 21st, 22d, December) thus furnishing himself, even in these unhappy circumstances, with subjects for useful meditation. (27th December) His highness arrived at Marienwerder, where he was occupied in collecting together all who remained of the fourth corps. After every research, we succeeded in collecting about eight hundred wounded, the miserable remains of forty-eight thousand warriors, all of whom had marched from Italy to Russia. They were the victims, not of the arms of the enemy, but of the fatal imprudence of their chief, who, not satisfied with having subjugated the best half of Europe, wished to contend with the elements, for a country which consisted only of deserts. The viceroy afterwards despatched towards France and Italy those officers and soldiers, whose infirmities would not permit them to undertake another campaign. He rewarded those soldiers who had behaved well, and punished, by the most sensible disgraces, those few who had dishonoured themselves by a cowardly and pusillanimous conduct.

Such were the dreadful calamities which annihilated a powerful army, which had rashly undertaken the proudest and the most useless of all expeditions. If we look into the annals of antiquity, we shall find that never, since the time of Cambyses, did so numerous a body of men experience such dreadful reverses. Thus were the boastful predictions of Napoleon at the beginning of the campaign, literally fulfilled, but with this difference, that not Russia, but himself 'hurried away by a fatality, had accomplished his destiny.' These calamities have had one happy result, by putting an end to a despotic influence; they have restored to Europe her liberty, and to France her happiness.

END OF THE NARRATIVE

Appendix I

Itinerary of the March of the Fourth Corps in the Russian Territory, during the Campaign of 1812

The emperor Napoleon passed the Niemen at Kowno, the 24th June; the 22d, being at Wilkowiski, he declared war against Russia. The fourth corps, commanded by the viceroy of Italy, passed the Niemen at Pilony; the advanced guard effected its passage the 29th; but the prince and the fifteenth division passed on the 1st of July. On the 28th Napoleon was at Wilna.

1 July, from Pilony to Kroni . . 2 leagues

2 July, Melangani 7

3 July, Rouicontoui 6

4 July, New-Troki 3

5 July, Halted.

6 July, Ditto.

7 July, Rudniki 6

8 July, Paradomin 3

9 July, Halted.

10 July, Paulovo 4

(At the castle of the count of Choiseuil)

11 July, Ochmiana 6¼

12 July, Smorghoni 8

13 July, Halted.

14 July, from Smorghoni to Zachkevitschi 3¼

15 July, Vileika 8

16 July, Kostenevitschi 6

17 July, Dolghinow 4½

18 July, Dokzice 7

19 July, Halted.

20 July, Berezino 6½

21 July, Pouichna, or Gloubokoé 6½

22 July, Kamen 6

23 July, Botscheikovo 3¾

24 July, From Smorghoni to Bezenkovitschi 4

25 July, Soritza (3 leagues on this side Ostrowno). 4½

26 July, Combat (bivouac at small castle Dobrijka) 5½

27 July, Bivouac before Witepsk 2½

28 July, Bivouac at Aghaponovchtchina 5½

29 July, Sourai. 5

30 July, Halted.

1 August, Ditto.

2 August, Ditto.

3 August, Ditto.

4 August, Ditto.

5 August, Ditto.

6 August, Ditto.

7 August, Ditto.

8 August, Ditto.

9 August, From Sourai to Janowitschi 4

10 August, Halted.

11 August, Velechkovitschi . 3½

12 August, Liozna 2½

13 August, Liovavitschi . . . 5¼

14 August, Rasasna 4

15 August, Siniaki 7¼

16 August, Katova 3

17 August, Bivouac (at a league from Korouitnia) 5

18 August, Bivouac (near the *chateau* of Novoidvor) 5

19 August, Suburb of Smolensk 1½

20 August, Passed the Nieper (bivouac above Smolensk) . . ½

21 August, Bivouac same place.

22 August, Ditto.

23 August, Volodimerowa . . . 5

24 August, Pologhi 7½

25 August, Zazélé 5½

26 August, Mikailovskoe . . 7½

27 August, Agopochina (passed the Niemen at Blaghove) . . 4½

28 August, Bivouac (round a *chateau* a league beyond Bereski) 4

29 August, From Agopochina to Novoe 9

30 August, Halted.

31 August, Pokron 6¾

1 September, Paulova 6½

2 September, Woremiewo . . . 2

3 September, Halted.

4 September, Louzos 5½

5 September, Encamped on the heights of Borodino 4

6 September, Ditto.

7 September, Battle.

8 September, Ouspenskoe, or Krasnoë 3¼

9 September, Rouza 6¼

10 September, Halted.

11 September, Alpalchtchouina 4½

12 September, Zwenighorod 3½

13 September, Buzaievo . . . 6½

14 September, Khorechevo . 4¾

15 September, Moscow 2

Total from Pilony to Moscow 263¾

Stopped in this city from 15th September until …

18 October, Village on the road from Kalouga, a league from Moscow 1

19 October, Little village, near Batoutinka bivouac. 5

20 October, Inatowo 7½

21 October, Fominskoe 3

22 October, Halted.

23 October, From Fominskoe to a village half a league beyond Borovsk bivouac 7¼

24 October, Battle of Malo-Jaroslavitz. Bivouac . 4¾

25 October, Halted.

26 October, Ouvarovskoe bivouac 4

27 October, Alféréva 4½

28 October, Village a league beyond Borisov, supposed to be Mitïaéva 2½

29 October, Ouspenskoe, called Krasnoë bivouac 5½

30 October, Village half a league on the right of the road between Kolotskoi and Prokofevo bivouac 6

31 October, Ghiat bivouac . 8¼

1 November, near Velitchevo bivouac 5

2 November, Foederovskoe bivouac 6¼

3 November, Battle of Viazma, bivouac half a league further 3½

4 November, Rouibki, a league beyond Semlovo 7

5 November, Jolkov Postoïa Door 3½

6 November, Doroghoboui bivouac 6

7 November, From Fominskoe to Zazélé bivouac. 7

8 November, Sloboda bivouac . 4

9 November, From Sloboda passed the Wop, bivouacked at a little village, half a league from this river 1

10 November, Doukhov-chtchina 4½

11 November, Halted.

12 November, Wolodimerowa bivouac 6¾

13 November, Smolensko . . 5¼

14 November, Halted.

15 November, Hamlet three leagues from Smolensko, supposed to be Loubna . . 3½

16 November, Krasnoë 7

17 November, Liadouï . . . 1½

18 November, Dowbrowna . . 8

19 November, Orcha 4

20 November, Halted.

21 November, Half a league before Kokhanovo bivouac . . 5

22 November, Bivouac around a castle, half a league this side Toloschin 5

23 November, Bivouac three leagues from Toloschin near Jablonka 4

24 November, Bobr 4

25 November, Little village, five leagues from Bobr, where there is an insulated church, bivouac. 5½

26 November, From a village at Nemonitsa, to two and a half leagues on this side Borisov, bivouac 5½

27 November, Studzianca, passage of the Beresina, bivouac. 4½

28 November, Zembin, bivouac 4½

29 November, Kamen 3¼

30 November, Niestanovitschi, near Zavichino 6

1 December, Iliïa 4½

2 December, Molodetschino . 6

3 December, Halted.

4 December, Village supposed to be Markovo bivouac 7

5 December, Smorghoni . . 4¼

6 December, Joupranoui . . . 5

7 December, Rovno-Pole bivouac 5

8 December, Roukoni
  bivouac 5½
9 December, Wilna 3
10 December, Evé bivouac . . 10
11 December, Zismori 6

12 December, Kowno 10

Total 256½

From Niemen to Moscow   263¾

Grand Total 520¼

A List Of all the Persons mentioned in this work, with their Rank, during the Campaign in Russia

Napoleon.

Jerome Bonaparte, king of Westphalia, commander of the 8th corps.

Joachim Murat, King of Naples, commander of all the cavalry.

Eugene de Beauharnois, viceroy of Italy, commander of the 4th corps.

Berthier, prince of Neufchatal and of Wagram, major general.

Davoust, prince of Eckmuhl, commander of 1st corps.

Oudinot, duke of Reggio, commander of 2nd corps.

Ney, duke of Elchingen, commander of 3rd corps, prince of Moskwa.

Prince Poniatowski, commander of 5th corps.

Marshal count St. Cyr, commander of 6th corps.

General count Regnier, commander of 7th corps.

Junot, duke of Abrantes, commander of 8th corps.

Victor, duke of Belluno, commander of 9th corps.

Duke of Tarentum, commander of 10th corps.

Prince Schwartzenberg, commander of the Austrian auxiliary corps.

Bessieres, duke of Istria, commander of the cavalry of the guard.

Caulincourt, duke of Vicenza, general of division, grand ecuyer.

Duroc, duke of Frioul, general, grand marshal of the palace.

Count Rapp, general, aide de camp to the emperor.

Count Lauriston, general, aide de camp to the emperor.

Count Lefebre Desnouettes, general of division, colonel of the horse chasseurs of the guard.

Count Friant, general of division, colonel of the grenadiers of the foot guards.

Count Nansouty, commander of cavalry corps.

Count Grouchy, commander of cavalry corps.

Count Montbrun, commander of cavalry corps.

General Dessoles, chief of the viceroy's staff.

General Danthouard, commander of the artillery of the 4th corps.

General Eblé, general of division of artillery, commander of the bridge equipages.

Count Gudin, general of division, 1st corps.

Baron Gerard, general of division, 1st corps.

Count Dessaix, general of division, 1st corps.

Count Compans, general of division, 1st corps.

Count Morand, general of division, 1st corps.

Count Verdier, general of division, 2nd corps.

Count Legrand, general of division, 2nd corps.

Baron Merle, general of division, 2nd corps.

Baron Ledrut, commander of a division, 3rd corps.

Count of Claparede, general of division, commander of the legion of the Vistula.

Baron Delzons, general of division, 4th corps.

Count Broussier, general of division, 4th corps.

Count Pino, general of division, 4th corps.

Baron Wrede, Bavarian general, 6th corps.

General de Roy, Bavarian general, 6th corps.

General Sierbein, Bavarian general, 6th corps.

Count Parthonneaux, general of division, 9th corps.

Baron Girard, general of division, 9th corps.

Baron Grandjean, commander of a division, 10th corps.

General Gravers, Prussian general, 10th corps.

General Kleist, Prussian general, 10th corps.

Count Charpentier, general of division, governor of Smolensko.

Count Baraguey d'Hilliers, general of a division.

Count Loison, commander of a division, from Koningsberg.

General Dombrowski, commander of a Polish division.

Count Sanson, general of a division, chief of the topographical bureau.

Baron Haxo, general of division of engineers.

Count Sebastiani, general of division of cavalry.

Baron Lahoussaye, general of division of cavalry.

Count Bruyeres, general of division of cavalry.

Baron de St. Germain, general of division of cavalry.

Baron Doumere, general of division of cavalry.

Count Preyssing, commander of a division of light Bavarian cavalry.

Prince Czartoryski, grand marshal of the diet of Warsaw.

Count Mejean, counsellor of state of the kingdom of Italy, and secretary of the viceroy.

General Poitevin (baron Maureillan), commander of the engineers of the 4th corps.

Baron Aubrey, commander of artillery of 2d corps.

Generals of Brigade - Barons Ricard, Rousel, Huard, Plansanne, Bonami, Nagle, Augereau, Marion, Compere, Villata, Fontane, Levie, Chastel, Berkheim, Colbert, Castex, Saint Geniez, Aug. Caulincourt, Pajol, Guyon.

Pouget, general of brigade, governor of Witepsk.

Lecchi, general of brigade, commander of the Italian guard.

Lepel, aid de camp to the king of Westphalia.

D'Hery, aid de camp to the king of Naples.

Klengel, general in the Saxon service.

General Jomini, governor of Orcha.

Baron Triaire, general of brigade, aid de camp to the viceroy.

Baron Gifflenge, general of brigade, aid de camp to the viceroy.

Baron Lacroix, colonel, ditto.

Count Louis Tascher Lapagerie, chief of squadron.

Count Charles Labedoyere, chief of squadron.

Count Maurice Mejean, chief of squadron.

Count Jules Desseve, chief of squadron.

Colonel Delfanti, officer of the ordnance of the viceroy.

Andre Corner, lieutenant, ditto.

Liedot, colonel of engineers.

Marboeuf, colonel of lancers.

Kliski, Polish colonel, with the viceroy.

Padzivil, colonel of the 8th Polish Hulans.

Durieu, adjutant commander, sub-chief of the staff of the 4th corps.

De Bourmont, adjutant commander attached to this staff.

Asselin, adjutant commander attached to this staff.

Forestier, adjutant commander attached to this staff.

Colonel Grosbon, of the 53d regiment.

Colonel Battaglia, commander of the Italian guards of honour.

Colonel Vidmann, commander of the company of the Venetian
  guards of honour.
Colonel Demay, commander of the artillery of the 13th division.
Colonel Banco, of the horse chasseurs.
Colonel Rambourg, of the 3d ditto.
D'Oreille, major of the Spanish regiment Joseph Napoleon.
Vives, major of artillery.
Coland, chief of battalion, wagon master-general of the 4th
  corps.
Sewlinge, ditto, attached to the staff.
Boutarel, captain of horse chasseurs, adjutant of the palais royal
  of Monza.
Trezel, captain, aid de camp of general Guilleminot.
Maisonneure, assistant captain of the staff of the 4th corps.
Jouard, assistant captain of the staff of the 4th corps.
Evrard, assistant captain of the staff of the 4th corps.
Morlaincourt, captain of engineers to the 4th division.
Bonardelle, captain of artillery.
Octave de Segur, officer of hussars.
Ferrari, officer of hussars.
Guyard, captain of the 9th of the line.
Savary, captain of the 9th of the line.
Bordoni, lieutenant in the Italian guards of honour.
Mastini, lieutenant in the Italian guards of honour.
Saint Marcellin de Fontanes, attached to the staff of the 4th
  corps.
Lesseps, French consul at Moscow.
Villeblanche, auditor of the council of state, intendant of
  Smolensko.

Alexander I, emperor of Russia.
Grand duke Constantine.
Prince Kutusoff, commander-in-chief of the Russian army.
Barclay de Tolly, commander-in-chief before the arrival of prince
  Kutusoff.
Prince Wittgenstein, commander of the 1st Russian corps.
General Bagawout, commander of the 2nd Russian corps.[1]

1   Second corps, called the army of the west.

General Schmoaloff, commander of the 3rd Russian corps.

General Tutschkoff, commander of the 4th Russian corps.

General Prince Bagration, commander of the 5th Russian corps.

General Doctorrow, commander of the 6th Russian corps.

General Tormasow, commander of the 7th Russian corps.

Admiral Tschikakoff, commander of the army of the Danube.

Platoff, Hetman of the Cossacks.

Platoff, son.

Orlow Dennisow, general of the advanced-guard.

Kamenski, general commander in Volhynia.

Ertel, general, commander in Volhynia.

Essen, general, commander in Volhynia.

Marcoff, general, commander in Volhynia.

Repnin, general, commander in the corps of prince Wittgenstein.

Stengel, general, commander in the corps of prince Wittgenstein.

Lambert, commanding a division of the army of the Danube.

Sicverse, general, employed in the second army of the West.

Ostermann, general employed in the centre of the Russian army.

Bennigsen, general employed in the centre of the Russian army.

Skallon, general employed in the centre of the Russian army.

Ouvarow, general employed in the centre of the Russian army.

Balla, general employed in the centre of the Russian army.

Koulniew, general of light cavalry.

Koff, general of cavalry.

Miloradowitch, commander-general of the advanced-guard of
   prince Kutusoff.

Archbishop Platon.

Bishop Augustin, vicar of Moscow.

Rostopchin, noble of Moscow.

Momonoff, noble of Moscow.

Orlow, noble of Moscow.

Saltikoff, noble of Moscow.

Shermitow, noble of Moscow.

Index

Also available from Helion & Company